The Minister
and the Murderer

The Minister and the Murderer

A Book of Aftermaths

Stuart Kelly

GRANTA

Granta Publications, 12 Addison Avenue, London W11 4QR

First published in Great Britain by Granta Books, 2018

A CIP catalogue record for this book is available from the British Library.

1 3 5 7 9 10 8 6 4 2

ISBN 978 1 84708 922 9
eISBN 978 1 84708 924 3

Typeset in Aldine 401BT and Rotis Serif by Avon DataSet Ltd,
Bidford on Avon, B50 4JH

Printed and bound by CPI Group (UK) Ltd, Croydon, CR0 4YY

To my nephews and niece, Danny, Frazer, Finlay, Angus
and Ailsa, in the hope that one day this makes sense
of your eccentric uncle, though you do not know it yet.

A Prayer for a Writer

*An Author, or a Journalist, for all whose craft it is to use
words which many will hear or read.*

O God, you gave me the gift and responsibility of using words.
Help me in all my writing and my speaking to be the servant of
goodness, of beauty and of truth. Help me never to write or to
say anything which would injure another's innocence or take
another's faith away.

Help me never to write or say anything which would make that
which is wrong more attractive, or which would soil the mind
of anyone who reads or hears it.

Help me never to pander to that which is low, never to seek
popularity at the expense of truth, never to be more concerned
with sensations than with facts, and always to respect the
feelings and the rights of other people.

Grant that all that I may write or say be such that it can stand
the scrutiny of my own conscience, and such that I could with a
clear conscience offer it to you.

This I ask for your love's sake. AMEN.

William Barclay, *More Prayers for the Plain Man* (1962)

The Book of Psalms 122:1

I was glad when they said unto me,
Let us go into the house of the LORD.

It is called, both accurately and ironically, the Black and White Corridor. This chequered vestibule lies at the top of an impressive flight of stairs, found in the quadrangle of Edinburgh's New College. From the outside, the building, like much of the city's finest architecture, looks medieval but is actually Victorian. Designed in the neo-Gothic style by William Henry Playfair, it seems as though it might have escaped from Mervyn Peake's Gormenghast trilogy or a Hammer House of Horror film. Below, on Princes Street, shoppers mill and bustle, or meander through the neoclassical serenity of the National Gallery; with New College like a vertiginously arched scowl of disapproval above, its twin towers almost critically perpendicular, uprightness in dark stone. In the quadrangle itself, entered through imposing gates that insist on how small humans are, stands a statue of John Knox, the great reformer of the Scottish Church, resembling an Old Testament prophet with his Bible tucked under one arm, the other raised and with fingers extended as if he were rebuking Heaven itself. The Black and White Corridor itself leads into rooms for clerks and ministers and eventually into the General Assembly Hall, where the Church of Scotland meets

1

annually. The General Assembly is the Church's highest legal, political and theological authority, under the leadership of the Moderator, a position filled each year by a different minister. I first heard of the corridor as I sat in the public gallery of the Assembly in 2013, listening to the debate about the ordination of ministers in same-sex relationships. I was trying at the same time to strip away twenty-nine years; to imagine the entire room filled with serious men in crepuscular suits, to airbrush out the jeans and jolly jumpers. The Church had allowed the Scottish Parliament to sit there between its being reconvened in 1999 and the completion of its permanent home at the bottom of the Royal Mile in 2004 – although, in an assertion of authority that reverberates throughout Scottish history, the Parliament had to vacate each year for the Assembly to sit. This meant, however, that there were curved pine desks with inbuilt microphones, rather than geometric lines of uncomfortable green leather benches. It was even carpeted, and you could barely catch the echoes of brogue on wood that must have once clattered throughout. As the various speakers made their points, a large digital screen flashed messages: would the Rev. McQuhat meet the Rev. Thrawn in the Black and White Corridor? Over the week during which the Assembly sat, I had become aware of the various factions ranged around the room, and wondered: whyever should McQuhat need to speak to Thrawn? I learned only later that the Black and White Corridor is not merely a description: it is where one discusses things in confidence, a place where deals are cut and alliances struck. It is the place where things are far from black and white.

It would have been, I supposed, in the Black and White Corridor that an agreement was eventually reached in the days before 19 May 1984, concerning the innocuous-sounding section 2.3–5 of the Board of Education Report. Or rather, an agreement was reached on the reporting of the debate around section 2.3–5. In an unprecedented step, all audio and video recording devices would be turned off during the debate; thirty years later and it seems inconceivable that interest in Church matters was so high up the media agenda that so much of the proceedings were actually broadcast, or that the decision not to would be so controversial. Print journalists were told they could cover proceedings, but only with a pencil and paper. The decision to hold a debate in secret was as contentious as the debate itself. Newspaper leader columns openly opposed the move. One former Moderator, the Very Rev. Bill Johnston, said, 'We are a court and we are more than a court. We are a Church which proclaims a gospel of forgiveness and reconciliation – which is on trial. Is it not right that we should be as open as we can be?' It may, of course, never have happened there at all. Those who would know are dead or silent.

What was the subject so divisive as to be held secretively? The Assembly of 1984 was set to be dramatic even before this turn of events. It was the second year of Margaret Thatcher's second term in office, and the Church had taken a trenchant position against her government's policies. Reports were due to highlight unemployment and worsening poverty and issue a call for the defence of 'one of the few signs that our society is truly Christian and civilised', the National Health Service. There were hands to be wrung over the prevalence of 'video nasties' and the proliferation of nuclear weapons. The vexed question of what was to be done with surplus communion plates was to be raised, and whether or not to invite the Methodists to join the World Alliance of Reformed Churches. The perennial problem of the Aged and Infirm Ministers' Fund was again on the agenda.

The Family Matters report into 'Christ in Childlessness' was to be presented. For the first time ever, a rabbi would address the Assembly. But neither politics nor theology was the cause of the Church's sudden need for privacy. The actual debate would cut to the core of what the Church believed and meant.

At the time I was eleven years old and a pious little shit. I still have my notebook in which I earnestly wrote up summaries of each of the books of the Bible, paying particular attention to the Book of Revelation and markedly less so to First and Second Chronicles – in fact, I am sure I just wrote out the section headings and skipped the actual text. I had been brought up in the Kirk. I would not say we were a God-fearing family: there was little brimstone and less hellfire. Our minister was a clever and gentle man with Mephistophelean eyebrows and a wry smile. We went to church on Sunday, to my mind, because that is what we did on Sundays, just as we had candy-floss only when the fair was in the nearby town and you wouldn't carve a turnip-head lantern in February. The Church simply *was*. It structured the year, from Advent and Christmas, to Easter, which was Mysterious, to summer outings in Borders valleys, to harvest and taking canned soup, chrysanthemums and windfall apples around elderly neighbours. My dad was the Session Clerk, *primus inter pares* among the laity, who wrote up the Session Minutes in a three-inch-thick leather-bound volume. He looked after the goblets, patens and white cloths used when the Kirk celebrated Communion, which seemed to me, being too young to participate, objects invested with some mystical significance. My mum played the church organ and took the choir, as my brother and I sat in the other room; so my earliest memories of the *Star Trek* episode with the Gorn are accompanied by a soundtrack of rather wavery voices singing 'Lord of All Being,

Throned Afar' and 'The King of Love My Shepherd Is'. As a birthday present, much later, my parents gave me a drawing I had done as a child, found in the back of a set of drawers as they redecorated. It was an order of service of sorts, announcing a church service in our house. I had written that there would be a prayer at '40 past 8, repet 40 past 8', and the 'bible redding' would be given by 'master sbk'. It was illustrated with a picture of the Trinity: an abstract cross, strangely notched; a bearded, berobed Son (or is it the Father?); and a Holy Ghost straight out of *Scooby Doo*. So much for the piety; as for the shit I was . . .

As will become clear later, the Church of Scotland is a very different entity to the Holy Roman Catholic Church, the Episcopal Churches or the Orthodox Churches. One aspect of its difference is a profound sense of the equality of all believers, an aversion to hierarchy – hence the annual election of a Moderator, rather than a sinecure or perpetual position. I could pay honeyed lip service to this idea as a child, while secretly believing that with my mum leading the music and my dad nothing less than the minister's deputy, his lieutenant, his right-hand man, I was born into ecclesiastical aristocracy. An asthenic, asthmatic and bespectacled child will seek out any system in which to insist on his superiority. That sentence's glut of ssss-es is probably the most eloquent way I can describe my childhood character. I was very good at propriety and much less good at goodness. Kindness eluded me for years. I could abide by with the best of them, but rarely reached out. There was a nagging resentment that by eleven I really should have heard the voice calling in the night like the prophet Samuel or have accomplished some modest miracle, in private. I was affronted when the minister posed a question during the children's homily: what was the last thing your mum said to you before you left for kirk today? I knew the answer was 'Have you remembered money for the collection?' but my brother answered truthfully and to peals of laughter, 'Did you go to the toilet?' When Christmas fell on a Sunday, and the minister had to tread cautiously as many parents wanted the nativity play the week before since 'Christmas was for the children, really', I priggishly pursed my lips, and argued that the Incarnation was more important than an AT-AT Walker, which I had also once wanted, and did not get. My untested virtue was my carapace and morning star.

This was exacerbated by having a riddling, questioning little mind. I asked questions more to see the discomfiture of my interlocutor than in expectation of an answer. 'Dad, what actually is your conscience?' 'A voice inside you that tells you if something is right or wrong.' 'But don't mad people hear voices? Is that their conscience?' 'No, it's a voice that you trust in your heart.' 'But you don't think with your heart, so how can it tell your brain if a voice is a conscience or being mad?' and on, and on, and on. One of the ethical dilemmas that occupied me a great deal in 1984 was the section 2.3–5 debate. I knew it at the time only through newspapers and television and overheard conversations. It is headed in the 1984 *Reports to the General Assembly* simply as 'The Candidature of Mr James Robert Nelson'.

The Assembly had originally been approached by the presbytery of St Andrews to give guidance over whether they should grant a licence to James Nelson, who had applied to be a probationary minister in one of their parishes, which would have allowed him eventually to become a full minister and be ordained. But events had intervened: in 'an emotion-charged 150-minute debate, during which frayed tempers reflected the widely divergent beliefs of the presbytery', as the *Scotsman* newspaper reported it on 12 April 1984, it had been decided by a single vote not to grant a licence. Before the Assembly now was not just their own investigation into the handling of the matter, but an appeal to overturn the decision of the presbytery. The merits and demerits of his case would have to be brought before the bar of the entire Church. It would be done so against a series of claims and counter-claims – of cover-ups, conspiracies, of members of the presbytery being put under undue pressure, of the moral rectitude of the individual in question and the Kirk itself. It had already become a cause célèbre, especially as some of the members of the presbytery learnt of the problem only through a newspaper scoop in the *Glasgow Herald* about 'the Kirk's best-kept secret'.

I had not thought about the case of the ordination of James Nelson for many, many years until a lunchtime conversation with colleagues over the question before the Assembly in 2013. Already, I had laid out my critique of what I thought was the Kirk's overcautious approach to the matter: the Greek word *arsenokoitai* used by St Paul in First Corinthians does not mean 'homosexual'; well, it certainly doesn't in Philo of Alexandria, where it clearly means 'temple prostitute' – the Church of Scotland recognises only baptism and communion as sacraments, so marriage is considered under civil law not Church law, and the whole problem of divorcees remarrying is theologically *much* more complicated but that was resolved – and anyway – they ordained Nelson for goodness' sake! Nobody knew who Nelson even was.

No, no: to be truthful, it was not to colleagues. It was to the woman who was not then yet my ex-wife. To tell this story as it should be told will require a degree of self-scrutiny I had not anticipated. How strange, I suddenly think, that to be an ex- is for ever, but to be a -wife might be temporary. The vote on homosexuality that day was a shameful fudge, a compromise that was touted as a turning point. As I walked out into the torrential rain, I overhead one man say to another, 'At least Someone is making his opinion known clearly enough.' If only, I thought.

What was the quandary that was tearing the Church apart in 1984? It was quite simple. James Nelson was a self-confessed murderer who had served ten years in prison for his crime. Could a murderer also be a minister? *Introibo ad altare Dei.*

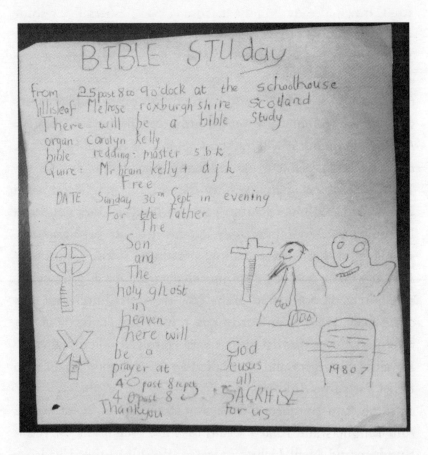

The Book of Nehemiah 9:38

And because of all this we make a sure covenant, and write it;
and our princes, Levites, and priests, seal unto it.

To understand the decision that was made, and its consequences, one first has to understand who was making the decision, and this necessitates a brief interlude into Church history. It may be that you are less interested in the intricacies of the 1697 Barrier Act than I am, but it will stand you in good stead for the rest of the book, and possibly the harder pub quizzes.

If people know anything about the Church of Scotland, they know it is even more fissiparous than radical left-wing politics. It seems wryly appropriate that a Church born out of schism should find itself riven by schism throughout its history. Although there had been previous demands for a different kind of Church, the formation of the Church of Scotland is usually dated from 1560, when Parliament ratified the demands of the reformers. After that date it has split between Covenanters and Royalists, Engagers and the Kirk Party, the Secessionists, the Relief Party, the Auld Lichts and the New Lichts, the Burghers and the anti-Burghers (further fractured into Auld Licht Anti-Burghers and Auld Licht Burghers and New Licht Anti-Burghers and New Licht Burghers), the United Presbyterian Church, the Reformed Presbyterian Church, the Church of

9

Scotland and the Free Church of Scotland, the United Free Church, the Free Church of Scotland Continuing (also known as the 'Wee Frees') and the Free Presbyterian Church of Scotland (also known as the 'Wee Wee Frees').

One of the most typical of Scottish jokes concerns a man rescued from a solitary existence on a desert island. As he and the captain of the ship that has saved him stand on the deck and watch the island recede, the captain points out a small hut. 'Ah, that was the house I built,' this McCrusoe says wistfully. As they round a headland, a larger structure appears. Prompted, he replies: 'That was the church I built and attended every Sabbath.' A little farther out to sea and an even larger, dilapidated building is visible. 'And that?' he is asked. 'That,' the solitary replies with venom, 'is the church I used to go to.' This welter of disagreement is easy to parody but harder to understand. Remarkably the Church has held itself together to this day – and there was even the Reconciliation between the Church of Scotland and the Free Church of Scotland in 1929, with the novelist John Buchan, the son of a Free Church minister, deputised by George VI as Lord Lieutenant to attend the Assembly when the rapprochement happened. Although the post-1929 Kirk contains Moderate and Evangelical wings, or Traditionalist and Progressive groupings, Alpha courses and Omega warnings, it has split over only one subject, albeit repeatedly: authority.

Understanding this means going back to the man whose statue glowers over the New College quadrangle: John Knox. Knox has been a cliché in Scotland for centuries; lauded as a pioneering, courageous speaker of truth to power on one hand, and lambasted as an intransigent, misogynist killjoy on the other. Knox was certain of one thing, about which he was utterly wrong: that he would be a martyr for Protestantism. There is an affecting anecdote of Knox, when he, as a trained Catholic priest turned apostate, was acting as the bodyguard to the reformer George Wishart and news came that the latter would soon be arrested. Wishart dismissed Knox, who was keen to stay, and even fight, with the words: 'One is enough for a sacrifice.' Wishart was then hanged and burned; Knox was thereafter a galley slave on a French vessel and a theological advisor to the English king, Edward VI. When he returned to Scotland in 1559, having studied with John Calvin in Geneva, his expectation was that he would die a brutal death on his native shores. Instead, he transformed the country in an unimaginable, wholescale fashion. The Reformation was as much a political revolution as it was a religious upheaval. Preparing to be a martyr, he ended up a state-builder.

Central to Knox's thought was a very simple proposition: equality before the eyes of God. He began restructuring Scotland with the frighteningly titled *The First Book of Discipline* of 1560, along with five colleagues, the so-called Six Johns: Knox, Willock, Winram, Row, Spottiswoode and Douglas – the visionary, the innovator, the Devil's advocate, the surprise convert, the steady hand and the academic forerunner. That it was written by committee, rather than a lone polemicist, meant not just compromise but the chance of implementation. Scotland was divided into parishes, parishes together made up presbyteries, and the Assembly would be comprised of representatives of the presbyteries, both lay and ordained, to determine Church policy. Bishops were demitted from office. Each parish had to provide education for the young, poor relief for the needy, and justice for the wronged when the cases were not so severe that the legal profession had to be involved. There were other considerations that would be of importance when the Assembly met later: the parish, and only the parish, had the right to choose its minister. The days of the monied and the propertied imposing some addlebrained nephew or a super-fluous third son on a living were over – of course, they persisted nevertheless, and the schisms thrived when the ideal and the actuality were obviously out of kilter. But the principle was there. The Church was governed by the congregation, not by vested interests, landed gentry or political appointees. The broadcaster Andrew Marr rightly says that the Assembly was the closest thing to a democratically elected sovereign power most Scots had between the Act of Union in 1707 and the re-establishment of the Parliament in 1999.

Knox's Reformation had another consequence. The Parliament had traditionally been formed of the Three Estates: the First Estate drawn from the prelates (bishops and abbots), the Second from the nobility and the Third from the burgh commissioners. With the Church entirely remade, one third of the Parliament could no longer sit in it. It allowed an influx of new members – the lairds and the minor nobility – to take their places on the benches. It meant something more than that. The aristocracy, loyal to the Crown mostly, could now be outvoted.

Who then had power? And what would they do with it?

I remember seeing the statue of Knox in St Giles' Cathedral in Edinburgh one Christmas and marvelling that it had been draped with purple tinsel. By then I was a strident atheist, and a buffoon of the first water. For the first time in my life I think I snickered. How, I smugly wondered, would he have felt to know that he was now a derisively bedecked figure? How much I would love to see those adamantine shoulders crumple and that lidless eye squeeze out a tear; no, a snowflake. The child who had thrilled at books – no, to be precise, a Book – on the backs of burnished eagles – had been a child. My eyes were open now, and Knox was no more part of me than Harry Lauder or William McGonagall or Stanley Baxter. He, being a statue, did not blink. And then, standing in a church with 'Hark! The Herald Angels Sing' faintly in the background, I wondered why I was there at all.

When James VI of Scotland acceded to the English throne as James I in 1603 and became the first king of 'Great Britain', he became the monarch of a single dominion with two distinct ecclesiastical forms of governance. Although both were ostensibly Protestant, they were very different forms of Protestantism. The Church of England had retained bishops and much of the aesthetics of Roman Catholicism; Scotland had outlawed bishops and preferred an austere simplicity without 'graven images'. Henry VIII had declared himself the head of the Church of England; in Scotland, the head of the Church could be only Christ. As Andrew Melville, Knox's spiritual and ecclesiastical successor, said to James,

> Sir . . . there are two kings and two kingdoms in Scotland:
> there is Christ Jesus the King of the Church, whose
> subject King James the Sixth is, and of whose kingdom he
> is not a king, nor a lord, nor a head, but a member . . . We
> will yield to you your place, and give you all due
> obedience; but again I say, you are not the head of the
> Church; you cannot give us that eternal life which even in
> this world we seek for, and you cannot deprive us of it.

Moreover, he rebuked the king as merely 'God's sillie vassal'.

But the fault lines ran deeper than questions of liturgy or

Church governance. George Buchanan was one of the intellectual powerhouses of the Reformation: a humanist scholar, perhaps the most widely read Latin playwright in Europe at the time, and tutor to James VI. He was, in that great Scottish word, 'thrawn': obstinate, intractable and stubborn. When he saw the English courtiers fawning on James he famously remarked, 'You may kiss his arse, but I hae skelped it.' He had also written an inflammatory work of political theory, *De Jure Regni Apud Scotos*, in 1579. It developed a contractual theory of kingship in which the king ruled by the consent of the people – and it is noticeable that while James was the sixth 'King of Scots', he was the first of his name as 'King of England'. The most provocative part of Buchanan's thesis was that the people had the right, even a moral duty, to remove, if needs be by execution, monarchs who became tyrants or ungodly. James's own treatise on the monarchy, the *Basilikon Doron* of 1599, was a refutation of Buchanan's ideas. In it, James set out what became known as the 'divine right of kings', as he had done in a work of the previous year, *The Trve Lawe of Free Monarchies: Or the Reciprock and Mvtvall Dvtie betwixt a Free King and his Naturall Subiectes*. Kings, according to James, were appointed by God and any attempt to depose or dethrone a monarch was not just illegal and immoral but a blasphemy: only God could withdraw his support for a ruler.

James, having grown up with the Kirk, knew he had to tread carefully in dealing with it. The constitutional settlement ettled on either side: the Catesby plotters, for example, were terrified that James would import Presbyterianism from the north, making circumstances even more difficult for recusant Catholics. The Kirk worried that James was seduced down south not just by episcopacy and his favourites, but by authoritarianism. James had written *Basilikon Doron* as a manual of instruction for his heir, Prince Henry. When Henry died in 1612, his younger brother Charles became heir apparent. Henry had once said that when he became King he would make Charles Archbishop of Canterbury. Charles might have kept his head if that had come to pass.

The First Book of Samuel 3:6

*And the LORD called yet again, Samuel. And Samuel arose
and went to Eli and said, Here am I; for thou didst call me.
And he answered, I called not, my son; lie down again.*

I was supposed to be a cleric and ended up a critic. In many ways
they are not such dissimilar vocations. Both are, in a way, forms
of self-abnegation.

As a child I wrote – well, I didn't: I imagined writing though
the actual pen-and-paper stuff was rather too much work – a
huge number of epic fantasies. Although I would like to claim
they were inspired by Tolkien, it is more likely they were
derivative of Terry Brooks's *The Sword of Shannara* and a series
of four novels about seven magicians which I borrowed from
Galashiels library and have never been able to trace again. (The
final volume featured one wizard trying to find a way to carve an
image of the soul, which impressed me no end at the age of
eight.) The only thing I remember about my works, apart from
the terribly detailed maps I drew, was that one of the stories
featured the usual cast – a warrior, an elf, a dwarf, a sorcerer, a
giant (possibly a cyclops), a princess and a priest. The priest –
who, of course, could not use bladed weapons – was leading
them to a portal to a Dark Lord's Dark Realm. At some point,
probably on a mountain top, the priest grabbed the warrior's

sword and sliced open his chest, then pulled apart his own rib-cage as if he were merely opening a cardigan: because he himself had been the gateway all along, and would sacrifice himself for questy reasons. I was awfully pleased with this idea. In almost every story I made up, a man of faith would perform some hugely altruistic act of suicide. I admit I was a strange child. I used to cry because I thought one half of the bed would be sad if I slept on the other.

The greatest benefit of being a sickly child is the amount one gets to read, and it taught me an invaluable lesson very early on: that I would not be a novelist. Unless I could write some-thing as good as – well, the list would change over the years from C. S. Lewis to Dostoyevsky to Mark Danielewski, there would be little point in even attempting a novel. Being readerly was an exercise in being humbled. It was the perfect training to become a critic.

Critics, as I would learn at university reading Matthew Arnold and F. R. Leavis, are secular clerics. They put others first. Their function is to interpret. They must begin with empathy, move towards discrimination and finally cast a judgement, and do all this while realising they are not the centre of attention. The service is more important than the servitor, just as the review is not about the reviewer. They persist in the limbo of being both blatant and covert.

In my time as a literary editor, the job changed dramatically. We all have to have 'portfolio careers' now, and an increasing part of that is the literary festival. The more I chaired events at literary festivals, the more I realised they were actually church services. Think about it: a congregation assembles. There is a reading from the Word, and then a kind of sermon. In place of beseeching prayers, there are audience questions. The chairperson/minister and the author/God are usually sitting on an altar above the audience, a raised dais. At the end there is a collection, in the form of book sales, and petitioners may touch the hem of the Lord, or take a selfie.

If Knox bequeathed one thing to the Church of Scotland, it was a profound reverence for the Book. Every Sunday, the Book was brought out, in front of any individual, and laid down as if it were a trembling newborn. The Book was both legible and inscrutable, a mystery and a commonplace, something both holy and open. The sermon was nothing more than an explication of a complicated text, a lit-crit analysis of only a few lines. It was a book with more than one meaning.

It all made utter sense. Of course, we would almost worship the Book. The Book was God in paper form, the Almighty in covers, the Ineffable in words. It was the solution to every problem if only one were clever enough to riddle out its hidden meanings. It was a book of secrets, and a book so transparent its pages could not be read in strong sunlight, when every word would be doubled recto to verso, a schizophrenia of vision. I knew profoundly that God didn't really have a beard, or hands, or footstools. But I did know he had His own Book as well as the one we placed on the pulpit.

God may have spoken the Universe into being, but he writes its ending. At Revelation 20:12 we read: 'And I saw the dead, small and great, stand before God; and the books were opened: and another book was opened, which is *the book* of life: and the dead were judged out of those things which were written in the books, according to their works.' He has been writing his Book since the outset. But God also edits. In Exodus 32:33 he makes this explicit: 'And the LORD said unto Moses, Whosoever hath sinned against me, him will I blot out of my book.' In the

Psalms we hear several different versions of God as editor: at 69:28, 'Let them be blotted out of the book of the living, and not be written with the righteous', and at 139:16, 'Thine eyes did see my substance, yet being unperfect; and in thy book all *my members* were written, *which* in continuance were fashioned, when *as yet there was* none of them.'

God is not just an editor of his own work: he is a termagant of a commissioning editor. He is perpetually telling people to get on with their writing: Moses is told in Exodus 17:14, 'Write this *for* a memorial in a book, and rehearse *it* in the ears of Joshua: for I will utterly put out the remembrance of Amalek from under heaven.' The priests in Numbers 5:23 are told to 'write these curses in a book, and he shall blot *them* out with bitter water'. At Isaiah 30:8 he is told to get on with it: 'Now go, write it before them in a table, and note it in a book, that it may be for the time to come for ever and ever.' The prophet Jeremiah, at 30:2, is given his upbraiding: 'Thus speaketh the LORD God of Israel, saying, Write thee all the words that I have spoken unto thee in a book.' He is also a rather good publicist according to Daniel 7:10. 'A fiery stream issued and came forth from before him: thousand thousands ministered unto him, and ten thousand times ten thousand stood before him: the judgement was set, and the books were opened.'

Writer, editor, critic: God was all of them. One of the quiet delights of the Second Epistle to Timothy is Saint Paul saying, almost randomly, 'The cloke that I left at Troas with Carpus, when thou comest, bring *with thee*, and the books, *but* especially the parchments.' Knox installed in me a specific vision, that the World is Word.

As I was attempting to resume my future, I used to go into the Church and just sit. Then I would go round the graveyard, and found more than one stone which affected me. One said AU REVOIR, NOT ADIEU and I sneered since I knew that *à dieu* meant 'with God', so the gravestone basically said, See you in Hell. Another was a strange TARDIS-shaped monument with a gooseberry bush growing out of it. Nobody would be brave enough to eat the fruit that bloomed on the dead. The final one, just down by the edge of the cemetery, had always drawn me. IN LOVING MEMORY OF MY DEAR FATHER, CHRISTOPHER LAUDER, WHO WAS KILLED BY LIGHTNING 14TH JUNE 1888 AGED 29 YEARS. Much later, and in a different place, I would stand before lightning, as it crackled and spilt and leapt around like an idiot in front of me. I was blind for a moment, holding a hedgerow of hawthorn. But in its blue and suddenness it was remarkable, and I wanted to be in it – it seemed divine. Instead I staggered home.

But the moment of being almost struck has never left me, that sort-of epiphany, that kind-of transcendence, that momentary joy. To have been in the sparkle and darkness, the insane whiteness and thunderous noise would have been – heavenly. I missed it by moments.

The Church after Knox would be about promises and commitments. I, like everyone, have broken many. But the promise is still the promise and the vow is still the vow. They would insist on that.

Haggai 2:5

According to the word that I covenanted with you when ye came
out of Egypt, so my spirit remaineth among you: fear ye not.

James, the 'wisest fool in Christendom', had managed to keep an
uneasy peace between his kingdoms' churches, by prevaricating
and temporising. Charles was far more reckless and feckless.
Along with the man who actually became Archbishop of
Canterbury, William Laud, he decided to homogenise the state
religion. In 1633, eight years after his accession, Charles travelled
to Scotland with Laud in order to be crowned with full Anglican
rites. Four years later, they attempted to impose the Book
of Common Prayer on Scotland. When James Hannay, Dean of
Edinburgh's St Giles' Cathedral, read the Collect for the Day on
23 July – 'O GOD, the protector of all that trust in thee, without whom nothing is strong, nothing is holy: Increase and
multiply upon us thy mercy; that, thou being our ruler and guide,
we may so pass through things temporal, that we finally lose not
the things eternal: Grant this, O heavenly Father, for Jesus
Christ's sake our Lord. Amen' – a market trader called Jenny
Geddes was having none of it. Purportedly, she threw a 'creepie-
stool', or folding chair, at the minister and shouted, 'De'il gie
you colic, the wame o' ye, fause thief – dare you say the Mass
in my lug?' It precipitated a riot in the church, and then on the

21

streets of Edinburgh. Negotiations with the Crown soon broke down. It led to the writing of the National Covenant of 1638, by Archibald Johnston (later Lord Warriston) and the theologian Alexander Henderson. This was a legal document that committed the Church to supporting the monarch as long as and if and only if the monarch supported the Reformed Church against 'superstitious and papistical rites'. Brought up to believe in the divine right of kings, Charles was learning how the Kirk could restrict his authority and countermand his commands. The National Covenant was as much a political as a religious document, and it insisted that obedience was not mandatory. It is no wonder that Robert Burns named his horse 'Jenny Geddes'.

The success of the National Covenant was unparalleled: around 60 per cent of the population of Scotland signed it. This in itself is remarkable, and testament to Knox's drive for literacy and education among the populace given that the document itself is a complex piece of legal writing, citing Parliamentary acts and General Assembly rulings as much as the Bible. The Covenant was the spark in the north for the ensuing internecine battles and civil war, just as the attempted arrest by Charles of the MPs Hampden, Haselrig, Holles, Pym and Strode in Westminster ignited the English Revolution.

But Scotland soon found that the Covenant bound it as much as it restrained the monarch. When Charles sought to surrender, he did so to Scottish troops and immediately insinuated he was willing to sign the Covenant himself. The Kirk found itself in a cleft stick: the very document which it thought would safeguard its interests now was used to protect the King's person. When Charles was executed by the English Parliamentary forces in 1649, the Scots were outraged – the King of Scots had been beheaded with nary a by your leave to the Scots themselves.

From a tentative alliance with Cromwell, the Scots took up arms against him, much to their misfortune. It is one of the ironies of history that the first time there genuinely was a 'United Kingdom', it was under the Protectorate of Cromwell.

Having pledged itself to the King and the House of Stuart, albeit with stringent conditions, the Church found itself embroiled in the political vacillations and turbulence of the seventeenth and eighteenth centuries. Scotland crowned Charles II as King before England did: they were, as they maintained, a Covenanted People. This put them in direct conflict with the Protectorate. When Charles II was returned to the throne after the 1660 Restoration, he unwisely continued his father's policy of creating uniformity between the Churches. Charles having broken good faith with them, many in the Church refused to countenance the new ruler's policy. A radical group of those who had signed the Covenant or believed in its doctrine – the Cameronians especially – resigned their charges and preached in the open air. (That the Church of Scotland is currently pursuing a policy called 'Church Without Walls', which seeks to galvanise the religious outside of the hour-long Sunday service, is in some ways a direct inheritance of the field-preachers of old: the Church is, as they say, a hospital for sinners not a refuge for saints.) The Church in the north still refused to accept the King as its head. Samuel Rutherford, one of the great theologians of his age, wrote a work called *Lex, Rex* in 1644, arguing that the king was bound by something greater than himself: the law. Charles II was so infuriated by it, he had it burnt by the public hangman when he regained power. Charles sent a loyal enforcer, the Marquis of Claverhouse, to suppress these dissident – in his eyes – conventicles, leading to a period in Scottish history still referred to as 'The Killing Times'. Of course, on the death of Charles II, the Church of Scotland would not accept James VII and II as monarch, given that he was a Roman Catholic; nor would even allies such as Claverhouse accept the Glorious Revolution of 1688, which put Charles II's daughter Mary and her staunchly Protestant husband, William of Orange, on the throne, and broke their contract with the House of Stuart. It meant that former foes fought alongside each other, some for the Kirk's independence and some for the House of Stuart's claim on the crown.

The period created some of the most memorable and ghastly figures in Scottish history. 'Peden the Prophet' must rank highly among them. Born Alexander Peden in 1626, he studied at the University of Glasgow and was ordained, in untimely fashion, in 1660 when Charles II took the throne. Refusing to comply with the Ejectment Act of 1663, he started an itinerant lifestyle, preaching in the valleys of the south of Scotland, and often wearing a mask to elude capture. It seems rather bizarre that the original of Batman might be a Scottish Presbyterian: a figure shrouded in darkness, whose disguise means he might be here, or there, or anywhere, or any number of people. The mask itself – or at least of the ones that have survived – is one of the most chilling objects I know: human hair and leather, as if it came from an Eighties slasher film. Yet when he was arrested and sentenced to transportation to the Americas, the captain of the boat released him on learning why he was being banished. When he died in 1686, and was quietly buried, government troops wanted to exhume his grave so that he, like Samuel Rutherford's book, would be subject to posthumous punishment. The 2nd Earl of Dumfries refused the troops the chance to desecrate the grave.

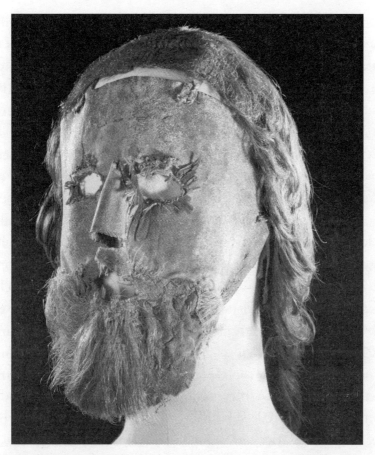

But the ways in which the Killing Times impacted were not always as theatrical as the career of Peden the Prophet. The parish in which I live now comprises many parishes which have been agglutinated together under one rubric as attendance declines. In one – Linton, notable for a medieval wyrm being defeated by a knight carved above the door – the Rev. Robert Boyd was 'outed', in the parlance of the time, under Charles II in 1662, having been minister since 1658. He was 'indulged' to the parish of West Kilbride and replaced by John Broune and then by a non-juror, John Wilkie, who was 'deprived' in 1689, after the accession of William and Mary. At that point the parish roll records that 'Robert Boyd (Restored)' is minister again. He would go on to serve the parish until his death in 1697. Five miles as the crow flies is the parish of Hownam, where their list of ministers records that the Rev. Matthew Ewing was relieved of office by the Privy Council when he refused to pray for William and Mary. Someone has decorated his name with forget-me-nots – he is the only minister whose dates are ornamented. Less than a half-day's hike apart were political and religious differences profound enough to make men be stripped of or give up on their livelihoods: their wives and children would follow them into poverty on principle or by obedience. They may have had less choice than I imagine.

The Kirk managed to be both authoritarian and the exemplar of the anti-authoritarian in the seventeenth century. It was rebellion and it was pure. It was unswerving while it tacked into the wind, buffeted by every dynastic disruption. The memory of it is not just nostalgic persistence, but an active ideology. In the nineteenth century, Sir Walter Scott, under the pseudonym of 'Jedediah Cleishbotham', wrote one of his best novels, *The Tale of Old Mortality*, which was a furious denunciation of the Covenanters as religious terrorists; basically, the Tartan Taliban. Scott's novel was introduced by the real-life Robert Paterson, nicknamed 'Old Mortality', who as late as the beginning of the nineteenth century tended the graves of the Covenanters. Indeed, the commemoration plinth to Peden the Prophet was erected only in 1866.

When I was seventeen, we had a different minister: the Rev. James Watson. I had been instrumental in his being proposed for the post, but that's a story for another time. James was much more 'fundamentalist' – a word he liked before it became tainted by grievance and grief. He meant that there were fundamentals to our faith, and so, on Easter Sunday when I was sixteen, we abandoned the church and headed into the hills, to preach and hear the Word as our Covenanting ancestors had done.

I remember the mist, and sore legs, and our picnic being rather subpar. I think it may have involved hard-boiled eggs and corned beef with pickle sandwiches. I may be wrong. I remember the Eildon Hills looking as if we had never had civilisation here at all, all cloaked in sulking mists and wisps of cloud tangled in the pine trees we never reached. Most of the congregation, to be fair, were quite elderly, and couldn't make it to the summit, so we had the service in a nook of the hill. It was, as Jim said, our return to our origins: a Church that did not involve architecture and did involve at least a rubbed-raw heel or a measure of metaphysical pain. I thrilled to it, and almost the next day decided I would not believe in God. I would instead force him to believe in me.

The Covenant has a simple synonym: a Promise. We promise to do things, and a breaker of promises is someone we shun later. I have made and broken oaths. On that hillside, I never considered the possibility that I was not of the Elect and Chosen. I was reading the Gospels in Latin and Greek, reading commentaries and works such as *Who Moved the Stone* and *Mere Christianity*. I was at the same time wrong in almost every belief I had. I went up the hill determined to reach the summit and was told in the sermon that the laggers-behind, the failures and the weak had as much right to aspire to the summit as I did in my arrogance that I would reach it first. We sang hymns, surrounded by frost and pale daffodils.

The Covenant left an indelible mark on the Church of Scotland. It enshrined a sense of independence, an unwavering and unremittent refusal to submit itself to the mores of the age. It also rooted the Church in both theological nicety and legal precision. When the Assembly came to decide if a murderer might be ordained, it would draw deep on that heritage. It would also refuse to be beholden to mere populist opinion.

The First Book of Kings 16:21

*Then were the people of Israel divided into two parts: half of the
people followed Tibni the son of Ginath, to make him king,
and half followed Omri.*

The village where I live – or villages, as the place, like Budapest,
is two distinct settlements divided by a river and united by a
name, into Town Yetholm and Kirk Yetholm – has two churches,
although only one is now in use. The main church is a striking
building of glossy, volcanic black andesite, threaded through
with red veins, built in 1836 to replace the old thatched building.
Within seven years the town started to build another church,
now a vaguely derelict shell on the edge of a caravan park. At the
time the village had a population of around 1,200; now it has just
under 600. But the closing of the second church had nothing to
do with the falling number of residents or church attenders.

The Disruption of 1843 may seem like a technicality turned
into a crisis. It was in fact a point of principle pursued to its
logical conclusion. The various splits in the church during the
eighteenth century – such as the Burgher and Anti-Burgher
controversy – were preambles to the main cataclysm, and concerned exactly the same sticking point. In short, Knox's *Book of
Discipline* had asserted that the congregation had the final say in
the appointment of a minister. The imposition of ministers

sympathetic to the more Episcopalian form of worship in the seventeenth century by the Crown had been the trigger for the Covenanters to light out for the hills. But even with the Protestant settlement under William and Mary, and then George I, land-owners, who often paid for the upkeep of the church buildings, attempted to circumvent the congregation and fill vacant posts with their preferred candidates.

I had direct experience of the methods of obtaining a new minister as a teenager. In 1988 Tom Donald retired from my childhood parish. Among his last duties was to prepare me to become a full church member 'by profession of faith'. It had meant two months of weekly Bible reading in the draughty manse of the parish to which we were linked. When he stood down, the church had to form a Vacancy Committee – as a new, full member, and the youngest in the church, I was asked to sit on the committee. I was not so secretly rather smug about the appointment. Over the following weeks, ministers from else-where in Scotland would intimate that they might be interested in taking over, and we would visit those whom we thought might be appropriate. It was a kind of ecclesiastical tourism for me, travelling over the country, observing different forms of worship and styles of sermon, and then questioning the minister over lunch. Once we had decided on a minister to call to the parish – the 'sole nominee' in the Church's terms – they would preach in front of the whole congregation, who would then vote on whether to invite them to be 'translated' to our parish.

It was not always so civilised and consultative a process. The seeds of the 1843 Disruption lay a decade earlier. In 1834, the Evangelical wing of the Church had put forward a ruling at the Assembly, called the Veto Act, which allowed congrega-tions not to accept a patron's candidate as minister. This was immediately tested in the case of Robert Young, who had been nominated and rejected for the parish of Auchterarder. He took his case not to the Assembly, but to the civil courts: to the High Court of Session itself, which ruled by eight votes to five that the Church had acted unlawfully in terms of the patron's nominee. The Evangelicals produced a *Claim, Declaration and Protest anent the Encroachments of the Court of Session* in 1842 which insisted that the Assembly took precedence over the Court in spiritual matters, the ordination and induction of ministers included. The Assembly itself – at the time more conservative in outlook and unwilling to set itself against the legal and political authorities – voted against the claim.

Then something unprecedented happened. On 18 May, led by the former Moderator David Welsh, 121 ministers and 73 elders got up and left. They took up temporary residence in Tanfield Hall in Canonmills, a working-class area of Edinburgh, elected the most eminent religious writer of the day, Thomas Chalmers, as their Moderator, and declared themselves the Free Church of Scotland. Within a week nearly a third of all the ministers in Scotland had joined the breakaway group.

It takes a degree of moral effort, nowadays, to realise the courage of those 474 ministers. Ministers lived in tied manses: they had just made themselves homeless. The Church paid their stipends: they had just made themselves unemployed. Their cause may have been just: but they had just relinquished the very pulpits from which they could plead their case. Chalmers, more in sorrow than in anger, expressed their position. 'Though we quit the Establishment, we go out on the Establishment principle; we quit a vitiated Establishment but would rejoice in returning to a pure one. We are advocates for a national recognition of religion – and we are not voluntaries.' 'We are not voluntaries'

31

summarises the sense of ethical obligation they felt. This was not done out of wilfulness or self-seeking. It was done because there was no other choice.

In Chalmers, the new Free Church found its ideal orator. So deep was his influence and so highly praised his commitment that a town in New Zealand is named after him. Just before he took the momentous step of becoming the Free Church's first Moderator, he had been a pillar of the establishment, serving for seven years as the Vice President of the Royal Society of Edinburgh. Born in 1780, he had left his childhood home in Anstruther, in Fife, to attend the University of St Andrews at the age of eleven; as well as holding a position as the minister of Kilmany and attending extra lectures in Edinburgh, he was assistant to the Professor of Mathematics at St Andrews. He became the minister of the St George's Tron Kirk in Glasgow in 1815, and devoted himself to reforming Poor Relief. He also realised that the rapid expansion of Glasgow in the earliest stages of the Industrial Revolution had outstripped the capacity of the parishes to minister to their congregations, and initiated a programme of church building to redress the problem. Chalmers, with the combination of enthusiasm and rationality that typified such nineteenth-century churchmen, applied Adam Smith's laws of supply and demand to the Church itself: without churches, it was understandable that there were low attendances. Before the Disruption he had been made Professor of Moral Philosophy at St Andrews and Professor of Divinity at Edinburgh.

Chalmers understood that if the new Free Church were to succeed, it needed infrastructure as much as the moral high ground. Drawing on his experience in Glasgow, he started an even more ambitious programme. Those seceding from the Church managed, within four years, to build 470 new churches.

A fund of £400,000 of voluntary donations meant that within a generation, the Free Church had created seven hundred churches, four hundred manses and five hundred parochial schools, as well as the 'New College', a training centre for new ministers of the Free Church, with Chalmers as the Principal. That New College would eventually become the seat of the General Assembly, where I would sit, decades later, through an interminable debate about who puts what where in the bedroom.

The Free Church – especially in the remnant that still persists – can be caricatured as the worst of Presbyterian intransigence; a Church devoted to tying up children's swings on a Sunday, being suspicious of organs, and excommunicating, as late as 1988, a figure like Lord Mackay of Clashfern for having the audacity to attend the funeral of a Roman Catholic friend. But in its origin it was not just standing up for democratic rights, it was Modernist in intent. It was engaged with the city when the official Church was still concerned with the village. Nothing conveys its strange modernity better than its use of technology. Two of Chalmers' colleagues and friends from St Andrews were the physicist and specialist on optics David Brewster (who, incidentally, also invented the kaleidoscope) and the artist and photographic pioneer David Octavius Hill. Brewster introduced Hill to Robert Adamson and together they collaborated on a series of photographs of the Free Church Assembly, which were then used to create a nineteenth-century 'history painting' of epic form and scale. Through engravings, lithographs and mezzotints, Scots knew what these successors to the Covenanters looked like.

If you spend any time in any part of Scotland, as you wander around even the smaller conurbations, you will see abandoned churches. The Disruption was the reason why even tiny Yetholm has two churches, one now desanctified. There would be a Church of Scotland and a Free Church of Scotland, as well as, elsewhere, Catholic and Episcopal buildings, Methodist and Baptist and Quaker meeting halls, and the 'tin tabernacles' of even smaller denominations. The abandonment of churches was not just the result of declining attendances. In 1929, the Church of Scotland had acceded to the Free Church's view on the rights of the congregation to choose and summon their own ministers. This led to the Reconciliation, the very outcome Chalmers had longed for in his statement on the necessity of the new Free Church. Suddenly, Scotland had twice as many churches as it needed. On the one hand, the newly harmonised Churches acquired the splendid New College site for the Assembly. On the other, those churches that were not simply demolished were turned into arts centres, rock-climbing facilities, eccentric houses, garage storerooms, ruins. I like the ruins best.

When my grandfather died, we had to sort out the things that had never been sorted out. There were shirts he had bought and never worn; records with no record player on which to play them; photographs of people whose names we'd never thought to ask. There was also a box of keepsakes my grandmother, who had died before him, had left. I doubt it had been opened in decades. But I dutifully went through it, and thrilled to discover certificates for proficiency in Bible reading and church attendance. All of them stated that she had been a member of the Free Church. It seemed a strange and uplifting link in such a melancholy task. She and her family had been on what I increasingly thought of as the right side: those who had sided against seigneurial imposition and for the equality of the plough-hand with the field owner, the factory worker with the factory owner. At the same time, I doubt she cared too much for the religio-political import her grandson put on it. After all, in one of her final conversations with me, she was concerned that there could be no place big enough to hold all the dead, and Heaven must be a crowded, uncomfortable place, if such a place existed at all.

The Disruption was about the equality of believers, as much as the Covenant was. It also gave as equal a voice and vote to the regular churchgoer who left school at fourteen and did the flowers or swept the church porch as it did to the university-trained elder who sat on committees and attended the Assembly. Who might choose whom should be their, or even a, minister? Not, even in a Church that believed in the Elect and the Damned, an Elite.

The Book of Psalms 45:1

*My heart is inditing a good matter: I speak of things which I have
made touching the king: my tongue is the pen of a ready writer.*

All churches have their calendars. Epiphany, Lent, Passion Week,
after Easter comes Pentecost and then Trinity and the other long,
long Sundays after Pentecost, as John Meade Falkner called
them, Advent, Christmas. They have their liturgies and rituals,
their god-clocks of adoration, confession, supplication, thanksgiving and intercession. They also, because they are human, all
too human, have their own little etiquettes and quaint traditions.
There is coffee and cake on every first Sunday of the month.
They stand as the Bible leaves, or they don't. One friend once
told me that at the school she attended, they played their own
little game: listen to the sermon and see if the minister or vicar or
leader of worship in the service says a word beginning with A, a
word beginning with B, a word beginning with C, and if you
ever get to Z – a difficult proposition, since X-rays and xylo-
phones and X-rated rarely occur in sermons – they would all
drop their hymnals. I used to play 'Spot the Sleeper' on occasion.

There are a lot of words that people would use about churchgoers. In one column one might perhaps put 'pious', 'holy', 'nice'
and even 'saintly'. In the other, one might have 'hypocritical',
'sanctimonious', 'fatuous' and 'gossipy'. During – and this is a

word I adore – a quinquennial visitation by the presbytery to our parish, we had to do that most awful of things: a group exercise. What is the best thing about your church? was the question. 'We are awfae welcoming.' 'We're richt open and welcoming.' 'It's a welcoming space here, so it is.' I wondered: if I were to turn up with thirteen heroin addicts from an Edinburgh suburb, how welcoming would these nice people be? If there is one thing I know about the Church it is that there is no such thing as a good Christian. A Christian who thinks themselves to be good is not actually a Christian at all.

These thoughts were badgering my brain as I took my daily walk over to the kirk of Kirk Yetholm. I sometimes sit in the graveyard and just allow space, if not silence. It's never silent. Plants rustle, birds chirrup and caw and cackle, the sheep, safely grazing, will stutter a muted baa. A bush will have bees like movable blooms buzzing. Tractors will thunder along the road and motorbikes will zoom. But with the dead is a space to think. It is a place where a slumber can your spirit steel, among the rocks, and headstones, and trees. I know somewhere in this municipally manicured place my ancestors are buried. I have never found their graves, so many of them are toppled and rotted.

I had a kind of vision involving andesite. Imagine the entire church separating, brick from brick, suspended in the air. The red streaks of the andesite would make it possible to rebuild the original rock, lacing up each stone to its former neighbour. Before the chiselling, before the quarrying, before the bevelling this was one thing and a thing alone. The church might disintegrate and reform as a rock.

But the church stands. It refuses to return to being a stone.

My history in churches: one where I was baptised and seemed faintly glad. Another where my brother was baptised and he screamed the place down as I observed proceedings through the legs of my teddy bear. The cavernous place of school end-of-year services; the beautiful Anglican chapels; the rural churches with flaking plaster and an air of imminent dereliction. A ghastly sermon about AIDS being a warning shot across the bows of promiscuity. A sermon about how there used to be loopholes to God.

I know how this story ends, but I do not know what it means.

The First Epistle of Paul the Apostle
to the Corinthians 1:20

Where is the wise? where is the scribe? where is the disputer of this world? Hath not God made foolish the wisdom of this world?

When the case of James Nelson came before the Assembly in 1984, it was clear there was a deep division between the Church's members as to the ethical, legal and theological evidence and import. The man tasked with chairing their debate was the Moderator, the Very Rev. John M. K. Paterson, a fighter pilot in the RAF during the Second World War who had qualified in insurance and worked in East Africa. It was there, in Nairobi, that he was inspired by the Rev. David Steel and eventually was ordained, serving in Bathgate in West Lothian and then the affluent Glasgow suburb of Milngavie. At the time, he was the Moderator who had served for the shortest period of time before taking the Kirk's highest office – and in some ways, he had been selected at this crucial juncture not because as a former member of the air force he had been complicit in causing death, but because of his facility with accountancy.

He had also served on the Assembly Council set up to inspire, manage and implement change within the Church, and so in himself balanced the more prudent and radical aspects of the

Church. After his moderatorial year, he devoted much time to the Church's policy on ethical investment (such as boycotting South African companies: a stance which always caused me some shame as our church used boxes of South African sherry as communion wine, as the village shopkeeper had a job lot he would sell at a discount), credit unions and debt cancellation. It was Paterson who decided that the audio and visual recording devices be turned off, but pen and paper allowed to the media, on the grounds that the Assembly was, at that point, a legally constituted court, and should be treated with the same reserve awarded to the civil courts. I imagine he also realised that a broadcast of the debate could be counterproductive, that it could overdramatise an already fractious situation. Although the *Scotsman* in its editorial of 21 May claimed that the Church had been bold in advancing Nelson's claim, it said that it had nonetheless been 'timid and intolerant' in refusing the recording, and while conceding that 'those who disagree with the decision . . . may be able to respect the Assembly's motives for making up its mind the way it did', it dryly noted that the Church had neglected 'an opportunity for worldwide publicity'.

The two factions were led by two eminent figures. Opposing Nelson's ordination was the Rev. Dr William Morris, the minister of Glasgow Cathedral. Born in Cardiff in 1925, he had completed postgraduate work at New College in Edinburgh and been an assistant at Canongate Kirk. Ordained into the Presbyterian Church of Wales, he had taken charges in Barry Island and Cadoxton before returning to Scotland. Like Paterson, he cut his teeth in challenging parishes – in his case, Buckhaven and Peterhead – before being offered the more prominent and prestigious role in Glasgow. His obituary in the *Herald* describes him as a 'pillar of the Establishment, but at a time when flexibility was more fashionable and establishments out of favour'. It would be easy to caricature his accomplishments as exactly that – he was from 1969 one of the Queen's Chaplains, and was chaplain to the Royal Company of Archers and (in a coincidence which linked him with Nelson) both Strathclyde Police and the Royal Scottish Automobile Club. He had a marked preference for 'Thou' over 'You', and was described, with all the sly litotes of any obituary, as 'neither by conviction nor temperament a media-minded minister'. He was the author of two books, *A Walk Around Glasgow Cathedral* and *Amazing Graces*. The latter captures a sense of a man of dryly irreverent wit and conservative inclinations – one of the graces is recorded on the website of the former Prime Minister John Major, when he was giving a speech to the Scottish Confederation of Business Interests: 'Oh, Lord, since these good things are of Thy giving / Help us to use them all for wiser living / Each use restraint, reduce inflation / To be a slimmer, fitter nation / And not be sunk in deep depression / When waist and hairlines face recession / Oh, Lord Thou dost with steady interest wait / Which of Thy family will devaluate? / Lord, guide us in our problems from on high / And, for this evening, bless the CBI.'

But Morris's adherence to tradition did not make him temporise or compromise in matters of the gravest importance. In 1968, just a year after he took up his position at Glasgow Cathedral, he established the first ecumenical service there. Given the sectarian resentment and violence then defacing Scotland's second city, this was an act of bravery, especially as it brought him to the attention of the notorious pastor Jack Glass. Glass looked like Svengali and preached like Ian Paisley – who reputedly once referred to him as 'a bit of an extremist'. He was a literalist, an evangelical, a contrarian and profoundly opposed to the Roman Catholic Church. While students in Paris were lifting paving stones and rioting to slogans of 'It is forbidden to forbid' and 'Be realistic, demand the impossible', a more unusual showdown was unfolding in Glasgow. Morris, to his credit, stood his ground, and nudged a process of, if not reconciliation, then at least mutual respect into action. One other facet of his life is of relevance: his wife, Jean, was the chair of the Scottish Parole Board, the very body which had sanctioned Nelson's early release, to which she herself had been opposed.

Supporting Nelson was the Rev. Dr James Aitken Whyte. Five years older than Morris, Whyte had studied philosophy rather than theology, and was an army chaplain before taking his first charge at Dunollie Road, Oban: another minister tested in the tougher parishes before moving to Mayfield in Edinburgh's leafy Southside. His career was mostly in academia, working as Professor of Practical Theology and Christian Ethics at St Andrews, as well as being Dean of their Divinity School, and lecturing at Glasgow and Edinburgh. He had a strong association with the Hope Street Church in St Andrews, and as principal of St Mary's College, St Andrews, had James Nelson as one of his students. Whyte was one of the few people who knew about this particular student's past. One word comes up again and again when reading about Whyte – that he was charming. Yet there is an ambivalence in that word. Is charm more of a virtue than sincerity? Is bonhomie more persuasive than rigour? There is much more to discuss about Whyte's later career, especially as it intersects again with Nelson's, but a sense of his character is easily gleaned from two volumes of sermons he published later, *The Dream and the Grace: Sermons on Healthy and Unhealthy Religion* and *Laughter and Tears: Thoughts on Faith in the Face of Suffering*. The introduction to *The Dream and the Grace* pitches its key with a self-deprecating anecdote about his Leith merchant father giving him Charles Sturgeon's *Metropolitan Tabernacle Pulpit*, one of those volumes of sermons that infrequently grace publishers' catalogues these days. It's amusing, but it has an aftertaste of pawky self-regard; as does a three-sentence letter he sent to the *Scotsman* about the privatisation of the Trustee Savings Bank, the year after the Nelson case: 'Bankrobbery is the word we use to describe the crime of stealing from a bank. But what word can we use to describe the stealing of a bank? Words cannot describe the crimes of government!' Some of the later sermons, with anecdotes about broken computers or golf rounds, have a vaguely wheedling desire to be relevant but casual, revealing but informal. That said, his finest sermons are masterpieces of the form.

Whyte may be characterised as representing a more liberal strand of the Church; but liberals are as capable as conservatives of digging in deep their heels. The conservative thinks that the liberal will breezily abandon centuries of accumulated wisdom; the liberal thinks the conservative blinkered and hidebound to truths derived from first principles. Yet their strategies reflect positions one might not have expected. Whyte organised a petition, signed by sixty-one ministers. He relied on his oft-mentioned charm, sincere though it was, while Morris argued from moral absolutes. Whyte had a campaign that was amenable to the media, even while they were sceptical of his position, while Morris was not given to soundbites. Whyte was thrawled to the Spirit of the Age, while Morris was attuned to the Unchanging Spirit; Morris would change only when change was absolutely necessary, Whyte thought change imperative.

Whyte was every bit as uncompromising as Morris. In one sermon he writes that 'the idealist is a revolutionary who wishes to destroy the present in order to build the perfect future. The reformer takes what we've got and tries to make it a bit better. The reformer usually does more good than the revolutionary.' I suspect that Morris thought Whyte more revolutionary than reformer. Looked at from one perspective, the Nelson case seems like a man who wanted a crusade pitted against a man who demanded proofs. Yet one of the Church's mottoes – raised during the debate about same-sex marriages – is *semper reformanda*, a snippet of a phrase which the thinker Karl Barth attributed, without much proof, to St Augustine: *ecclesia semper reformanda est* – 'the Church is always to be reformed'. The Reformation initially undertaken in Scotland had been a Revolution as well.

Morris, Whyte and Paterson were all men of integrity. Their integrity took different shapes, was focused on different aspects of the case, was aligned to different visions of what the Church ought to be, could be and would be. Their own words best encapsulate their differences and similarities. In the opening sermon of *Laughter and Tears*, Whyte tackles an age-old Christian problem: is this world a vale of tears to be endured or a gift to be enjoyed in all its serendipity while we walk but lightly on its sward? (As the novelist Horace Walpole put it, 'a comedy to those who think, a tragedy to those who feel'.) Whyte resolves the sermon, about a friend's funeral, with these words: 'I had a strong sense then that he was enjoying it too, and that already we were sharing with him in the laughter of heaven.' Morris told *Who's Who* that he endeavoured 'to be good, careful and happy, not always simultaneously'. All three men – and Nelson – are now dead. To have interviewed them would have been a privilege. I suspect, however, there are some things that all four would care to say only to the Almighty.

Deuteronomy 17:8–9

*If there arise a matter too hard for thee in judgment, between blood
and blood, between plea and plea, and between stroke and stroke,
being matters of controversy within thy gates: then shalt thou arise,
and get thee up into the place which the LORD thy God shall
choose; And thou shalt come unto the priests the Levites, and unto
the judge that shall be in those days, and inquire; and they shall
shew thee the sentence of judgement.*

'Facts', wrote Robert Burns, 'are chiels that winna ding / An
downa be disputed.' But the interpretation of facts is a rather
different proposition altogether. What were the events of which
the Assembly could be sure?

The *Scotsman* reported on 7 January 1970 that James Robert
Nelson, then aged twenty-four, had been sentenced to life
imprisonment for murder. The crime was committed on
30 October 1969. The *Evening News* adds in its report of the
same day that he was employed as a joiner and that the murder
took place at 92 Barrachnie Road, Garrowhill, now a suburb of
Glasgow, then in Lanarkshire. The trial took place at Airdrie
Sheriff Court, under Advocate-Deputy Donald Macaulay. The
accused was reported to have agreed with the Advocate-Deputy
that he had 'lost his head'. Newspapers, like the Bible in some
respects, are inventories of unintended surrealism. Above the

story about the murder Nelson committed, the *Scotsman* ran a story – admittedly much smaller – about the Cinematograph and Television Technicians Union being refused a pay increase, and so the Scottish Television serial adaptation of Walter Scott's *Redgauntlet* would, unfortunately, be transmitted in black and white. Were these of equal importance?

Scots law has a similar distinction to English law regarding murder and manslaughter, although in Scots the latter is referred to as culpable homicide. For a charge of murder to be brought meant establishing the state of mind – *mens rea* – of the accused. In involuntary culpable homicide, the *mens rea* is not present; in voluntary culpable homicide it is, but there are mitigating circumstances. Nelson had been interviewed on 14 November by Dr Leonard Cook, the consultant psychiatrist at Hartwood Hospital in North Lanarkshire, who determined that he was a 'perfectly normal individual'. The killing was an 'act carried out in cold rage rather than with ungoverned fury', but noted it was also 'the end and result of years of deprivation of affection'. A plea of diminished responsibility was rejected by the jury. Nelson was detained at HMP Edinburgh, commonly but unofficially known as Saughton.

Although he had been brought up in a religious household, it was in Saughton that Nelson felt drawn to the Church: the reasons for this and motives are not established facts, and will be considered elsewhere. The prison chaplain at the time was the Rev. Tom Downie, and he encouraged Nelson to study the Bible and to sing in the prison choir; he was latterly helped by another chaplain, Rev. Malcolm Rew, who taught him New Testament Greek. Nelson did not talk much about his time in Saughton, though he did refer to it as 'more Dickensian than Victorian' – an odd distinction – and said he had to defend himself only twice from attacks. One former prison officer mentioned that Nelson had a 'reputation as a hard man', but this is not corroborated in any of the other statements. It was also in Saughton that he first met the Rev. Stewart Lamont, who was then recording a radio programme for the BBC's Religious Affairs Department. Although he was a 'lifer', Nelson successfully appealed for parole after ten years in prison.

When he was released in 1979, he had already started to preach. He made his way to Roseheartie in Aberdeenshire, where the Rev. Rew had taken up his first charge, and helped out with manual tasks and driving the church minibus. Although some of the congregation knew that the minister's guest had been serving a life sentence, it does not seem to have attracted any resentment or concern.

In the same year he applied to study divinity at St Mary's College, St Andrews. At least three people, tutors at the college, knew about his past: the Rev. James Whyte, Professor Bill Shaw and the Rev. William Henney, the minister of Hope Park Church. While there, he met another student, Georgina Roden, thirteen years his junior, and also studying for the ministry. Professor Shaw was to be best man at their wedding in 1983.

The Church has rigorous and confidential interviews for its 'selection schools' for ministers, including psychological assessments. Nelson applied to enter into the ironically entitled 'probationary period', which meant applying to the presbytery of St Andrews for the equally ironically entitled 'trials for licence'. This licence could be denied for various reasons – the presbytery could turn him down on the basis of 'life, literature or doctrine', or if its members were unimpressed by his preaching. The meeting in Cupar in April 1984 was, in the words of a source to the *Herald* newspaper, 'a shambles', with 'members embroiled in procedural complexities and disagreements about the rules'. There were fourteen objections laid before the presbytery, some of them simply placed on the table and not read for fear they were defamatory. On the first vote the presbytery divided, with 41 voting he should not be sent for trials for licence, and 41 maintaining that he should. A motion was put forward that members not be allowed to abstain in the vote, and it was held again, resulting in 43 against and 42 in favour. At this point, Nelson did not know if he would take his appeal to the Assembly himself, or whether the Rev. Whyte would do so on his behalf.

Prior to the meeting of the presbytery more details about Nelson's life had become public, and the means by which they had done so exacerbated an already difficult situation. On 17 November 1983, the *Glasgow Herald* had a scoop: 'Kirk Secret Out: A killer set to become a minister'. The story ran over several days, with both reporting and opinion pieces by the same Stewart Lamont who had spoken with Nelson in Saughton. The Kirk Session of Hope Street Park had decided on 17 November to appoint Nelson as a probationary minister, conditional on their presbytery agreeing to the licence the following year.

The newspaper articles revealed that Nelson had voluntarily handed himself over to the police at the scene of the crime on 1 November 1969, two days after the killing. It mentioned that at the time he 'liked to be a big spender' and had a 'flashy car'. There were financial difficulties and he recalled he had 'been burning the candle at both ends'. Even in terms of his post-prison academic career, it was noted there had been 'a couple of resits'. But there were voices more supportive of his application. The Rev. Ronald Blakey, Secretary to the Church's Education and Ministry Committee, said, 'His story underlines the very dramatic way the power of the gospel of Christ can make and remake an individual human life.' Nelson's new wife said, 'If facing this situation makes people face their Christian commitment then it's a good thing.' In a follow-up profile Lamont described Nelson as a 'tragic and sad figure who is now a happier and wiser man', as well as revealing that he had agreed with Nelson that should he ever wish to tell his story, he would write it.

Revealing the story on the day of the Session vote was a provocative and risky strategy which had immediate consequences. One elder, and former session clerk, Malcolm Black, resigned from the Church, citing the 'moral pressure put on them to come to a quick and favourable decision' and 'an atmosphere where people felt obliged to conform'. There were allegations of undue secrecy and that the presbytery provided 'a completely inadequate statement'. The Church was forced to deny a 'conspiracy'. There were also technical objections: although it was normal for the congregation and the Session to provide the funds to pay for a probationer's stipend, the Church itself had offered to pay instead from central funds. If not exactly blackmail, it looked very much like pecuniary inducement.

Black's resignation may have rested on technicalities and a clandestine suspicion of the 'high heid-yins' of the Church manipulating the congregation. In an astonishing letter from his wife to the *Scotsman* a few days later, more strident reasons were advanced. Blame was apportioned to the State – 'life imprisonment should mean life imprisonment. We are forever reading in the newspapers of crimes re-committed by those who have been released after serving only a fraction of their sentence' – to Nelson himself – 'could he not have gone to Bangladesh to help the poor and the starving, or done some Christian work among the misguided and hopeless youth of our own cities, without putting himself into a pulpit?' – and the Church itself – 'The Bible is being quoted by the Kirk with regard to forgiveness and "a second chance" but what about the Ten Commandments? On the radio on Saturday was heard an adulteress who was not even allowed to have a blessing on her second marriage. Where is the forgiveness here?' It ends hoping that those who 'sumpathise [*sic*]' with her 'daring' husband should speak up, as 'secrecy should not merely be the privilege of the Kirk'.

When the Church report was published, it was felt necessary to include in section 2.3.10 that 'The Kirk Session accepted the provisional proposal albeit that information about the circumstances came to them in the first instance through the press and not through the Committee and Mr Henney. The Committee and Mr Henney sought, but were not able to avoid this and regret, albeit they cannot accept responsibility, that inconvenience and embarrassment were caused to interested parties.' Indeed, the scoop in the *Herald* estimated that only twenty people knew the secret that James Nelson was a convicted murderer: twenty people knew beforehand, but on publication of the story, hundreds of thousands did, whether they were churchgoers or not. The article even noted that Ronald Blakey's brother, Bill, who taught religious education at Madras College in St Andrews, was not privy to the secret, though it noted that he 'will be recommending Jim Nelson to take the next step toward a dog collar'.

One of the strangest features of the role of a minister in a community is an unspoken sense that, despite the equality of all believers and the centrality of the belief sometimes called 'the doctrine of total depravity' or 'radical corruption' – St Augustine's view that we are all contaminated by original sin – the minister must somehow be morally superior to the congregation. Moral infractions by ministers – from exorbitant expenses to adulterous affairs to slighting the convenor of the flower circle – are regarded as more transgressive, and more culpable; and these instances are not even criminal actions. The minister in some ways is a scapegoat to the community: they are judged more harshly, and such condemnation almost acts to alleviate the guilty consciences of their condemners. If even the pious fall short, the middlingly unworthy can breathe a sigh of relief. Who among you, readers, can with hand on heart honestly claim they have never found in a pop-singer's coke habit, a comedian's tax evasion, a newsreader's fling or a foot-baller's thuggery a tiny glimmer of moral elevation? Of course you are not perfect; but you are delighted you are better than that. You may have faults, but they have failings; you may have done a wrong thing, but they did the bad thing.

The articles set a number of the facts about the case before the general public. How these facts were to be interpreted and judged would be played out in the Assembly by serious theologians and biblical exegetes, as well as in opinion pieces and editorial columns in newspapers, in pub conversations and family discussions. I do not remember what I actually thought of the case, other than that it intrigued me. I suspect, given I had once referred to a local bully as 'not the sort of person who should come to church' to my piano teacher, that my views were fairly inchoate and reactionary.

But it was only the Assembly that would have responsibility for the final decision. For the Church of Scotland, there was only one authority that could be appealed to directly: the Bible itself.

THE FIRST SERMON

The Second Book of Samuel 16:7

And thus said Shimei when he cursed, Come out, come out, thou bloody man, and thou man of Belial.

The Bible, one might assume, is unequivocal about murder. It is one of the big Thou Shalt Nots. But even that unambiguous commandment is a vexatious and problematic injunction, so much so that it is probably best if we go through all the evidence, slowly, and – like a detective in a drawing room with the assembled suspects nervously gasping at their cigarette holders and swirling their pink gins – spell out the entire story while keeping an eye on whomever might dart for the French windows.

The first murderer is the third human being: Cain, the firstborn son of Adam and Eve. He murders his younger sibling, Abel, and yet everything about the narrative is counterintuitive. Cain is the 'tiller of the ground' and Abel 'the keeper of sheep', but this conceals a crucial difference. Abel is not some kind of merry shepherd, lolling on grass knolls and tootling on a rudimentary flute while his poor brother ploughs and furrows and scatters and reaps. Abel is the first person in the Bible with blood on his hands. He slaughters his flock to make a sacrifice to the Lord, and the Lord prefers the smell of firstling fat to the wheat, beans, kale

52

and turnips that Cain offers. The disgruntled Cain ignores God's chastisement over his sulking, and attacks his brother with fatal consequences. Most people, I would wager, think that at this point the Bible says, 'Whoso sheddeth man's blood, by man shall his blood be shed: for in the image of God made he man.' Those lines actually come later, just after God has reduced the population of humanity to precisely eight with the Flood. Cain's punishment is banishment and – which is strange in the light of the later retributive demands in Numbers and Leviticus – an absolute command that no one harms Cain. Cain is sent to the Land of Nod, and cursed for seven generations. As a child I was always told, as the night drew in, that it was 'off to the Land of Nod' (when it wasn't 'Up the Wooden Hill to Bedfordshire'), and I wonder if my mum condemning her own firstborn to Cain's place of exile hasn't been a factor in our relationship ever since.

Who is the second murderer in the Bible? is a good, and annoying, question. The answer is Lamech, Cain's great-great-great-great-grandson. He is also the first polygamist, and what scholars sometimes describe as a 'culture hero'. His wives are Adah and Zillah, meaning 'dawn' and 'shadow', and Adah has two sons, Jabal and Jubal, whose names mean 'shepherd' (again) and 'musician'. From his other wife, Lamech has a son, Tubal-Cain, and a daughter, Naamah, whose names might mean 'blacksmith' and 'pleasure'. As a culture hero, Lamech is responsible for bringing into being all the things we think of as civilisation: agriculture, culture, technology, easefulness. Lamech – slightly out of nowhere – sings or laments, 'Adah and Zillah, Hear my voice; ye wives of Lamech, hearken unto my speech: for I have slain a man to my wounding, and a young man to my hurt. If Cain shall be avenged sevenfold, truly Lamech seventy and sevenfold.'

Now: who was the second murderee of the Bible? The text is curiously silent, and, just as nature abhors a vacuum, hermeneutics abhors a hiatus. The Rabbi Shlomo Yitzhaki, a millennium or six later, came up with a brilliant explanation. Lamech was blind, and Tubal-Cain helped him hunt. Tubal-Cain saw something on the horizon and his father unleashed an arrow. The thing on the horizon was none other than Cain, and Lamech then killed Tubal-Cain – bizarrely, by clapping. Tubal-Cain was the seventh generation after Cain, so the prophecy is fulfilled, the bloodline extinguished. Significantly, the Bible at this juncture tells us that Adam and Eve had a third son, Seth.

Murder stalks the rest of Genesis, but more often it is deferred or threatened. Abraham, in his test of faith, is brought to the brink of murdering his son, Isaac, only for, metaphorically, God to blink first and provide a ram caught in a thicket instead. Is Abraham a murderer? The twentieth-century philosopher Bernard Williams's concept of 'moral luck' is useful here. Williams argued that chance plays a greater role in ethical judgements than we might care to admit: the person driving at eighty miles an hour through night streets is less culpable than the person driving at eighty miles an hour through night streets who hits a pedestrian. It depends, in part, on the difference between intention and consequence: neither person intended to kill a passer-by; one, unluckily, did. Abraham's absolute intention was to kill Isaac. Imagine instead that God gave a gun to Abraham and told him to put it to Isaac's temple and pull the trigger. Abraham does just that, only God has not put any bullets in the gun. The intention was there; the consequence different. Einstein held the belief that 'God does not play dice.' Indeed he does not: he plays with loaded dice.

There is only one other murder in the book, in Chapter 34.

Dinah, the daughter of Jacob and Leah, has been raped by Shechem, the heir apparent of Prince Hamor the Hivite. In one of the more ghastly juxtapositions, after the rape Shechem decides that 'he loved the damsel, and spake kindly unto the damsel'. Jacob and his sons learn of the rape, but keep silent even when Shechem's father arrives to plead for Dinah's hand in marriage on Shechem's behalf. The sons, Simeon and Levi, 'deceitfully' propose that they will agree to the match on the condition that the Hivites circumcise themselves. So in love is the rapist that the Hivites agree to this, and then, 'when they were sore' from doing so, Simeon and Levi arrive at the city and kill Shechem, and every other man for good measure, before taking their children, wives and livestock as spoils, as well as retrieving their sister. Jacob is furious – not because his daughter has been raped, or because his sons have just committed the first genocide by humans, but because their political situation in Israel is still precarious, and the massacre has 'troubled me to make me stink among the inhabitants of the land, among the Canaanites and the Perizzites: and I *being* few in number, they shall gather themselves together against me, and slay me; and I shall be destroyed, I and my house.' The brothers' question in response – 'Should he deal with our sister as with an harlot?' – goes strikingly unanswered. Simeon and Levi are mentioned later, in Chapter 49, as 'instruments of cruelty *are in* their habitations'. Having already committed a city-wide slaughter, it is perhaps surprising that they only throw their brother Joseph in a pit a few chapters later. Commentators on this passage are gloriously at odds with each other. Shechem is at fault, not just for sexual abuse, but for undergoing the circumcision purely for gain. Simeon and Levi are at fault for using the covenant of circumcision for their own nefarious ends. Matthew Henry, the seventeenth-century divine, harrumphed, 'See what became of Dinah's gadding!' What is conspicuous in this story – between Jacob's cold pragmatism, the belligerence of Simeon and Levi, the actual assault on Dinah and the queasy behaviour of Shechem and Hamor – is that God is utterly silent. There is no condemnation from on high, nor is there any demand for vengeance. According to the Midrash, a text which explicates the thornier aspects of the Torah, Simeon and Levi were fourteen and thirteen years old at the time.

After Abraham, the most significant of the Old Testament patriarchs is Moses, and there is no ambiguity about his rap sheet. At the end of Genesis, the sons of Jacob join their brother Joseph in Egypt, to escape the famine afflicting the land. They have subsequently prospered, to the extent that Pharaoh has decreed that all male Hebrews are drowned at birth, as a means of controlling the population. Moses is saved by Pharaoh's daughter and, although a Hebrew, has been brought up in Pharaoh's palace. In Chapter 2 of Exodus, he sees an Egyptian beating a Hebrew and after 'he looked this way and that way, and when he saw that *there was* no man, he slew the Egyptian, and hid him in the sand'. As was the case with his great-grandfather, Levi, the murder is not unprovoked; but nor is it commanded. But Moses is not, like most murderers, particularly good at murdering, since in the next two verses, when he intervenes in a dispute between two Hebrews, the aggressor upbraids him, saying, 'intendest thou to kill me, as thou killedst the Egyptian?' So much for him seeing that *there was* no man. The news reaches Pharaoh, who orders that Moses is to be killed. Moses escapes into the land of Midian, where he will encounter God in the form of a bush which burns but does not turn to ash – the symbol of the Church of Scotland – and where his destiny as the saviour of the

Hebrews, the one who will take them into the Promised Land of Israel, will be made known to him.

There will be many, many more deaths over the next forty years when the Hebrews are in the wilderness; but none of the deaths, strictly speaking, can be considered a murder. Moses twice oversees the judicial execution of lawbreakers: in Leviticus, a blasphemer whose father was Egyptian and whose mother was called Shelomith of the Tribe of Dan is stoned to death on Moses' orders; and in Numbers, a man who was found picking up sticks on the Sabbath receives a similar punishment. In each case, God himself sanctions the act.

The most blood on Moses' hands is that of his fellow Israelites. When he discovers that in his absence they have made a golden calf and are worshipping it, Moses turns to his family – the Levites, who have a certain expertise in these matters – and orders them to 'go in and out from gate to gate throughout the camp, and slay every man his brother, and every man his companion, and every man his neighbour'. In total, three thousand are killed. One conspicuous survivor is Aaron, who had ordered the construction of the golden calf, and was dancing naked around it when Moses returned. Aaron instead became the first high priest. Two of his four sons, Nadab and Abihu, were burnt to death on the day of his investiture, for not correctly making the offerings to God; his grandson, Phinehas, is later commended for spearing through a man called Zimri and his Midianite lover Cozbi with a single javelin. In Phinehas's defence, the double murder does stop a plague God has sent because of the consorting with Midianites. It kills only twenty-four thousand Israelites.

What makes the story of the retribution against the golden calf worshippers so deeply strange is why Moses had been absent. He was on Mount Sinai, seeing God face to face, and receiving

the Ten Commandments. After the four 'theological' commandments – have no other God but me; do not make graven images
of God; do not take God's name in vain; remember the Sabbath
and keep it holy – Moses is given six 'ethical' commandments, in
order: honour thy mother and father, thou shalt not kill, thou
shalt not commit adultery, thou shalt not steal, thou shalt not
bear false witness, and no coveting of your neighbour's wife,
manservant, maidservant, ox, ass or, indeed, anything of his
whatsoever. The Israelites dancing down below have not, at this
point, even heard of making graven images, although they
have been told often enough that their God requires undivided
worship. Moses smashes the tablets with the commandments in
his anger at their idolatry, which prevents any of them seeing
that the Levites are about to break commandment six in a rather
dramatic fashion. Or are they?

It seems so clear. 'Thou shalt not kill' in the older King James
Bible; 'You shall not murder' in the New International Version;
'Do not commit murder' in the Good News Bible; 'Do not kill' in
the Common English Bible. Even in translation, the difference
between 'kill' and 'murder' is vast, but most definitions can
sketch out a line of division. It is impossible to murder uninten-
tionally. The eighteenth-century legal theorist William Blackstone
defined murder under common law as being 'when a person, of
sound memory and discretion, unlawfully kills any reasonable
creature in being and under the king's peace, with malice afore-
thought, either express or implied'. So a mad murderer is not a
murderer (not being 'of sound memory and discretion'), nor is the
hangman a murderer (since it is not done 'unlawfully'), nor are
members of the army guilty of murder (the enemy being, quite
literally, not under the king's peace), nor is an act of unthinking
temper or self-defence resulting in death a murder (so Moses,

seeing the overseer beat the Hebrew, might be accused of culpable homicide, but Levi and Simeon's cunning plan counts, definitely, as murder). The Greek and the Latin versions of the Bible continue the difficulty: the Greek Septuagint uses *phoneuo* – which means 'kill' or 'murder' – and the Latin Vulgate uses the verb *occidere*, which can mean anything from 'to kill', 'to murder', 'to slay', 'to perish', 'to fall down', 'to torture', 'to smash' or even 'to set', like the sun.

Going back to the original Hebrew is even less enlightening. The verb used in the sixth commandment is *ratsach*, which is generally taken to mean 'to murder' or 'to slay'. What is rather more surprising is that the sixth commandment is the first time the word *ratsach* is used in the Bible. It never occurs in the Book of Genesis, despite the multiple murders: instead, the verb *harag* is used when Cain kills Abel, when Lamech kills the young man, when Simeon and Levi slaughter the Hivites, and when Joseph's brothers plot to kill him. *Harag* occurs 163 times in the Bible; *ratsach* a mere 46 times. *Ratsach* tends to be used in very specific contexts, most notably in the rules concerning 'cities of refuge' in which people who have inadvertently or accidentally killed someone might seek sanctuary. The most frequent term used is *nakah*, with over five hundred occurrences. Like the Latin *occidere*, it has multiple and metaphoric uses, including 'to smite', 'to defeat', 'to wound', 'to slaughter' and 'to strike'. It can also mean 'to clap' or 'to applaud', which perhaps explains the surreal idea that Lamech clapped Tubal-Cain to death. When Cain worries that any man might now kill him, he uses the verb *harag*; God uses *nakah* when outlining his plan for a universal deluge. *Ratsach* seems to have had a specific, almost legal, nuance, but the precise nature of that nuance is lost to us.

Immediately after God gives Moses his ten-step moral

programme, he expands and extrapolates on this new ethical universe, adding a further 613 positive and negative *mitzvot*. These range from not muzzling an ox while ploughing and not having sexual relations with your own father, to ensuring that scales and balances are honestly calibrated, only making toilets outside the camp and wiping out the Amalekites. Sometimes the point has to be made strenuously: you are not to love the idolator, you are not to cease hating the idolator, you are not to save the idolator and you are not to say anything in the idolator's defence. There are also specific rules and regulations regarding punishments, many of which, on the face of it, completely contradict the sixth commandment. Capital punishment is invoked with surprising frequency: sorcerers, adulterers, murderers, contempt of court, disobeying parents, human sacrifice and picking up sticks on a Sunday are all to be punished with death. The text vacillates between *harag* and *nakah*. The more precise *ratsach* is never used. If we were to find a term to translate it, 'non-lawful killing' might be the best approximation.

The story of the judges and kings of Israel (and latterly the kings of Judah, when the kingdom fractures in two) requires another shift in preconceptions. First, it is crucial to remember that when the Israelites ask for a king, to be like their neighbouring nations, God is adamant that it is not a good idea. He nevertheless capitulates to the demand, with the warning that having a king might not be all that they expect; and the litany of feeble, idolatrous and vicious brutes that comes later bears him out. Second, the judges – men raised up by God in a time of warfare to protect Israel – are 'heroes'; but our idea of heroism is far too coloured by the chivalric and knightly notions of the Middle Ages. Heroes in the Ancient World – whether Gilgamesh of Mesopotamia, Achilles and Herakles in Greece, Aeneas in

Rome or Joshua and Samson of Israel – are a very different proposition. Archaic heroism is a ruthless affair, and the judge is the man who will do what must be done, regardless.

About some of the judges we know no more than a name. Othniel, we are told, killed Chushan-rishathaim. Ehud's little narrative reads like the Bible's first excursion into noir fiction. Israel has again strayed from the path of the Lord, and as a result the Moabites have conquered it. God raises up Ehud, a left-handed man. He conceals a dagger half a metre long against his right thigh and is sent to give the king of the Moabites, Eglon, a gift, and tells Eglon he has a secret message to be passed on to him in private. In Eglon's summer chambers, the servants dismissed, Ehud pulls out his weapon (which, one presumes, startles the king because it is in an unexpected hand as well as because it is there at all) and stabs him. The reason for the inordinate length of the dagger is revealed: 'Eglon *was* a very fat man'. Indeed, the folds of Eglon's belly even cover the shaft of the blade, and 'the dirt came out' of him, or, in modern English, he shat himself. Ehud then escapes to the hills. This is biblical heroism. There is no indication whatsoever that Ehud is anything other than a character to be admired and emulated.

Later judges form a similar pattern. Shamgar kills six hundred Philistines with an ox-goad. Gideon kills the princes Zebah and Zalmunna, but not before offering his son Jether the opportunity to do the deed. Jael, the wife of Heber the Kenite, kills Sisera, the general of the Canaanite king Jabin, by driving a tent-peg through his temple. An unnamed woman smashes the skull of Abimelech, the tyrannical bastard child of Gideon. Much later, in the Book of Judith the eponymous heroine decapitates the Assyrian general Holofernes, after feigning to seduce him and plying him with wine.

Of all the judges, Samson is the most famous and the most incomprehensible. His birth is miraculous, since his parents were infertile, and they are told that he must be raised as a Nazirite. The word 'nazir' means 'consecrated', and Nazirites were not a clan or a tribe, but those who took a series of special vows. Samson breaks all but one of those vows: he drinks alcohol, he touches dead bodies, he marries a non-Israelite. However, he does not voluntarily have his hair cut, one of the signs of a Nazirite: his mother is told 'no rasor shall come upon his head'. He is, for a hero, an out-and-out hooligan. When he teases his new in-laws with a riddle and a bet, they persuade his new – and oddly unnamed – Philistine wife to wheedle out of Samson the answer to his puzzle. (The Philistines even threaten to burn Samson's wife and her parents if she cannot accomplish this.) On being given the correct answer, Samson has to kill thirty men from Ashkelon in order to pay the wager. Samson's wife is given to his friend, and his ex-father-in-law offers him her younger sister instead. This really aggravates Samson, who ties together 150 pairs of foxes with a burning firebrand between their tails, and lets them loose on the Philistines' crops. In retaliation, the Philistines really do burn his ex-wife and former father-in-law. Samson's revenge is to kill one thousand Philistines with the jaw-bone of an ass (which miraculously doubles up as a source of water when his strength flags). The Philistines have to wait another twenty years to settle their score with Samson. They employ a prostitute, Delilah, to discover the origin of Samson's divine strength. Three times he gives her a false answer; three times the Philistines who are tasked with implementing the stratagem are unceremoniously killed. One would think that, having three times had evidence that his lover is collaborating with his enemy, Samson would be extra careful not to tell Delilah that his strength derives from his unshorn hair – the only Nazirite vow he had not broken. Nevertheless, in true fairy story fashion, that is exactly what he does. Captured, blinded and made to drive a treadmill in the prison, Samson's final humiliation is to be the entertainment at a festival to the Philistine god Dagon. When they allow him to rest by holding the pillars of the temple, he pulls it down in an act of suicidal retribution, killing three thousand men, women and children.

Samson is the third-last Judge of Israel before the period when kingship is established and the last to be mentioned in the Book of Judges. But the end of that book moves from the grisly belligerence of war to a kind of ancient torture porn, a story so inexplicably horrific it would test the faith of the most literal-minded fundamentalist. In Judges 19, a Levite goes to Bethlehem to bring home his concubine, who has 'played the whore against him' and for four months has been living at her father's house. Her husband seems to get on well with her father, and she consents to return with him. There does not appear to be any bad blood or recrimination between them. They decide not to stop in Jerusalem but to press on to Gibeah, a city of the Tribe of Benjamin. No one is about, except for an old man who gives them shelter. At this point, 'certain sons of Belial' turn up, beating at the door, and demanding the old man send out the Levite so that they can have sex with him: an exact repetition of the story told about Lot, the angels and the inhabitant of Sodom. The old man refuses, and offers his daughter. The sons of Belial are not appeased, and so the Levite's concubine is sent out. She is raped all night, and staggers back to the house at dawn, expiring on the doorstep. The Levite then takes her home and dismembers her body into twelve parts and sends one part to each of the twelve tribes of Israel. The twelve tribes meet and decide that the Tribe of Benjamin must be punished for their lack of hospitality. A civil war ensues, with the Israelites led by Phinehas, the grandson of Aaron. After two days, when the Benjamites seem to be gaining the upper hand (each man could 'sling stones at an hair *breadth*, and not miss'), God allows the Israelites to win. A tenth of the 400,000-strong Israelite army is killed, and of the 26,000-strong Benjamite force, 25,100 are killed. In the aftermath of the Battle of Gibeah, the Israelites lament that the Benjamites have been driven to the brink of extinction, especially since, over and above the military conflict, they have sworn that no daughter of any of their families can marry into the Tribe of Benjamin. To redress the situation, the Benjamites are, at first, allowed to pillage and massacre the city of Jabesh-Gilead, slaying all the men and non-virgins and carrying off the virgins. This, however, is not sufficient, so the other eleven tribes sanction the raping of their daughters when they are dancing at the Feast of Shiloh. The moral of the story? 'In those days *there was* no king in Israel, *but* every man did *that which was* right in his own eyes.'

What on earth can be made of this passage? Flavius Josephus, the first-century AD Romano-Jewish historian, wrote in *Antiquities of the Jews* that the 'certain sons of Belial' had always intended to rape the concubine as they had been struck by her beauty. That she was a concubine and that she had 'played the whore' vexed most Christian commentators: Matthew Henry, a theologian on the verge of the Enlightenment, noted that, as an adulteress, she ought to have been stoned to death under Mosaic Law. Her rape and murder show that even when her husband has forgiven her, God has not and '*culpa libido fuit, poena libido fuit*' – since lust was her sin, lust was her punishment. Indeed, Henry is so shocked at the implication of homosexuality, he seems positively relieved to be able to conjure up this piece of ethical algebra. The prize for the most tendentious reading must go to the seventeenth-century bishop – and satirist – Joseph Hall. With reference to the rape of the daughters at Shiloh, he observes 'the ambush of evil spirits carry away many souls from dancing to a fearful desolation'. The perpetrators of the original crime are 'sons of Belial'. Although the word 'Belial' would later be used for a variety of demons and evil spirits, its etymology means 'worthless' or, perhaps more pertinently, *beli ol*, 'without yoke'. They are, literally, unfettered.

It does not seem coincidental that this story comes at the end of the Book of Judges and just before the account of the transition to kingship – indeed, Saul, the first King of Israel, comes from the city of Gibeah, an early coded warning that his rule might not be as idyllic as the Israelites hope. The entire narrative is the culmination of the Book of Judges' exploration of moral paradox. If the first five books of the Old Testament – the Pentateuch – were about the revelation of the law, the Books of Joshua and Judges are about the revelation of the limits of the law. In Chapters 19 to 21 of Judges we see that overlooking transgression leads to transgression; that attempting to avoid transgression leads to transgression; that punishing transgression leads to transgression; and that making amends for transgression leads to transgression. The oath of the tribes is a metonym for the operation of the law: in order not to break it, the Israelites allow their daughters to be taken by the Benjamites, rather than given. The law reveals its structural inability to instil the very virtues it was designed to inculcate. To abide by the law is, at a moral level, to break its very reason for existence.

Moving to the First and Second Books of Samuel, the First and Second Books of Kings and the First and Second Books of

Chronicles is to move from the semi-mythical to the semi-historical. There is no less warfare, and no less murder, but it is braided around court politics and dynastic struggles. If figures like Joshua and Samson recalled heroes like Achilles and Hercules, then Saul and David, Joab and Adonijah resemble the imperial families described in Tacitus and Robert Graves's *I, Claudius*.

With the rise of the kings comes the rise of the prophets. Eli, the penultimate judge and high priest, blesses Hannah, the wife of Elkanah, who then conceives and gives birth to the last judge and first of the major prophets, Samuel. Samuel will anoint Saul (and later David) as king, but their relationship is not unequivocally harmonious. God had warned the Israelites through Samuel that 'ye shall cry out in that day because of your king which ye shall have chosen you; and the LORD will not hear you in that day'. Nevertheless, because they do not wish Samuel's dishonest sons to become judges, they persist in demanding a king. Saul's reign soon deteriorates. After his victory over the Amalekites, and forgetting the specific *mitzvot* regarding that people, Saul does not kill their king, Agag. Samuel upbraids Saul, tells him that the kingdom is 'rent' from him and 'hewed Agag in pieces'. Saul is condemned for not killing; later in the book he is condemned for wanting to kill David, the young man whom God has selected as his successor.

David seems self-evidently to be morally superior to Saul. Despite Saul's frequent plots against his life, David soothes him in his God-inflicted madness and twice refrains from assassinating Saul. These moments seem to prefigure the ethical universe we associate with the New Testament. But the unholy war between Saul and David for the kingship of Israel, and the external war against the enemies of the Israelites mean he has plenty of blood on his own hands. The story of David defeating the giant Goliath is part of general culture; his slaying of one hundred Philistines to provide the dowry for Saul's daughter (said dowry being one hundred Philistine foreskins) less so. The tensions between the dynastic feud and the ongoing conflicts lead to very morally ambiguous decisions. Saul tries to commit suicide on the battlefield when the Amalekites have defeated him. When an Amalekite soldier brings David the crown and tells him how he finished Saul off, David has no compunction in killing him.

Amid this welter of conspiracy and vendetta, one act of moral turpitude stands out. Narrated in the Second Book of Samuel, Chapters 11 and 12, it concerns David's seduction of Bathsheba, the wife of Uriah the Hittite. It was sufficiently heinous an offence that, in the First Book of Kings 15:5, we read, 'Because David did *that which was* right in the eyes of the LORD, and turned not aside from any *thing* that he commanded him all the days of his life, save only in the matter of Uriah the Hittite.' Having made Bathsheba pregnant while Uriah is away on a military campaign, David resorts to various ruses to conceal the matter. Uriah is recalled, and urged to sleep at his own home (and, one assumes, with his wife). The noble and non-Israelite Uriah instead sleeps outside, honouring the troops in the field who are still under canvas. David then gets him drunk, but still Uriah will not return home. David then takes more drastic action, and has Joab put Uriah where the fighting is at its fiercest when he returns to the front line. Uriah is killed.

The underhanded nature of Uriah's death is almost more despicable than the death itself, and David's sin is soon brought to light by the prophet Nathan. David – unlike so many of the biblical murderers – repents. His punishment is sadistically appropriate. Just as he murdered by proxy, he suffers by proxy:

God's vengeance strikes down the child he had with Bathsheba rather than the guilty king himself. David's guilt was supposedly expressed in Psalm 51; his regret over the child's death has sometimes been discerned in the background of Psalm 9. The unnamed child is, bizarrely, replaced: David and Bathsheba's second child, Solomon, will inherit the kingdom. He in turn will harbour murderous thoughts about Jeroboam, his chief super-intendent, who would be responsible for the ten tribes breaking away to form the Northern Kingdom on Solomon's death and breaking the unity of Israel. Proverbially wise and just, Solomon could nonetheless be ruthless: his half-brother Adonijah would be killed on his orders.

With the splintering of the kingdom, the Bible ushers in a sequence of variously brutal, hedonistic, vainglorious and intemperate monarchs in both Judah in the south and Israel in the north. Some, like Ahab and Athaliah, have become bywords for vice; a few, notably Josiah, who reformed the temple and rediscovered the scrolls of Moses, stand as out exemplars in an otherwise unremitting cycle of coups d'état. The focus changes, and the voice of moral authority moves more and more to the prophets. Even the prophets, however, can be men of blood. Elijah, the greatest of them, brought down fire on the troops of King Ahaziah and killed the prophets of Baal whom Ahab had allowed to worship their god. His successor, Elisha, is teased by children who call him 'bald head', angering God so much he sends two she-bears which kill forty-two of them in the Bible's most baroque homicide. But the poetics of the book are, subtly, shifting. Ezekiel makes skeletons come back to life in a vision of the restored Israel. As the prophetic books end, with Malachi saying, 'And he shall turn the heart of the fathers to the children, and the heart of the children to their fathers, lest I come and smite the earth with a curse,' one can almost imagine that the New Testament will be less bloodthirsty.

Before going on to exceptions and qualifications, it is of singular importance to stress that in the life of Jesus as it is presented in the Gospels, he does not kill anyone. There are numerous reasons why texts such as the Gospel of Thomas and the Syriac Infancy Gospel are not considered canonical: that they depict the infant Jesus as peculiarly prone to sudden miraculous murders is not the least of them. In the Gospel of Thomas, jostling Jesus, throwing stones at him and spilling water he has carried all earn immediate death, although most of the divine deaths are reversed. Even here, the emphasis is on resurrection rather than retribution. One part of the Gospel of Thomas, where the boy Jesus breathes life into clay birds, is repeated in the Qu'ran, at Sura 5:110, the Sura of the Table (which is also the sura which exhorts peace between Muslims and the other 'People of the Book', Jews and Christians).

Although Jesus does not commit any murders, the two people who did most to establish the Church in his name are far less than spotless. Simon Peter, the future St Peter, is always depicted as rash, and in the Garden of Gethsemane, where Jesus is arrested before his crucifixion, Simon chops off the right ear of Malchus, the servant of Caiaphas the High Priest. His name is recorded in John's Gospel; the fact that Jesus immediately reattached the severed ear is recorded only in Luke's Gospel. Mark and Matthew record the ear incident, but not the perpetrator, and only Matthew has Jesus then saying, 'for all they that take the sword shall perish with the sword'. But Simon Peter is more than just an attempted murderer, albeit one with the supreme moral luck of attempting the murder while standing next to the Son of God.

The other pillar of the Early Church, and in many ways Peter's rival, was originally Saul of Tarsus. Saul, in his own words, was a Pharisee – a member of one of the four strains of Jewish thought and belief after the end of the Kingdom, the Exile in Babylon, the Return to Israel and the Roman occupation. They were most noted, in the first century AD, for their opposition to the 'Jesus Cult'; and after the Second Destruction of the Temple by the future Roman Emperor Titus in AD 70, their codified writings – the Mishnah – became the basis for Rabbinical Judaism. As a Pharisee, Saul tells us that he studied under Gamaliel. The Mishnah itself says, 'Since Rabban Gamaliel the Elder died, there has been no more reverence for the law, and purity and piety died out at the same time.' Acts of the Apostles speaks of Gamaliel reverently and approvingly as one who was considered and thoughtful towards these new 'apostles'. Despite this, his student, Saul, was vehement and vengeful towards these new followers of 'The Way'. Saul never met Jesus in the flesh. When he was travelling to Damascus, he met Jesus as a blinding light that asked, 'Saul, Saul, why persecutest thou me?' He answered, 'Who art thou, Lord?' and the reply came, 'I am Jesus whom thou persecutest: *it is* hard for thee to kick against the pricks.' Saul became St Paul: we will discuss his conversion more fully later. But as Saul, he had not just been a zealous propagandist against Christianity. In Acts of the Apostles, Chapter 7, Saul is present when Stephen makes his long speech before being stoned to death. The opening of Chapter 8 is even more explicit: 'And Saul was consenting unto his death.'

Simon Peter and Saul, or St Peter and St Paul, the two most influential men in the life of the Early Church, are revealed as an attempted murderer and an accessory to murder. They are the culmination of a tradition running through the history of the Church. From Abraham to the brothers of Joseph to Moses to

Joshua to Gideon to Samson to Samuel to Saul to David to Solomon to Elijah to Peter and Paul, murder is not a stumbling block which prevents an individual from participating in God's unfolding plan: it is practically a precondition, a qualification for such a role.

Yet the three humans who, for Christians, are the epitome of perfidy are not murderers in the strictest sense. Judas Iscariot, Pontius Pilate and Joseph Caiaphas may have set in place the motions that would lead to deicide and the crucifixion of Jesus, but none of them dealt the fatal blow. The hiatuses in these sections of the Gospels are intriguing. Why would the name of the Roman who actually hammered in the nails or who thrust the spear into Christ's torso not be recorded in the text? Although we learn that Judas dies – in two different versions: in Matthew he commits suicide; in Acts of the Apostles, 'falling headlong, he burst asunder in the midst, and all his bowels gushed out' – nothing is said of the fate of Caiaphas or Pilate. In Dante's *Divine Comedy*, Judas is at the centre of the Inferno, but alongside the murderers of Caesar, Cassius and Brutus (who at least wielded the knives themselves), not alongside Caiaphas and Pilate: Pilate has to support the whole of Limbo on the shores of the River Acheron; Caiaphas is crucified and trampled on by others in the Circle of Hypocrites. Judas, Caiaphas and Pilate have responsibility and deniability. Judas merely organises the arrest, Caiaphas demands the trial, and Pilate washes his hands. The miasmic nature of their guilt became spiritually toxic. It metastasised, so that the rest of the Sanhedrin, the baying crowd, the Roman occupiers, all became tainted. The long and inglorious history of Christian anti-Semitism begins with a non-murder.

Schoolboy debaters and professional campaigning atheists can easily point to any number of verses of the Bible that narrate

acts and behaviours we would deem morally culpable, from Lot's
incest with his daughters, to the vituperative horrors of the Book
of Revelation, to the Psalmist exhorting 'happy *shall he be*, that
taketh and dasheth thy little ones against the stones' (a line
curiously omitted from Boney M's version of 'By the Rivers of
Babylon'). But in the entire text, one crime goes unmentioned.
Nobody in the Bible kills their own mother. It was this crime
specifically, matricide, that James Nelson had confessed to on 1
November 1969.

The Book of Joshua 1:8

This book of the law shall not depart out of thy mouth; but thou shalt meditate therein day and night, that thou mayest observe to do according to all that is written therein: for then thou shalt make thy way prosperous, and then thou shalt have good success.

The Bible made me an atheist (for a time, at least). Having been admitted into the Church, having served on the vacancy committee, I wanted to teach at the Sunday School for younger children. That meant, I decided, not just skimming the Bible and knowing key passages, but really reading it; reading it in the way I was reading Camus' *L'Étranger*, Shakespeare's *King Lear* and T. S. Eliot's *The Waste Land* at school. I soon realised why churches have lectionaries of weekly and daily recommended reading. The Bible must be the book that most people – believers as well as non-believers – 'know' in the most fragmented, aleatory, non-linear and decontextualised form. It is a truism often trotted out that the Bible is not a book but a library; I would argue that the 'Bible' we have in our heads rather than on the shelves is more akin to a text produced by William Burroughs's cut-up technique.

I was already having doubts, not about the book, but about its believers. I had gone along to the lunchtime introductory meeting being run by the Christian Union, which endeavoured to provide answers to commonly asked questions and reassurance for needling doubts. One of the very first topics they tackled was 'How do we know that the Bible is true?' The needlessly jolly sixth former leading the discussion explained that in the Second Epistle to Timothy 3:16 it is stated that 'All Scripture *is* given by inspiration of God.' Even at that age I could recognise a circular argument. And there is another problem that a close reading of the Bible begets. There are numerous books to which the Bible refers – such as the Book of Jasher, or the Book of the Wars of the Lord, or the Book of the Chronicles of the Kings of Judah, let alone the missing 1,825 Proverbs of Solomon, or his lost 1,004 songs. The Bible memorialises its own incompleteness.

The Gideon Bible, in its preface, stresses that although the Bible was written in different times and different places by very different people, it 'perfectly agrees in doctrine'. I had quickly realised that this simply could not be true. Why, for example, does Matthew 12:30 exhort 'He that is not with me is against me', when Luke 9:50 is equally clear that 'he that is not against us is for us'? There were plenty of logical inconsistencies that I could think I was thinking deeply about: for example, when Jesus prays on the Mount of Olives and an angel appears to him, we are told the disciples are all asleep – so who witnessed the visitation? Did Jesus just tell them about it later? How could Moses be the 'author' of the first five books of the Bible when they include the story of his own death? These were scarcely original thoughts, and I was not in any way really perturbed by them. I was perfectly accustomed to reading books symbolically, metaphorically and allegorically. That was what we were learning to do in the five hours and twenty minutes of compulsory English lessons we had each week.

It wasn't even that the Bible was so monstrously blood-thirsty – it was no more or less bloodthirsty than the *Iliad* and the *Odyssey*, or Livy's account of the Punic Wars. Teenagers are, anyway, slightly fascistic I have always felt, intrinsically drawn to gore, to certainty, to strength: they adopt lunatic convictions because they have no power. They adore purity and hate shams, backsliding and hypocrisy despite their fumblings and swither-ing affections and affectations; they are creatures of fundamental will and constrained action. I was unlike most teenagers and an exemplar of what I now think of teenagers. No, it was – though I could barely articulate it to myself – that it wasn't as well written as, say, *Paradise Lost*. *Paradise Lost*, for example, had far more convincing and better described monsters (at the time I avidly read *Dungeons & Dragons* rule books; not to play the silly game with other silly children – I was fairly solitary and certainly judgemental – but to pore over the detailed accounts of Demo-gorgon and Baphomet and Azathoth). I felt an almost blas-phemous thrill to read in the introduction to my Penguin Selected Poems of Milton that another poet, William Blake, had said of him that he was 'of the Devil's party without knowing it', and, moreover, that all true poets were. True poetry, in my then unwavering opinion, did not consist of dull and contradictory genealogies, sententious and often flat-out-wrong apothegms – Psalms 37:25 for example, which was carved around the hall of the college I later went up to ('I have been young, and *now* am old; yet have I not seen the righteous forsaken, nor his seed begging bread') is just clearly inaccurate – non-sequiturs of no possible relevance, venomous tirades and simply primitive shards of myth (what on earth was that business about the Israelites defeating the Amalekites – always on about the Amalekites, our Jehovah – only if Moses could keep his staff held aloft in

Exodus 17? Some form of proto-phallic imagery? If so, having his brother and the mysterious Hur help him keep his arms up seems even more bizarre). I decided to read the Bible as Literature, and as Literature the Bible let me down. That now I find many of those passages the most fruitful to contemplate is a sign, if not of maturity, then at least of the possibility of change.

No, that is not strictly true. I would like to think that as a literary critic, literary criticism was instrumental in all the decisions I made, whether naïve or considered. To an extent it was, and the only part of being a teenager that seemed to make it worth the acne, the bullying and the underestimation was that pleasing plasticity of mind. I could believe – and understand, I thought – anything for the duration of the time I was reading a book. Two books made an abiding impression on me, and I do remember in my prayers the public library in Galashiels, in the days before computers, when I came across them in the capacious stock. One was Malcolm Muggeridge's *A Third Testament*. It introduced me to St Augustine, Blake, Pascal, Tolstoy, Bonhoeffer, Kierkegaard and Dostoyevsky. They would form the core of any emergency library I might need to this day. The other was Malcolm Bradbury's *The Modern World*, a study of Dostoyevsky, Ibsen, Conrad, Mann, Proust, Joyce, Eliot, Pirandello, Woolf and Kafka. They would form the rest. One unsettled me in the idea that there could be a continuing revelation about the nature of God; the other, that in the absence of God, Art could make meaning for us instead. I also thought Virginia Woolf was almost unbearably beautiful: in a way, my first crush. One name appeared in both books, but not as a subject – as a kind of *éminence grise* that haunted these figures whose work I was devouring. Nietzsche.

This all sounds very high-minded, and it was. At exactly the same time, I was indulging in the kind of futile, self-centred, pique-fuelled and absurdly embarrassing practice most teenagers do, and I don't mean *that*. I mean blasphemy. I would, with an internal smirk, silently say the Lord's Prayer backwards. Or I would replace it all with antonyms and opposites: Your Mother, Who Aren't in Heaven, Damned Be Your Name – and such childishnesses. When I neither was struck down by lightning nor managed to summon a figure of smoke and darkness, I smirked the more. You could say 'I don't believe in God, the Father Almighty, Maker of Heaven and Earth' in church and *nothing would happen at all*. You could even mumble it when everyone else was saying the Creed. Instead of taking this to be proof positive that all this was just an etiolated superstition, I took it to be being overlooked and shunned by the immortal realm, deliberately disparaged and pointedly ignored. As I say, the teenage years are egomania at a cellular level. What I didn't know then is that those who meddle with darkness make themselves known to darkness.

In 1986, having been engrossed in the BBC's *I, Claudius*, I decided to watch a new programme with its star, Derek Jacobi, in it: Channel 4 had adapted *Mr Pye*, a 1953 novel by Mervyn Peake (I had, of course, read the Gormenghast trilogy, and bored people about how much better it was than Tolkien). The plot is simple: Mr Pye is a genuinely good man who travels to the island of Sark, which is small enough for him to conduct an experiment in reconciling old foes, promoting happiness and generally creating a more benevolent world. This he does, with such success that he grows wings. Mortified by this development, he resolves to do bad deeds to make the wings recede, which they do, at the cost of two nubs of horn emerging on his forehead. Stranded between angel and devil, he becomes the outcast, the scapegoat, the sacrifice: the harder form of good. I gloried in it and was furious at it, because reality was so insufferably less strange and more enstranging. This is not this book's most awkward confession: after watching it one night – I had the supreme luxury of a television in my bedroom – I fashioned a pair of wings out of paper, sellotaped them to my back, slept the whole night wishing the world was, well, more imaginative, and then peeled them off in the morning, secreted them under my bed, and put on my school uniform. I wanted the world to be operatic and apocalyptic. I would have sold the soul of mine I increasingly doubted existed for just one glimmer of it being anything other than rather predictably mundane. *Mr Pye* was my first heartbreak. The paper feathers never took in the night. They were also quite uncomfortable.

The Bible had promised drama on a cosmological scale and delivered duty on a quotidian level. That was what eroded my faith, a simple sense of being slightly bored in a nondescript Borders village, with loving parents and annoying brothers, and taking tea with old ladies with whom you had to forgo, politely, a second slice of cake before graciously accepting it nevertheless. Looking back, I see it was one of those old ladies who gave me a kind of golden thread that linked the pious little shit me to the bumptious atheist me to the fractious believer me. At school we had had to watch Willy Russell's *Educating Rita* – which I rather enjoyed, truth be told – and a persistent tease of me became Maureen Lipman's exquisitely drawled 'Wouldn't you just *die* without Mahler?' It seemed to squeeze every poisonous drip of philistine inverted snobbery into just six words. Having heard 'Stuart would just die without Mahler' for the umpteenth time one day, I decided to seek out this Mahler and like his work whether or not I did. (A better definition of 'thrawn' I cannot give.) One of the elderly ladies of the village had a very good record collection – she once advised me that you have to listen to Schoenberg several times before the liking sets in. I took Mahler's Eighth Symphony, the Symphony of a Thousand, and it opened a little chink in me that has never closed. At the time it was perfect: a hymn to the Holy Ghost that was also a panegyric to creative endeavour. 'Veni, veni Creator Spiritus' it begins – 'Come, come, Spirit of Creation' – and whether that spirit was brooding over the unformed waters before the making of the world or a quill scratching in Austria made not one jot of difference.

There was not a single, unique, Damascene moment when my faith frayed. It was like a Victorian butterfly pinned behind glass, or a slightly gauche child's sampler left in a chest, or a set of crocus petals pressed in a family Bible – most likely around the Second Book of Chronicles, which nobody really likes or reads. My faith was perfect and preserved, intact and entire. Nothing of it had decayed except everything. Only pressure kept it pure. But unseal the mounting, open the box, let light fall upon the page, and a slight miracle happens. What seemed to be exquisite and intricate turns out to be nothing but ash, in the blink of an eye.

The Book of the Prophet Isaiah 49:15

*Can a woman forget her sucking child, that she should not have
compassion on the son of her womb? yea, they may forget but
I will not forget thee.*

The person whom James Nelson murdered was his mother, Elizabeth. Although Nelson had moved out of the family home to live first in digs and then with his older sister, Anne, in Glasgow, the financial difficulties he had run into meant he was again living with his parents. His mother was fifty-eight at the time of her death. According to a different report, she was sixty-two. It is not the only point on which those closest to the affair disagreed about fundamentals.

On the night of 30 October, Nelson came home while his sister and his father, Robert (who as well as being a joiner was the church organist), were at choir practice. The sequence of events is simple enough to record, although the atmosphere which pervaded the Nelson home is more difficult to reconstruct. According to the earliest newspaper reports, a row developed when Nelson sat in his mother's chair and was told 'to get the hell out of it'. Later, Nelson would say that as the argument escalated, his mother been 'very rude about my girlfriend's character'. The earlier version is far less genteel: she referred to his girlfriend as a 'dirty whore' and a 'lazy bitch'. Nelson claimed to be 'staggered' at her tirade. Something, he later said, 'just snapped'.

While the *Herald* reported that the court was told Elizabeth was struck 'with a metal rod or similar instrument', the *Scotsman* was more specific. Nelson went to the kitchen and took down a baton from the wall of the hallway. This perplexed me until I found a later reference to the weapon being his grandfather's police truncheon. This perplexed me even more: what kind of family has such an item as a decoration or ornament? Nelson battered his mother about the head until she fell to the floor, and the baton itself broke. He then went to the garden to get a brick, but in his testimony says that does not remember using it: 'I remember I came to my senses with the brick in my hand and it was obvious that I had used it.' When the full details of his case became public knowledge in 1983, the phrase 'demonic rage' is used; moreover, he told Stewart Lamont that it was 'as if an outside force were motivating him'. In the actual moment, 'He felt no horror at what he had done.'

Nelson dragged his mother's corpse into the garage, which, he later claimed in a newspaper interview as the Assembly was assessing him, was to 'reduce the shock' for his father and sister when they returned. This does not to me seem rational: it might reduce the time between their realising she was not there and discovering the body by minutes at most. He then washed, changed his clothes, packed an overnight bag, put £25 in his wallet and left into the night. The verb 'put' is curious as well. Did he select that amount from a larger store of cash he had? Why not take the entire amount? It seems a euphemistic alternative for 'stole'. Moving the body was a key fact that led to the charge being murder rather than culpable homicide, because it indicated a degree of rationality and planning. He was 'clearly aware what he was doing and knew the nature and quality of his acts'.

In an interview in 1998 with the *Daily Record*, his sister described the scene. 'When we opened the living room door there was blood everywhere. It was all over the walls and the carpet. There was a huge six-inch pool of blood near the settee and a trail of blood to the kitchen, then to the garage. Our Labrador dog was hiding under the settee. My father and I followed the trail of blood to the garage and my mother was lying there on her stomach. Her head was to one side and I could see her brain where it was caved in at the back.' Her mother's body, she noted, was still warm.

At the trial, Nelson had claimed diminished responsibility, and the psychiatrist had described 'years of deprivation of affection' and mentioned that 'only two people in Nelson's life had given him affection – his sister and his girlfriend'. In the *Glasgow Herald* in 1983, Nelson clarified much of this. The murder was the 'culmination of a long, unhappy childhood' and he felt 'a hopelessness that there would ever be any end to the tension'. It transpires that he had to work for his father from a young age, something he clearly resented. He recalled 'being thrown out of the house when I was eight because I wanted to go and help a friend instead of working. I was told to go and live there if I was not prepared to work.' At the age of twelve he ran away from home. Both son and daughter describe their father as an authoritarian figure: 'a classic Calvinist' according to Nelson. 'It's true ours was never a happy household,' said Anne. 'The tension in the house was terrible.' Nelson referred to his father's reaction when the wife of their local minister 'ran off'. Rather than feeling any sympathy for the minister, he was 'against him'.

When the news of Nelson's attempt to become a minister broke, his public statements were very cautious about the dysfunctional nature of his family. He says that he felt unwanted, that he was a 'mistake' – the sense is of a joyless, stern and stifling background, devoid of warmth and fondness. His sister was far more explicit when she spoke to the media fifteen years later. She admitted there were 'persistent beatings' and that the father 'often took a belt' to both children. 'If social workers had been as vigilant as they are now we would have been taken away,' she ruefully remarked. 'When my father lost his temper he really lost it. When he started to hit us he forgot when to stop.' It cannot be a coincidence that this describes exactly how her brother behaved on the night when he killed their mother.

It puts Nelson's earlier words in a very different context. He said in the 1983 *Glasgow Herald* article, 'Normally you would expect your mother to defend you against parental aggression.' This is peculiar again: Nelson says 'parental' not 'paternal'. The articles emphasise his mother's 'vitriolic' outbursts, and, in cataloguing his complaints, Nelson's gripes can seem peevish: being made to work, not being allowed to see friends, even at one point saying the money he received 'was never a gift. I was paid a full wage, but I suppose I was underpaid in the sense that I was his son and was making his business a profit.' Nowhere does Nelson mention being physically brutalised and assaulted by his father. Yet if he lived under such cruel conditions, it would make things like running away much more explicable. But it raises a question I cannot answer: why did Nelson not kill his father? If I were a betting man, and having such facts before me as I do, I would certainly wager that the psychomachia being waged at 92 Barrachnie Road would have ended in the son killing his father, not his mother. Was his mother a substitute victim, because it was easier, and more cowardly, to kill her?

In her interview, Anne had an almost throwaway line that lingers: 'But my mother defended Jim at every turn.' Does this mean that she physically defended him during the beatings, or that she stood up for him when he was being berated? It is starkly at odds with Nelson's own condemnation of his mother's failure to intervene in the 'parental oppression'. Memory is always something reconstructed rather than retrieved, and every member of that family would have replayed certain memories until the prick of consciousness drove a deep groove into their minds, even obliterating the original sensation. A story retold and retold and retold to oneself becomes something stronger than the truth.

When he told the story in public again, around the same time as his sister was giving her account, Nelson gave another version of the events that took place. On Channel 4's late-night programme *After Dark*, alongside a very interesting panel to be met later, Nelson said in leaden, mostly monosyllabic words, 'There was a police baton hanging in the hallway. I was under a tirade and I just lost my temper and smashed her skull with this baton.' There is a lot to unpick here. Why does he use the deictic 'this' baton? It was not in his hands when he spoke, and, in a way, it quite clearly still was. The use of 'skull' is eerie. One might say he smashed his mother's head, or face, or countenance, or visage, but a skull is something you are really aware of only when someone is already dead. Then there is that little word 'just'. I just missed you. Just what I needed. Just as usual. Didn't he just? 'Just' is a weaselly little word with a lot inside it: it is both 'barely' and 'exactly', 'narrowly' and 'thoroughly', 'merely' and 'utterly', 'possibly' and 'perfectly', 'rightly' and 'quite'. With all these ambiguities, there is another horror: he has just killed her. Again. He is always killing her. 'I think of it infrequently,' he said at the time of the Assembly, 'as a nightmare.' His sister said she was 'haunted by nightmares'. One of those sentences is a simile, distancing, the other an actuality, reliving.

During the Channel 4 programme Nelson also said, 'I reckon it would be a sustained attack over possibly five minutes.' Much to untangle here too, not least that the sentence contains two modifiers that introduce ambiguity: 'reckon' and 'possibly'. But the tense is odd as well. Why does he not say, 'I reckon it *would have been*'? The crime is in the future as well as in the present. It is a moment out of time and therefore throughout time. Why this is hell, nor am I out of it, as Marlowe's Mephistopheles says in *Doctor Faustus*. Yet he goes on in the very next line: 'Think'st thou that I who saw the face of God . . .'

One delightfully frosty morning in late autumn I sat in my garden with a turnip – a swede or a rutabaga depending on where you are reading this – a watermelon and a hammer. I didn't have a police truncheon to hand. I set the timer on my phone for five minutes, and, well, to use the parlance of some of the rougher bits of Hawick, set aboot the turnip. I suppose I could have Googled which root vegetable or fruit is closest to the mass and density of a human head, but the idea of someone in Cheltenham having to review my Internet search inquiries seemed unfair, and it was too much bother anyway. Then I did the same with the watermelon. It was not a pretty sight by the end, with pink and yellow splatters everywhere, like a bad abstract expressionist painting, including all over my boiler suit (I had been prepared for that eventuality at least). Overall, the watermelon was relatively uncomplaining and the turnip far more resilient, but

STUART KELLY

the latter was pretty much mash by the end as well. I learned
nothing from this experience at all. I thought the exertion and
the effort would give me a sliver, a glimpse into what Nelson had
done. Instead it taught me that local horse riders can be spooked
by a bespectacled man pulverising greengrocery in his garden.
To be completely truthful, it did teach me something. Five
minutes is a long time.

Stupidly, I hadn't needed to do it at all. A few years ago my
brothers were badly beaten up after asking some chaps – *'chaps'?
Can you hear yourself, Kelly? – just say it, they were neds, chavs, gadgies,
scum* – to stop swearing on the bus. They were attacked from
behind by a bunch of cowards, and luckily two off-duty policemen
were also alighting at the same time. 'They were kicking his head
like it was a football,' one testified. Their defence was that they
'thought they were up for a square-go'. So square, two held one
of my brothers back while another one pummelled his head
with his trainers. I did not recognise my brothers when they
came home: lips, eyes, teeth, noses, even hair all made wrong.
That had been seconds.

Given that my childhood was – asthma and melancholy aside
– as close to idyllic as I can imagine, it is a pompous intrusion to
imagine that I could ever empathise with Nelson, or magically
make engrained rage by battering a wersh fruit and a tough tuber.
But I might be able to sympathise with him nevertheless. There
is also one other piece of information which it would be wrong
not to divulge at this point. In her interview, Nelson's sister
repeatedly states that she cannot forgive him, and that subject is
so fretted and fraught and friable, it will require another sermon.
But she does say several things that deepen the mystery. She
visited him just after his arrest, when he was detained in Barlinnie,
a prison that would contain an eldritch analogy to his own

incarceration, and 'the conversation was strained and there was no mention of what had happened'. She went to see him again before the trial, and asked him why he had killed their mother. 'He just never answered. I have never had an explanation.' Once he was sentenced and moved to Saughton, she persisted in trying to maintain their relationship. She 'visited a few times over the next seven years but we never really spoke of my mother. On the one occasion we did he called her a whore and that is just not true. That was when I stopped visiting.'

The actions rhyme with the father and the words rhyme with the mother. So what did the father say?

The Gospel According to
St John 15:1–3

I am the true vine, and my Father is the husbandman. Every branch in me that beareth not fruit he taketh away: and every branch that beareth fruit, he purgeth it, that it may bring forth new fruit. Now ye are clean through the word which I have spoken unto you.

It would have been supremely unlikely if Robert Nelson wholeheartedly agreed with his son's self-representation as an unloved and exploited child driven to an act of furious aggression by intolerable circumstances. Nevertheless, there is much between the lines in his public statements. 'We were not gushing parents,' he said, 'but we did love him and went out of our way to make him happy.'

When Nelson's story came to light, he was at pains to correct one impression that had been given. At the trial, it was claimed that his father had said, 'I never want to see my son again.' In fact, Nelson claimed, his father had visited him in prison between 1971 and 1978 and had even helped him in buying his theology textbooks. (His father's recollection is somewhat different: he said that if Nelson passed his exams 'that would be repayment' – so they were a loan disguised as a gift.) But something happened in 1978 which meant that an already strained relationship became to all extents and purposes irreconcilable. According to Anne they had a meeting when Nelson was released on parole, 'but they had a huge falling out about something. Dad never told me about what.'

'She was a faithful, dutiful wife and mother,' his father claimed. 'In no way was she unfair to her family. The only friction was caused by my son's behaviour.' Some of his descriptions chime with his son's own confessions about his life at the time. 'He always wanted to look big, to be above others. That got him into trouble as a flashy, big spender, living above his means. It's a very bad story . . . we both got sickened by his rebellious nature.' He argues against many of son's claims: 'A lot of people have told me I was too soft with him and gave him too much. But I often warned him that he would get into serious trouble if he carried on the way he was doing . . . We tried to talk him into leading a better life, including seeking professional help. It did not work. He said he suffered total subjugation for twenty years, but it was my wife and I who suffered and I am suffering still.' I wonder what kind of 'professional help' is meant here. The family do not seem the type that might have considered counselling or psychotherapy; indeed, there would have been very few practitioners in the Scotland of the 1960s. The Presbyterian virtues of self-reliance and self-discipline seem far more in keeping with the image of the family the various interviews give. The Church, perhaps, which plays such a strong role in their lives? Would being 'forced' into the ministrations of the minister be a factor in Nelson's eventual crime?

In Anne's interview she mentions that, as well as the physical beatings, there was a great deal of psychological belittlement. They 'would never amount to anything', her father had said.

Throughout all their interviews there is a perceptible yearning for approval. When Nelson discussed his father breaking ties with the local minister when his wife left him for someone else, he gave an example of how this breach manifested itself. 'He ordered me to come out of the Scouts attached to that church (Parkhead East). It was just prior to me receiving my Queen's Scout badge, for me a tremendous achievement. The Scout-master could hardly believe it when I told him.' In his interview, Robert begins by saying, 'I have never wished him to be a failure.' One can detect a note of almost blighted admiration when he says, 'His acceptance to the ministry should be a joyous and proud day for me – but it's not. It must have been a very high calling – if it was a calling. I thought he might have given up the ministry because of what has happened between us . . . if only he had chosen another job. He has picked the worst one as far as I'm concerned.'

Another oddity is his father's insistent claim: 'I am no Calvinist.' This is clearly a retort to Nelson's phrase 'classic Calvinist'. This is very strange indeed. The Church that Nelson was attempting to become a minister of is self-confessedly and proudly Calvinist. As the religious historian Jane Dawson observes, John Knox is the only non-Frenchman in the heroic monument of the reformers in Geneva, the Reformation Wall, alongside William Farel, Theodore Beza and John Calvin himself. Moreover, after Robert Nelson's disenchantment with the Church of Scotland's decisions about his son's potential ordination, he left it to join the even more Calvinist United Free Church. The word 'Calvinist' here has little to do with any of Calvin's actual thoughts on predestination, justification by faith alone or the self-authentication of Scripture. Rather, it is a kind of shorthand to refer to a vehemently authoritarian, pleasure-hating, judgemental and self-righteous form of religion; the kind which the political theorist Tom Nairn had in mind when he declared that Scotland would not be free 'until the last minister is strangled with the last copy of the *Sunday Post*'.

It is evident from Robert Nelson's testimony how raw and palpable his grief is, and one should not underestimate this in any way. 'He has given so much hurt to so many people . . . He lost his freedom for less than ten years. I lost my wife after 28 years of marriage and have been virtually alone ever since.' Although the picture that emerges is of something of a self-controlled martinet, Anne's account of the discovery of her mother's body is quite different. Robert Nelson simply went to pieces: 'My father was screaming and screaming. He was incapable of phoning 999 so I went back into the kitchen to do it. I went back into the garage to look for signs of life but my mother was dead.'

So what happened in 1978? Referring to the theological textbooks, Nelson's father said, 'Because of his attitude in 1978, and at our meeting today, he has not passed in my eyes. I cannot forgive him until he clears up some statements.' Nelson told the *Glasgow Herald* that he was 'pessimistic' about any reconciliation. 'I will never be in the situation where my father can regard me as a valid and equal human being.' His father's response was: 'I cannot forgive and forget. I do not believe in his behaviour, but I also cannot forget that he is my son. I have tried to forgive him, but things have happened over the last year that have left me dissatisfied.' In a classic piece of deference he added, 'I am not against the Church finding him a suitable person. They know better than me.' Anne Nelson said that the attempt at restoring their relationship was in part precipitated by her father's 'finally realising how authoritarian he had been'. But the subsequent meeting was 'a disaster' according to her father, though the reporter noted he 'declined to elaborate'.

One clear sticking point is that Nelson's father said his son 'had never asked for forgiveness from me'. This is just a facet of an incredibly complex set of moral and theological arguments, which another sermon will explore. It is sufficient for the moment to note that this is not just a refusal to forgive, it is predicated on Nelson's failure to plead for forgiveness. It leaves absolutely intact a power dynamic by which the father's withholding of forgiveness is in proportion to the son's being required to ask for it.

The other point of disagreement is hinted at rather than explicit. Robert Nelson claimed he needed two apologies: the first for the murder, and the second for the 1978 row 'over how they both remember Mrs Nelson'. In describing his life with his parents as one of unbearable tension, with violence being almost inevitable, Nelson does put part of the blame for the situation on to his mother. He admitted that 'it could as easily have been' his father whom he killed. Yet it was not. Nor, when pleading for mitigation, did he raise his father's attacks on him. It seems as if he was protecting his father as much as he was condemning him; and the full extent of the family violence would not come out until Anne's interview fifteen years later. If we trust Anne's account of her breach with her brother, the thing which stands out is Nelson's referring to his mother as a 'whore', at roughly the same time as the meeting with his father. Did he say the same thing to him? Given how Robert Nelson characterises her, such an insult would certainly be an impediment to any rapprochement.

Faithful and dutiful. Not loving or kindly. Robert Nelson even pointedly refers to her as his wife first and a mother second.

When discussing running away from home, James states that his 'parents' concern seemed to be for themselves, not me. Only for the worry I'd caused.' Robert Nelson also insisted that 'his son's criticisms of his mother on that day should have been left in the past'. Ostensibly, 'that day' refers to the 1978 meeting which led to a cessation of all contact. But it also seems to refer to the day of the murder. It seems as well that what Nelson's father is objecting to is not the criticisms themselves, but the public revelation of them. Did he feel some guilt about the language she had supposedly used about Nelson's girlfriend? Did it, in some way, crack the façade of a respectable, church-going family?

Two other things about this case which keep rattling around my head are very *unheimlich*, and both concern Robert Nelson's career. On the night of the murder he was at choir practice, and every article about him mentions that he is a church organist. For some reason this brings to mind the character of John Jasper in Charles Dickens's unfinished *The Mystery of Edwin Drood*. Jasper is Drood's uncle and guardian; he is also the choirmaster of Cloisterham Cathedral and an opium addict. At the end of the opening chapter, as Jasper hurries to Vespers with the choir in their 'sullied white robes', the words are intoned, 'When the Wicked Man—'. Although we cannot tell how Dickens intended to end the novel – whether Drood is dead or alive, for example – it is clear that the villain of the book was to be Jasper. In her interview, Anne refers to her father as 'a church saint and a house devil. He was unbelievable.' The other part is that he was a joiner: 'Is not this the carpenter's son? Is not his mother called Mary?' is how Jesus is identified in Matthew 13:55 (although Mark 6:3 has 'is not this the carpenter, the son of Mary'). Early anti-Christian polemicists frequently resorted to mockery of Joseph as regards the doctrine of the Virgin Birth. As W. H. Auden memorably puts it in his Christmas Oratorio, *For the Time Being*, 'Joseph, have you heard / What Mary says occurred? / Yes it might be so / But is it likely? No.' Satirists referred to Joseph as a simpleton cuckold and Mary as a duplicitous woman of negotiable affection: a whore. When I first started to look into Nelson's story, what struck me was the sheer abundance of a diverse range of mythological, cultural and literary resonances it had. It seems self-evident that a news story appearing about the first-ever convicted murderer to be ordained into any part of the Christian Church would attract a great deal of attention: Stewart Lamont even referred to it as the ecclesiastical equivalent of a 'man bites dog' story, writing that 'while "dog collar murderer" or equally "murderer dons dog collar" are both sensational stories, there is a difference in the moral quality between the two. James Nelson's story is the latter and clearly preferable to the former.' What kept it in the news was not just prurient interest, but a whole host of archetypal forms braided throughout the story. We shall, in turn, look at some of the most pertinent.

Robert Nelson died in 1987. It was five years after his son gave his side of the story. It took ten years for his daughter to give her side of the story. Father and son never reconciled, even though the former had said, 'Before I die I would like to get all this resolved. Today is not the time.'

He also said, 'I don't want him made into a hero.' It might have surprised him that one of the most important classical heroes – one of the aboriginal 'culture heroes' – was also a matricide.

The Gospel According to
St Luke 2:34–5

And Simeon blessed them, and said unto Mary his mother, Behold, this child *is set for the fall and rising again of many in Israel; and for a sign which shall be spoken against; (Yea, and a sword shall pierce through thy soul also,) that the thoughts of many hearts may be revealed.*

When one thinks about them, almost all crimes of violence become unthinkable. Although the Bible is quite uncompromising about sin, in that there is a sense in which no sin is more sinful than any other sin – as the Epistle of James puts it, 'For whosoever shall keep the whole law, and yet offend in one *point*, he is guilty of all' – humans naturally create, for both judicial and moral reasons, gradations of wrong. We tabulate and taxonomise criminality, in terms of both the penal consequences for the action and the moral revulsion we feel for the perpetrator. Despite the Bible's almost inconceivable notion that stealing a penny chew from Woolworth's when you were seven is no different from stabbing a random stranger to death, the Church quickly established hierarchies of wickedness. Evagrius the Solitary is credited with the first inklings of the Seven Deadly Sins (pride, envy, wrath, sloth, greed, gluttony and lust, in order of worst to least worse) in the fourth century, which were popularised by his pupil John Cassian and inform literary works such as Dante's *Purgatorio* and Chaucer's 'Parson's Tale' in *The Canterbury Tales* and continue in popular culture up to *Whiz Comics #2*, when Billy Batson meets the 'Seven Enemies of Humanity' before becoming Captain Marvel (in which lust is replaced by injustice to keep clear of the Comics Code), and David Fincher's film *Se7en*. Not all sins are crimes – Lord help us if every instance of pride or lust ended in a court appearance – and not all crimes are sins: one could consider some acts of civil disobedience as morally right if legally wrong, or the horrors of what happens when the law itself becomes immoral, as it did in Nazi Germany.

Yet there are some crimes which are visceral taboos as well, and matricide ranks highly among them. The idea of taking the life of the individual who gave you life seems abhorrent on a different level to Othello's insane jealousy or Brutus's political misgivings or Titus Andronicus's furious vengeance. As Susan Sontag writes in her essay 'Piety without Content', 'Matricide is of all possible individual crimes the most insupportable psycho-logically', going on to compare it to deicide, to which 'entire cultures' saw it as equivalent. We must, however, be careful in the definition of 'matricide'. I am excluding from mine examples where the entire family is killed – such as the case of Ronald DeFeo Jr, who slaughtered his parents and siblings in the event that would be immortalised in *The Amityville Horror*. Likewise, the murder of a mother as part of a wider killing spree, such as with Kip Kinkel in Oregon in 1998, or the serial killer Edmund Kemper in 1973, who had already committed six sexually motivated murders, seems to be a different kind of case. There are many dynastic matricides, from the Emperor Nero's killing of Agrippina to the Crown Prince Dipendra of Nepal who, in

2001, massacred his entire family, rather than specifically target-ing his mother. Nor would I consider killings with pecuniary motive to be archetypically matricidal; and again, in most cases, such as the Menendez brothers in 1989, the mother tends to be part of a 'familiocide'. Matricide is even rarer if one limits it to the killing of a mother by a son. Perhaps the most famous – and in some ways problematic, as who inflicted the mortal wound is ambiguous – is the Parker–Hulme murder case of 1954, in which a teenage girl and her best friend killed the mother. It is the subject of Peter Jackson's film *Heavenly Creatures*, and the friend, then called Juliet Hulme, is now known as the crime writer Anne Perry. In a twist that may be significant, Perry later converted to Mormonism, or the Church of the Latter Day Saints, after having served five years for the crime. But, in a technical sense, she is not a matricide either. It was Pauline Parker, the elder of the two, whose mother was the victim. She latterly became a Roman Catholic. Their case inspired Angela Carter, who wanted to make a film called *The Christchurch Murders*; Beryl Bainbridge, whose debut novel, *Harriet Said . . .*, drew on it; and the contemporary novelist Evie Wyld's *All the Birds, Singing*. I will note now: there is no equivalent literary and cinematic interest in the Nelson case.

There is one 'precise' matricide which also had a cultural afterlife: the case of Antony Baekeland, whose story informed the 2007 film *Savage Grace* written by Howard Rodman and directed by Tom Kalin. Baekeland's mother, Barbara, was a socialite, whose dinner party guests included Tennessee Williams, William Styron and Greta Garbo. She had modelled for *Vogue* and *Harper's Bazaar*. Her father had committed suicide; she herself would attempt to do so on more than one occasion. Her son by Brooks Baekeland, a scion of the dynasty that invented

Bakelite, was bisexual and a heavy user of hallucinogenic drugs. One of the few women with whom he was involved then started an affair with his father, after his parents' divorce. Baekeland attempted to murder his mother in July 1972 by pushing her into oncoming traffic; he succeeded in November of that year by stabbing her with a kitchen knife. Baekeland's reasons for these horrific actions stemmed from an equally horrific one. Disgusted by her son's preference for same-sex partners, Barbara had first of all paid for female prostitutes to 'cure' him, and when this seemed to have little impact on his choice of lover, she took even more drastic and caustic action. Somehow – the mechanics elude me on almost every level – she forced or seduced her son into having sex with her to curtail his more homosexual leanings. If there is any taboo more deeply engrained than killing either of one's parents, it must be incest. Having thrust a knife though his mother's heart, he waited for the police. Sentenced to the psychiatric prison Broadmoor at the age of twenty-five, Baekeland served seven years before being released after a campaign orchestrated by friends. By then thirty-three, he travelled to New York to stay with his mother's mother. Seven days later he had attacked her with a knife, inflicting eight wounds and breaking several bones. He committed suicide in prison on Rikers Island. In almost every respect, Baekeland's case bears no comparison to Nelson's. Almost. They were of different classes altogether, and there was a history of mental illness in the family – Baekeland's grandmother, who was almost his second victim, had also had a breakdown. There was the misuse of alcohol and the use of narcotics, neither of which was a trait of the Nelson household as far as one can tell. The only thing – the little niggle – is that Baekeland had been, somehow, sexually involved with his own mother. There is no evidence that Nelson was a victim in this regard, but the trigger for the night of horrors was a reference to his sexual activity and his girlfriend's sexual morality. And he called his mother a whore.

If reality cannot enlighten us much about matricide, might culture? Patricide is deeply studied and endlessly theorised about in many forms of text. It is the basis of Freud's Oedipus complex. Why did Freud choose Oedipus when the origin myths of the Greeks all involve fathers trying to exterminate their sons, and sons bound to supplant their fathers? Ouranous is slain and emasculated by Kronos for power; Kronos eats all his children except Zeus, who dethrones him after being hidden; Zeus, in later imaginings of his pre-eminence, is anxious about which son will force him from power. Oedipus had an angle to the story which the hierarchy of resentment, consummation and vilification lacked: he had, albeit inadvertently, slept with a woman who was his mother, though he did not know it. Freud's extrapolation – that all male children wish to castrate the father and sleep with the mother – is a very weak reading of the texts by Sophocles. Oedipus did not want to have 'knowledge of' his mother, as more prim versions of the Bible would have it. Having achieved what Freud thinks of as an ambition, Oedipus is disgusted and blinds himself with his mother's dress-pin. (An aside: Oedipus revenges himself upon himself using a family totem or token, just as Nelson's first choice of weapon was a family bibelot.) His mother, Jocasta, commits suicide.

Carl Jung, Freud's friend, pupil and enemy, tried to establish an 'Elektra complex', the psychic under-structure by which a young girl would resent the mother and desire the father, as a gendered opposite to the Oedipus complex. It is worth mentioning, in passing, that Jung turned to the tragedy of the House of Atreus for his mythological archetype. In part this is because of the specificity of Elektra's psychosis; but there were other female figures in the Oedipus cycle – his daughter/sister Antigone, for example – or from other legend sequences – the infanticidal Medea or Phaedra, who developed an incestuous passion for her stepson – who might have served as metaphors.

Jung and Freud are ironically perfect examples of Freudian theory, in that the younger Jung sought to castrate, intellectually, the patriarch Freud, especially by removing libido as a key drive and force of the subconscious. His 'Elektra complex' is simmeringly rivalrous, and developed the concept of penis envy. I don't know any woman who has penis envy, or who believes that her mother somehow took away her masculinity. I do know that my mum, who is among the sanest people I have the fortune to know, told me about when she once saw a boy younger than her taking a widdle behind some bushes on a Sunday School charabanc. She ran back to her father and told him what she'd seen, with the wonderful conclusion that she would like one of them too, as they'd be awfully handy if you were caught short on a trip away. I think that might be better defined as 'penis covetousness' than anything to do with Jungian theory. Jung and Freud both believed, in some manner, in the impossibility of matricide. Their psychodynamics were chauvinistically gendered and hetero-normative, and the idea of a man killing his own mother was somehow beyond the beyond. They may even have a point.

There are susurrations and hisses, whispers and stutterings around matricide. But its silence speaks and its absence howls in turn. The only major, 'canonical' novel to deal with matricide by a son is *The Family of Pascual Duarte* by the Nobel Prize for Literature winner and Franco loyalist, Camilo José Cela. First published in 1942, it exemplified and founded the Spanish school of *tremendismo*, a cousin of existentialist writing. In his introduction to his 1964 translation, Anthony Kerrigan aligns Cela, judiciously, with two other right-wing nihilists, Louis-Ferdinand Céline and Curzio Malaparte.

Matricide is the culmination of Pascual Duarte's crimes. His life is one of unremitting suffering: his father dies of rabies, his younger half-brother Mario is mauled by swine and kicked to death by the individual who cuckolded his father, his sister becomes a prostitute, his first wife miscarries their first child and the second dies at the age of eleven months, before his wife too dies. He variously shoots his own dog, stabs his horse, gets into a knife fight with his friends on his honeymoon and batters the man who pimped his sister and seduced his wife. Throughout, Pascual talks about the inevitability of his actions, even when he readily admits he does not know why he enacts them. The description of Pascual's feelings towards his mother is genuinely horrific:

> I wanted to make a clearing in my memory which would
> allow me to see when it was that she ceased to be a mother
> for me and became an enemy, a deadly enemy – for there
> is no deeper hatred than blood hatred, hatred of one's own
> blood. She became an enemy who aroused all my bile, all
> my spleen, for nothing is hated with more relish than
> someone one resembles, until in the end one abominates
> one's likeness. After much thought, and after coming to no
> clear conclusion, I can only say I had already lost my
> respect for her a long time before, when I was unable to
> find in her any virtue at all worthy of imitation, or gift of
> God to copy, and I had to be rid of her, get her out of my
> system, when I saw I had no room in me for so much evil.

> I took some time to get to hate her, really hate her, for
> neither love nor hate is a matter of a day.

Pascual's mother is unnamed in the narrative. She constantly humiliates her son, doubting his masculinity. The final attack on the mother is unbearable: at first Pascual is immobilised, unable to stab her in her sleep; when she awakens to find him above the bed, knife in hand, they struggle, and his mother bites off Pascual's nipple in an inverted parody of maternal suckling. It is no wonder that the novel was banned the year after it came out. Pascual, at one point, muses that 'sooner or later everything comes in this life, except forgiveness from those one has wronged, and that seems to hold off perversely'.

What is so powerful about Cela's novel is its almost anti-psychological refusal to provide reasons for Pascual's fury. The corroborating letters are contradictory and the transcriber of Pascual's prison manuscript ends the book seeking in vain for other pages which might provide some form of explanation. It is at its most Gothic in its sheer meaninglessness. While patricide can be contained in narratives of usurpation and power, matricide is a void: it is that which must be avoided, the primal taboo. A nothing, a not thing, a knotting. A word about which more later.

Most commentators on Cela's work note that it appeared in the same year as Camus' *L'Étranger*. While Cela is baroque, almost stilted and gaudily explicit, Camus is deliberately mono-tone, affectless and restrained – the famous 'writing degree zero' which Roland Barthes identified as radical in his work. It is a novel in which the ghost of matricide flickers on the margins. It famously begins 'Mother died today', and at the trial the defence lawyer says, 'But after all, is he being accused of burying his mother or killing a man?' The prosecutor responds that 'between two such actions there existed a profound, tragic and vital relationship. "Yes," he exclaimed violently, "I accuse this man of burying his mother like a heartless criminal." This pronouncement seemed to have a considerable effect on the public.' Meursault's failure to grieve for his mother is an act of unfilial rejection that is the moral equivalent of matricide. This might explain, as John Robert Maze argues in *Albert Camus: Plague and Terror, Priest and Atheist*, why Meursault is sentenced to be guillotined, rather than to life imprisonment. The shooting of the Arab on the beach is not arbitrary or random. Its meaninglessness is a consequence of Meursault's having already eroded the fundamental moral order of society by his impious apathy.

The most famous matricide in contemporary culture is probably Norman Bates in Alfred Hitchcock's 1960 film *Psycho*, based on the 1959 novel by Robert Bloch. In the film, the psychiatrist Fred Richmond analyses Bates thus:

> To understand it the way I understood it, hearing from the 'mother' . . . that is from the 'mother' half of Norman's mind . . . you have to go back ten years . . . to the time when Norman murdered his mother and her lover. He was already dangerously disturbed, had been since his father died. His mother was a clinging, demanding woman . . . and for years the two of them lived as if there was no one else in the world. Then she met a man . . . and it seemed to Norman that she threw him over for this man. That pushed him over the line and he killed them both. Matricide is probably the most unbearable crime of all . . . most unbearable to the son who commits it. So he had to erase the crime, at least in his own mind.

The most significant difference between the film and the novel is that in the novel Norman is already interested in transvestitism, the occult and pornography while his mother is still alive, whereas the film concerns itself only with the transvestitism, which is a direct result of his schizophrenic fissuring. Both share the idea that the 'mother' persona dislikes it when Norman is attracted to other women.

Again, we have a situation in which the impetus towards matricide is a domineering mother who attempts to police her son's sexual conduct. Cela and Hitchcock both share a vision in which the key condition for a matricide to occur is the unmaternal conduct of the mother: adultery, sleeping with someone other than the father, the use of filthy language or emasculating statements towards the son. In other words, matricide is possible as a crime only if the mother is un-mothered. Even in depictions of daughter–mother matricide there is a highly sexualised component to the crime. In Stephen King's 1974 *Carrie*, the provoking occurrence is the daughter's first menstruation, which her Christian fundamentalist mother believes is a sin, and unclean. In the reporting of the Parker–Hulme case, unfounded insinuations of disapproved-of lesbianism were offered as motives for the murder.

There is also a blame-shift in all these cultural and real-life versions of matricide. The mother in some way causes the matricide: it is a crime so beyond the pale that something worse than itself must have caused it. Matricide is the crime that is not a crime and that cannot be a crime. It is this moral conundrum that is central to the most famous depiction of matricide, which appears in a foundational text of Western civilisation: Aeschylus's *Oresteia* trilogy.

Leviticus 16:21–2

And Aaron shall lay both his hands upon the head of the live goat,
and confess over him all the iniquities of the children of Israel,
and all their transgressions in all their sins, putting them upon the
head of the goat, and shall send him *away by the hand of a fit*
man into the wilderness: And the goat shall bear upon him
all their iniquities unto a land not inhabited: and he shall
let go the goat in the wilderness.

There are no examples of matricide in the Bible. Although one might have thought that the concept of matrilineal descent – you are of the Chosen People if and only if your mother was of the Chosen People – might be the reason why both the Old and New Testaments shudder at matricide, this cannot be the case. It is never mentioned as a precondition of Jewishness in the Tanakh – what Christians might think of as the Old Testament, its name an acronym from the three traditional subdivisions (Torah, teaching, Nevi'im, prophets, Ketuvim, writings) – and was only codified in the Mishnah, the cornerstone of Rabbinical Judaism. Matricide seems to have been a deep taboo for the Semitic peoples of the seventh to fifth centuries BC. It was equally taboo for their neighbours in Greece, but for very different reasons.

Between them, the Greek playwrights Aeschylus, Sophocles

105

and Euripides wrote around three hundred tragedies, of which thirty-five have survived. Among those thirty-five, we have only one intact trilogy (all the plays were originally in trilogies): Aeschylus's *Oresteia*, comprising his *Agamemnon*, *Choephoroi* and *The Eumenides*. It was first performed in Athens in 458 BC, originally with a satyr play, a kind of burlesque tragicomedy, at the end: we know the *Oresteia* ended with *Proteus*, of which only two lines survive: 'A wretched piteous dove, in quest of food, dashed amid the winnowing-fans, its breast broken in twain.' The three plays tell of the aftermath of King Agamemnon's decision to have his daughter Iphigenia sacrificed to secure favourable winds as he and his fleet embarked towards Troy, in order to wage war and retrieve his brother Menelaus's errant wife, Helen, who had eloped with the Trojan prince, Paris. When the plays open, the ten-year war is over, and Agamemnon is returning home, where his wife Clytemnestra has, as Robert Burns put it in a different context, been 'nursing her wrath to keep it warm'.

Clytemnestra has taken a lover, Aegisthus, her husband's cousin, and has not forgiven her husband for sacrificing their daughter. The play opens with a series of signal fires announcing that Agamemnon is returning to Mycenae, and the watchman rues the 'manly hearted rule of a woman' under which he has languished 'like a dog' (almost as if Kafka had time-travelled to include the end of *The Trial* in the first stirrings of literature). Agamemnon walks across vermilion carpets into his palace like a true conqueror, and is slain by Clytemnestra and Aegisthus as if he were the same kind of sacrificial offering he consented for his own daughter to become. The triumphant lovers return to the stage brandishing the bloody ceremonial axes with which they have exacted revenge. 'Let us not be bloody now,'

Clytemnestra declaims. In a rare moment in Greek tragedy, the Chorus almost surge against the criminal couple to warn them that Agamemnon and Clytemnestra's son will not allow this to go unpunished.

The *Choephoroi* or *Libation Bearers* introduces that son, Orestes, who, along with his cousin Pylades, is visiting his father's grave. Unobserved, he sees his sister Elektra with a chorus of women there to pour libations on the grave. They have been sent by Clytemnestra herself to 'ward off danger'. After he announces himself to his sister, she reveals to him that Clytemnestra is troubled by nightmares in which she gives birth to a snake that suckles milk and blood from her. To appease the gods she is sending funeral rites for Agamemnon. It is 'too late an atonement for a hurt past cure' for Orestes, and he travels incognito to the palace, where he takes his revenge on both his mother and Aegisthus. At that moment the Erinyes, or Furies, appear, supernatural spirits who seek out the worst of criminals for punishment. As a matricide, Orestes has been brought to their attention.

In the final part, *The Eumenides* or *The Kindly Ones*, Orestes has reached Athens, harried and driven mad by the Furies. The ghost of his mother spurs them on, though the god Apollo, who first instructed Orestes that his duty was vengeance, has tried to put a check on them. But there is dissension in the heavens. In killing his own mother, Orestes has certainly committed an act deserving of punishment; but he has simultaneously fulfilled a moral obligation in that he has avenged the death of his father. The code of vendetta has created an ethical paradox whereby the same intervention might be both deplorable and commendable. To solve this problem, the goddess Athena convenes the first court to determine the question of Orestes' guilt. When it splits with six in favour and six against, she uses her casting vote to exonerate Orestes and to turn the Erinyes into the Eumenides who will ensure the prosperity of Athens. Furthermore, she establishes that in cases of a split jury, the finding should always err towards justice rather than retribution.

Orestes is therefore a 'culture hero' in two senses. He is the equivalent of the Hebraic scapegoat, but it is not the transgressions of the community that he takes upon himself. Rather, he incarnates the conflict between irreconcilable moral codes and reveals the instability and contradiction at the heart of things. He is also the symbol of the rule of law overtaking mere retaliation, of law supplanting revenge. But this is a deep and subtle text, and the 'triumph' of reasonable justice over choleric blood feud is not as simple as a summary of the plot might indicate.

Orestes' crime is so outwith the moral spectrum that it requires, by way of the institution of judicial courts, a reorganising of society to deal with its outcome. It is a crime beyond crime; and at the same time it is a crime of which he is found innocent: matricide, in this instance, turns out not to be a crime at all. Again, this chimes with later accounts and reports. The primal villain is yet again the mother, and the murderous child is unburdened of his guilt. There is another parallel in the ancient world, in the Babylonian creation myths narrated in the *Enuma Elish*. One of the very earliest goddesses was Tiamat, a primordial ocean deity. After she had produced seven generations of offspring, whose luxury and arrogance meant humanity was servile, a civil war broke out between the younger and older gods – seven generations, which recalls the Lamech and Cain story. Tiamat has now taken the form of a dragon, and Marduk, a new god of storms, takes up the challenge of defeating her – she represents the watery abomination over which, in another mythos, the Spirit moved. Marduk is associated with lightning, fire, spades, nets, arrows, maces, chariots, horsemanship and medicine: he is culture and technology to her chaos and nature. Her dead body becomes the building blocks and raw materials from which Marduk will create a new heaven and earth. It is one of the few myths in which an ancestor goddess is overthrown by an emergent god. Marduk, naturally, does not suffer any censure for defeating the primal mother.

To begin with, we have the *Oresteia*'s parallels with the other narratives of matricide discussed beforehand. Again we have a mother whose sexual mores are problematic, and who unmans her son by making Aegisthus the heir to the House of Atreus in his place. There is also the question of the seemingly expendable Iphigenia, whose death does not seem to unleash the Furies. It is strikingly similar to the biblical story of Jephthah, narrated in Judges 11–12, but without the irony that often marks the biblical texts. Jephthah's rash promise rebounds on him; Agamemnon is simply following orders. But the mother of Agamemnon, Aerope, was also condemned for promiscuity, having been found in bed with a slave and sentenced to death by her father, Catreus. She escaped her fate, and later sources, particularly Apollodorus, contain the story that she was exiled rather than ordered to be killed because of an oracle that claimed a child of Catreus would kill him. Aerope married into an equally disastrous family: her husband, Atreus, was the son of Pelops, whose own father had boiled him up to serve as dinner to the gods at a banquet. Realising his atrocity, the gods refused to eat and reassembled Pelops. Intergenerational murder seems to be a speciality of the House of Atreus. Atreus himself, in ousting his brother Thyestes, also fed him a meal made up of the latter's sons (save for Aegisthus). But only Orestes inverts the order from child-killing to parent-killing.

STUART KELLY

Athena's decision to use her casting vote to pardon Orestes is not all that it seems. In part, it is justified by her as a preference for clemency rather than punishment. But it is also biographically nuanced. In the Greek pantheon, Athena was supposedly born, fully grown and armed, from her father Zeus's head. In *The Eumenides* this 'genealogy' is described. Apollo says, 'A father can father forth without a mother / Here she stands, our living witness. Look – / Child sprung full blown from Olympian Zeus / Never bred in the darkness of the womb.' Athena herself replies, 'My work is here, to render the final judgement. / Orestes, I will cast my vote for you. / No mother gave me birth / I honour the male in all things but in marriage / Yes, with all my heart I am my Father's child.' So Athena's decision to clear the matricide is predicated on the fact that she has no mother; that mothers are in some ways superfluous. This is more than poetic licence. Aristotle believed that male semen was in effect identical to a seed, in that the full pattern for the future human lay in it – as a form of homunculus. The woman was merely the soil in which the seed quickened; a kind of biodegradable incubator. Although we now see paternity as a legal fiction, to the Greek mind a logical corollary of their biological belief was that a father's offspring would be *his regardless of which woman bore the child*. Motherhood was interchangeable. In significant ways, it actually did not exist.

This narrative conceals an older one, found in the *Theogony*, Hesiod's seventh-century BC epic poem. Hesiod records that Zeus lusted after one of the Titans, called Metis, whose name means 'wisdom', 'skill' or 'craft'. There was, however, a prophecy that a child of Metis's would be stronger than the father (in keeping with the cycle of divine supplantings), so, having slept with her, Zeus tricked Metis into turning herself into a fly, which he swallowed. Metis was already pregnant: she gives birth

110

inside Zeus, and fashions Athena's weapons and armour. This causes Zeus incredible migraines, and the god of blacksmiths, Hephaestus, uses an axe to split Zeus's head, whereupon Athena springs forward. (Zeus is remarkably unharmed by this.) So Athena does have a mother, and Zeus usurps the female generative power in a consolidation of patriarchy. Much of the best research on this has been done by Amber Jacobs, in one of the very few critical works to scrutinise matricide and its myths, *On Matricide: Myth, Psychoanalysis and the Law of the Mother*. Athena excuses the matricide because she herself is a kind of matricide, certainly symbolically: no one seems to have recorded what happened to Metis after the cleaving of Zeus's skull – another, almost complete, erasure. Jacobs's observations lead to further fruitful parallels. Agamemnon is struck down in what might be seen as a parody of the 'freeing' of Athena, using the same weapon.

Euripides, a generation after Aeschylus, rewrites him several times. His *Orestes*, dealing with the same material as *The Libation Bearers*, has a scene in which he explicitly questions the moment when Orestes and Elektra recognise each other, by means of a lock of hair Orestes has left on Agamemnon's tomb. In Euripides' version Elektra mocks the notion that such articles would 'prove' Orestes has returned; in other words, we have moved from a debate about justice to one about proof and evidence. In *Iphigenia in Aulis*, Euripides presents the sacrifice narrated in retrospect in the *Agamemnon*, giving a far more sympathetic role to Clytemnestra. In *Iphigenia in Aulis*, it is the husband-abandoning Helen, Clytemnestra's sister-in-law, who represents deviant sexual behaviour. The sacrifice of Iphigenia is 'buying what we detest with what we hold most dear'. At the end of the play, it is revealed to Clytemnestra that the goddess Artemis spirited away Iphigenia at the moment of the sacrifice, replacing her with a deer. The substitution seems to parallel the sacrifice of Isaac in Genesis 22, although Abraham knows of the replacement, whereas Agamemnon continues to think he has dutifully killed his daughter. That he would have gone through with it anyway is sufficient grounds for Clytemnestra still to want revenge. Euripides makes more of the substitution in the earlier *Iphigenia in Tauris*, where Iphigenia has become the priestess among the Taurians. Orestes and Pylades arrive there while being pursued by the Erinyes. Local custom dictates that Greek visitors must be sacrificed, and Iphigenia – not recognising her brother – is due to perform this, an inversion of her own previous (non-)sacrifice. The siblings recognise each other at the last minute, and Athena extends her protection specifically because Orestes was willing to lay down his own life. There is yet another strange substitution in Euripides' *Helen*, where it is revealed that, before the Trojan War, Zeus requested that his wife create an image or 'eidolon' out of clouds to replace Helen (who is his daughter by an adulterous liaison with Leda, whom he seduced in the form of a swan). So the entire bloodshed of the Trojan War is for the hand of a mirage. These transpositions and replacements and deferrals create a merry-go-round of myths of the feminine. The victim becomes a killer; the whore becomes a virgin; the childless monsters become protecting maternal figures. The Atreides tragedies are not an aboriginal myth of misogyny, but an account of the emergence of multiple misogynies.

An early tradition about the play is that the appearance of the Erinyes in *The Eumenides* was so terrifying (they begin to awaken, and hum rather than speak to begin with) that a woman called Neaira miscarried and died on the spot. A play about matricide not only causes a mother to die, it turns the unborn child into the weapon by which she is killed.

With such a heady, mephitic discourse around matricide in both culture and reality, it is no wonder that the case of James Nelson drew such aghast attention. As a crime it is singularly ambiguous. It is a crime which can be committed only because of prior crimes on the part of the victim; it is not a crime at all; it is beyond justice and the origin of the need for justice. Although the Bible does not feature matricide, one of the most striking moments is a rejection of the mother. In Matthew 12:47–9, Jesus is told that 'thy mother and thy brethren stand without, desiring to speak with thee'. His reply is devastating: 'Who is my mother? and who are my brethren? And he stretched forth his hand towards his disciples, and said, Behold my mother and my brethren!' Just beforehand, Jesus had been elaborating on the only sin that could not be forgiven.

The First Epistle of Paul the
Apostle to Timothy 1:15

*This is a faithful saying, and worthy of all acceptation, that Christ
Jesus came into the world to save sinners; of whom I am chief.*

The question of Nelson's proceeding to ordination was not just
about the fact that he was a sinner – the Church is certain that we
all are – nor was it just about the fact that he had been convicted
of a crime (Nelson has a strange shadow throughout this case:
there was another convicted criminal seeking to become a
minister at precisely the same time). It was also about the nature
of the crime and the sin. One word on many lips was 'unnatural'.
A member of the presbytery told the press it had been said that
'after the hours of dark, no women between the ages of seventeen
and seventy would open their door to him'. Nelson's new wife
received a poison pen letter saying, 'Murdering thug Nelson, you
are being hogwatched.' A friend of mine recalls his mother
discussing the case along the lines of: 'Well, what will happen if
someone goes along to him saying they're having problems with
their mother? Will he just tell them to stove her head in?'

Although the phrase had been used since the beginning of the
nineteenth century, the writer and jurist Oliver Wendell Holmes
gave its most well-known iteration: 'Great cases like hard cases

make bad law. For great cases are called great, not by reason of their importance . . . but because of some accident of immediate overwhelming interest which appeals to the feelings and distorts the judgment.' Nelson's was both a great and a hard case, and in some ways the Church had to proceed with the debate because it was a case of extremes. If the question was about fitness for office, about the preconditions for forgiveness, or, even if there were preconditions, about the efficacy of 'grace abounding to the chief of sinners', then this was a test case like no other. It was a kind of moral brinkmanship.

It was not just a discussion of the particular theological angles and arguments. It was an estimation of character, of a nebulous quality between morality and politeness, etiquette and ethics. The minister was an individual who would be there at your family's marriages, baptisms and funerals, who would take the midnight service on Christmas Eve, when many people who'd never cross the door of the church from year-end to year-end would boozily turn up for some sentimentality and soup, who would open the coffee mornings and sales-of-work and judge Women's Guild chutney competitions. The theology was happening in the most rarefied of intellectual realms, and the final decisions would be taken by people who just might not take to the cut of the jib. One of the reasons for the overture about Scottish Church history was that the higher echelons of the Church also had a get-out clause. A minister could not be imposed on a parish. Nelson might apply to be a minister, but a parish would have to invite him as sole nominee to be not just their minister, but an intrinsic part of their community. There was always the chance that Nelson would not be called. At the opening of the Assembly, it was noted that there were 902,714 communicant members on the rolls of the parishes of the Church of Scotland – 20 per cent of the population. The Church might be able to secure a moral victory and allow Nelson to become a minister, while knowing that declining rolls and amalgamating parishes might mean he would never actually be a minister. Many are called, after all, but few are chosen.

By chance, I came upon a strange volume of memoirs in a bookshop in Innerleithen while thinking about the idea of the 'character' of the minister. It is called *No Better Than I Should Be: The Making of a Minister*, by the Rev. James L. Dow. It was published in 1975 by Hutchison of London as they were then called, and has a handsome dustjacket showing Dow in his robes, outside a white-painted church. The foreword is by William Barclay, Professor of Divinity and Biblical Criticism at Glasgow University, and a noted exponent of pacifism, evolution and universal salvation (the heresy that meant that my favourite theologian, Origen, the second/third-century Greek writer, has never been made a saint: he believed that even Satan would be redeemed in the end). Among many books, Barclay was the author of *The Plain Man's Book of Prayers* and *More Prayers for the Plain Man* and *The Plain Man Looks at the Beatitudes*. I remember these on our shelves in my childhood, and not the least of his virtues was that the Plain Man was himself, and these were not prayers for people judged either plain or necessarily masculine. (The tang of slight stuffy unthinking sexism is there though.) In his dustjacket portrait, Dow looks uncannily like the fascist Oswald Mosely. I should state, for the avoidance of all doubt, that Dow is in thinking nothing like Oswald Mosely. In earlier photographs – the book has eight plates of photographs! – he looks like a young Basil Rathbone.

The Church of Scotland, unlike the Church of England – or indeed Episcopalian Churches around the world – does not have a notable tradition of ecclesiastical memoirs. We have no *Apologia Pro Vita Sua* by Cardinal Newman, no range of eccentrics like the Bensons (Edward Benson was the only Archbishop of Canterbury to have a biography of his wife published later on entitled *As Good as God, as Clever as the Devil*, let alone to be the father of the author of the *Mapp and Lucia* novels), no wistful Richard Holloway with his faith-ebbed *Leaving Alexandria*, no Richard Coles with his striking lack of self-censorship. My first girlfriend, once I went to university, was from an Anglican background, but was, shall we say, non-practising. I ditched atheism for High Anglicanism straight away, but kept my Nietzsche, Sartre and Heidegger in full view in my rooms, in one of the chameleon tactics I am ashamed and afraid of now. But it did mean I imbibed a great deal of affection for High Anglican autobiographies.

Kirk memoirs, or at least as many of them as I have read, tend to have certain common features. They insist that – despite all the clichés of glowering, grim-faced and grey-haired grouches – they are actually quite a jovial bunch these days. Many of them were in the war, and speak little about it, except to say how humbled they felt. They do not mention shooting people. Dow's book, which is actually rather wonderful, is paradigmatic: here he is on his nativity, when a christening mug (does anyone even have such things now?) was falsely inscribed. 'The mistake is that I was born not in February 1908 but in March, which makes me a Piscean and not an Aquarian, and this, no doubt, has had an important bearing on many events and tendencies.' I love this: it is both sarcastic and sincere, coy and forthright. 'I do not know what trouble Grandfather got into for getting the month wrong. I cannot remember Grandmother, but from a picture of the two of them which stood on the bookcase, I would think that the trouble was considerable.' There is something delightful about this, and something almost desperate. At points, Dow can be as uncompromising as one would wish. Speaking about sitting with terminally ill people and their families in the aftermath, he records an anecdote that inspires me. 'I've heard at second-hand, or even at third-hand: "You know, Mr Dow came in to see her when we were there and he never offered up a word of prayer." I'll have prayer with the bereaved. But not with an audience.'

Leafing through the book again, I find the thing that surprises me most about it is that there was a time when such a book could exist. To say it evokes a bygone age is a vast underestimation. It is difficult to imagine that such an era ever was – a time when *Songs of Praise* was not shuttlecocked around the schedules but an immovable part of Sunday programming, when pubs closed between two and six on a Sunday and you could buy a newspaper but not a Bible because of the Sunday trading laws. Theodore Beza, the colleague of Calvin, once said that the Church was 'an anvil that has worn out many hammers'. It might have seen off the hammers, but it can succumb to the drip-drip-drip of barely noticed rain.

Nobody would think the Rev. Dow a sinner, and his book is full of kindly advice to new ministers (start saying the Lord's Prayer loud and then tone it down so the congregation take over) and examples of his righteous intransigence when he thinks something is wrong, but never when he thinks he is in the right. But it begs to be liked, as likeable as I find it. As he writes, 'If ever I attain to being a saint, which, even if remotely possible, is highly unlikely, I will be honest when they come to canonize me. I will tell them that any pretensions I have to sanctity are due to the fact that early in life I concluded I was plainly not cut out to be a sinner. I always got found out.' Dow was one of the first ministers to use mass media – his author biography describes him as 'widely known as a broadcaster on radio and television, as a journalist and novelist, as a Burns expert, and as an accomplished amateur actor'. There was a forward-looking element to the Church exploring how new media might broaden their message; there was also an etiolation of the message as they aligned themselves to the key of the day. It became a three-minute pop song with some Jesus-y bits, rather than a thirty-minute exploration of belief. It found its grotesque ideal in the comedian Rikki Fulton. At home, at Hogmanay, from when I was a child to when I was a twenty-something, Rikki Fulton would appear and do a sketch in which he played a character called 'the Rev. I. M. Jolly'. It was a scathing satire on the Scottish minister's perceived gloominess, depression and faux profundity (one of his best gags was: 'And my son said to me, Daddy, did Jesus play for Rangers?' – the Protestant Glasgow football club – to which he replied, 'In a strange way, son, He did.'): I have sat through many sermons about the 'strange way' in which black is white, doubt is faith and three is one. Fulton also wrote a book under the I. M. Jolly persona, with the wonderful title *How I Found God and Why He Was Hiding from Me Anyway*). By adopting a couthy, wry and self-deprecating style, the new-media ministers tried to undo the image of an inflexible, doctrinaire Church. It was lowest common denominator niceness rather than abrasive and sometimes unfashionable virtue.

This has a bearing on Nelson's self-presentation as a ministerial candidate, one which troubled me for a long time. He does not play the card that many American Evangelical preachers play, and berate himself as the worst of sinners, the vilest offender, the most wretched of transgressors. This would inform the Assembly's debate. In the wider media maelstrom, Nelson said many things which led to questions about his sincerity. The Church required a psychological assessment of the candidate, as had the judicial system in terms of what charge was to be brought. About this, Nelson said, 'I'll be the only Church of Scotland minister who can show two certificates to prove his sanity.' At St Andrews, Nelson applied for a single room because 'he had a dust allergy and . . . his room mate might not take kindly to sharing with a convicted murderer' – which nearly breached the university's desire for confidentiality at the outset.

When Nelson approached the Kirk's officials at 121 George Street in Edinburgh to enquire about entering the ministry, he claimed the reason was 'that he was in it for the money'; in another gaffe, on being asked about what kind of parish he would ideally serve, he said, 'One with a salmon stream at the bottom of the manse garden.' Taken together, these do not form a good impression. Scattered across several interviews and articles over a period of time, they might also be interpreted as rather gauche attempts at wit, perhaps caused by nervousness, perhaps in imitation of the very register of pawky humour with which ministers with public profiles tried to emolliate the Kirk's unsmiling stereotype.

The Book of Judges 5:7

*The inhabitants of the villages ceased, they ceased in Israel,
until that I Deborah arose, that I arose a mother in Israel.*

In 2013, the novelist Iain Banks revealed that he had terminal cancer. He asked that I conduct the final print interview. He had just finished his last novel, *The Quarry*, in which the protagonist is suffering from incurable cancer: all the time he was imagining what it would be like to have cancer, he had cancer. In the interview he was his usual witty, irreverent and fascinating self; and it didn't even seem as if he were having to make an effort to be so. Apropos of the truly ludicrous irony, he said, 'Only real life can get away with the really outrageous stuff. The trouble with writing fiction is that it has to make sense, whereas real life doesn't. It's incredibly annoying for us scribblers. A lot of the time you're simply deciding how far down the path of unlikeliness you can go.' I have often thought about Iain's words since, especially when considering non-fiction. Were this a novel, this section would stretch improbability to incredulity.

Before the debate about Nelson was scheduled to take place, there was another report due before the Assembly into a topic which was generating as much heat and as little light in the letters pages. It was higher up the agenda not because it was more pressingly serious; rather, it was immemorial custom that reports to the Administration and Special Interests Department took precedence over reports to the Department of Education. Before the Church had the opportunity to discuss the advisability and feasibility of ordaining a man who had killed his mother, it was to hear from the Women's Guild/Panel on the Doctrine Study Group on the Motherhood of God.

Two years beforehand the Church had got itself into something of a fankle when it was revealed that the National President of the Women's Guild had, some weeks earlier, convened its annual meeting with a prayer in which she referred to 'God, our Mother' and 'Dear Mother God'. That the prayer had actually been written by a man, the Rev. Dr Brian Wren, seemed only to increase the momentum behind the calls for clarification on the matter. The Rev. James L. Weatherhead suggested that 'the concept of the "Motherhood of God" which this usage implied deserved some study; for it represented a problem which had faced the Church for centuries'. As the reforming Humanist Erasmus has it in his early-sixteenth-century *Adages*, 'The mills of God grind slow but exceedingly fine', and the report was now complete. The panel comprised six members of the Guild, all office bearers, and four ministers – three men and one woman. It was a model piece of work, thorough, closely read, open about disagreements and precise about distinctions. In the published volume, it takes up twenty-six pages – but bearing in mind that the average page of *The Church of Scotland: Reports to the General Assembly* had nearly eight hundred words, it was a small volume in its own right (and duly published as such. I found a copy in The Bookshop in Wigtown, much to my delight). Such is the reputation of the Kirk for being painstaking and meticulous in such matters, it can sometimes call to mind the anecdote of the philosopher Hastings Rashdall (author of *Is Conscience an Emotion?*) walking with his new wife in the University Parks in Oxford and being overheard saying, 'And seventeenthly, my dear . . .'

It was 'not the sort of committee in which politeness has stifled frank talking' the report says, and at least one (unnamed) member was appointed to it 'as a direct result of voicing strong objection to the addressing of God as Mother'. The report begins by dealing with the issues in abstract, admitting that the question might not have come about but for the rise of 'secular philosophies' and noting that 'our very insistence upon Scripture as the sole written form of God's revelation intensifies the perplexity of those who cannot straightforwardly agree with what it is that Scripture "says"'. This does not prevent the report's authors from drawing on non-biblical but theological writings from the outset, such as the saying attributed to the Early Church Father Cyprian of Carthage, that 'no one can have God as Father who does not have the Church as Mother'. In true Enlightenment style, they raise the question of what kind of God a person might envisage if, being told God is a Father, their own was an 'absent or unloving earthly parent'. That the Church had used its patriarchal imagery for misogynistic ends was admitted and regretted, and forgiveness was asked for it. In the third section, the analysis of language becomes even more diligent. The entire panel agreed that it would be erroneous to assume God has a gender and a sexual differentiation, and that to call him Father is to attribute a quality of 'maleness' to a transcendental deity. I am quite in awe of the authors when reading this – not just for their open-mindedness, but for their assiduity and gracious carefulness:

> Because we believe there is some resemblance, a
> relationship, a correspondence, between human and divine

reality, we draw pictures, tell stories, adopt analogies, construct doctrines, confident that while these are only finite expressions of the infinite they are not wholly inappropriate or misleading. The emphasis today upon the use of narrative, parable and metaphor as the most effective, though indirect means of communicating the incommunicable, only echoes what most theologies have always known about the incompleteness of theological statements, which necessarily fall short of their Object.

They then, in true Presbyterian preaching style, move from the abstract to the specific. By calling God a Shepherd, we do not mean that he shears sheep – unspoken and unwritten is the idea that by calling God a Father we do not mean he has a penis and a healthy sperm count. It is pleasing to see the Church of Scotland catch up, in 1984, with the theology developed by Islamic scholars of the Mu'tazalite school which flourished in Basra and Baghdad between the eighth and tenth centuries AD, and whose name means 'those who withdraw' or 'those who set themselves separate': 'reformers' might have been as good a synonym. They had pioneered more metaphorical and sophisticated readings of the Qur'an, parts of which concerned the meaning of physical attributes given to a deity who pre-existed space and time. To put it bluntly, if we say Allah, peace be on his name, has a throne, it is not a logical consequence that he has a gluteus maximus.

The report looks into the difference between Fatherhood as something we ascribe to God, and as a manner of addressing God. Section 4, headed 'Re-affirming the Tradition: The Fatherhood of God', is magnificently subversive: God is not a Father in the way that Zeus had concubines, mistresses and victims of divine sexual assault; 'only-begotten Son of the Father' stresses the unlikeness of Christ and God's relationship to earthly fatherhood and is 'the antithesis of biological repro-duction'; and it wryly notes that Adam and Eve 'male and female he created', 'in his image'. They even find a lovely paradox in a seventh-century Church Council at which Jesus was described as being made '*de utero Patris*', 'from the womb of the Father'. Most important is the accurate translation of Jesus instructing his disciples how to pray, the 'Our Father' which had caused such consternation. The word translated as 'Father' is *abba*, and a more precise rendering would be the less imposing and more loving 'Dad'.

Turning to their explicit brief, they catalogue all the undeniable metaphors that have God as a Mother: a protective mother bird (Isaiah 31:5), a mother eagle (Deuteronomy 32:11), a midwife (Psalms 22:9), a mother conceiving (Numbers 11:12), a mother pregnant (Isaiah 49:15), a mother giving birth (Isaiah 42:14; cf. Deuteronomy 32:18), a hen gathering her brood beneath her wings (Matthew 23:37; Luke 13:34), Christ as the Bride of the Church (Ephesians 5:27), the ambiguous Woman Clothed with the Sun (Revelation 12 ff.), and many more. If that were not enough, after some provisional findings on the question of what it would mean to address God as a shield, or a fortress, rather than describe God as one, the committee moves from biblical exegesis to the 'devotional legacy', selecting examples from Clement of Alexandria, Gregory Palamas, Count von Zinzendorf, Anselm of Canterbury, Aelred of Rievaulx, Christina of Markyate and Dame Julian of Norwich.

The report loses its admirable lucidity only when it comes to dealing with Mary, or rather Mariolatry. The Church of Scotland may have made steps towards a respectful, if disagreeing, relationship with the Roman Catholic Church, but there were limits. It breaks into italics: *'To be a mother and to have a mother are not one and the same!'* Even here, however, less strident voices prevail and the overall sentiment of their rejection of 'the Mary Cult' is an opposition to 'the Marian ideal of female submission to the male Master'. Concluding their report, they reject that any of their proposals would constitute '(a) a surrender to secularism, (b) a return to paganism, (c) a flirting with Roman Catholicism or (d) an abandonment of the Father'.

To read the report after a period of thirty-odd years is a melancholy experience. It is so cautious and conciliatory, so clear-sighted and so complete, that it is a wonder the topic is still discussed at all. Yet it is, and done so with less grace than might be. On other related issues – the clergy in civil partnerships, for example – a hectoring and wheedling and hair-splitting attitude prevailed. That the new Pope, Francis, can achieve something as simple as having Mary Magdalene politely and deferentially referred to as 'the Apostle to the Apostles' – given she was the first to find an empty tomb on the first Easter Sunday – is a sign of how slowly Churches actually move. The captain may set the direction, but the arms to pull the oars are out of his command. Yet in 1984, the Assembly's acceptance of the 'Report into the Doctrine of the Motherhood of God' seemed to show a groundswell: not of liberalism, not of relativism or postmodernism or concession to the *vox populi*, but of a subtle and sensitive range of thinkers within the Church. Or one would have thought so. It was the work of ten people, one of whom clearly did not agree with some of the findings.

The report into Nelson's application to overturn the presbytery ruling is only four and a half pages of the same cyan-covered volume. In part, this is for honest and well-meaning reasons. In part, it is for procedural particularity and in keeping with the remit of the Report. In part, it is to let the Assembly itself speak on the actual and urgent matters, without television cameras and microphones which might record things that would later haunt the participants or warp the debate.

There is no Black and White Corridor in the press. We have the Black or White Corridors. In an age of trolling and below-the-line columns, the idea that to express one's opinion meant writing, in inks green or otherwise, having an envelope to hand, buying a stamp and going to a letter box seems arcane as well as archaic. No wonder so many novels of the Golden Age of Crime rely on poison pen letters and individual characters in various fonts snipped and glued: it took effort to be nasty. But nasty they were.

The *Scotsman*'s letters page of 25 May 1984 devoted more column inches to the Motherhood of God than to the possible ordination of a murderer. A previous column by the Rev. Mary Spowart had suggested that women being denied the chance to fully participate in the life and thought of the Church diminished all, male and female alike. It provoked the following responses. (The first two correspondents quoted are women. The third is a man. I will not place their names on the record.)

> Sir – It is with amazement and the gravest concern for the future that I have followed by television and reading the national Press the debates of the General Assembly of the Church of Scotland this week but surely the remark of the Rev. Mary G. Spowart in your 'This morning' column must take the biscuit when she suggests that 'The domesticating of the female is to no one's advantage'.
> Oh God, where are they leading us?

Or:

> I cannot agree with the Rev. Mary G. Spowart's final
> comment in 'This morning' today . . . Surely many
> husbands, children and women would disagree also.
> Would the opposite of 'domesticated' be 'unbridled'?
> Sometimes when women are 'allowed a say' that is how
> they portray themselves. What a pity she should tag such a
> comment on the women of the Bible, many of whom
> came across as godly, careful and contented home-makers,
> fulfilling a much needed ministry.

One correspondent, of Camelon Road, Falkirk, snidely remarks, 'Had the committee which reported decided to report on the Full Personality of God rather than something which is a "nothing" they might have got further.' One of the other parts of my brain is reminding me that 'nothing', according to *Shakespeare's Bawdy* by Eric Partridge, is an Elizabethan euphemism for female genitals. Nothing will come of nothing, much ado about nothing, Hamlet thinks that a 'fair thought to lie between maids' legs' is 'nothing'. I doubt the correspondent had it consciously in mind.

Other voices were present – a letters page needs balance, however spurious and specious. One Elspeth Strachan wrote that since the debate on God's Motherhood she was 'an outsider in the church', because the 'tawdry pettiness' of 'uncontrolled and aggressive clapping' from even some women in the public gallery let alone the Assembly itself disgusted her. This despite revealing she is the wife of a minister. She contrasts the bullying with the 'understanding and compassion shown to one who killed his mother'. Wherever she is, in this world or the next, I salute her.

In such a febrile and fractured environment, the Kirk would then have to debate two things: one man's soul and its own.

Before leaving questions of mothers and their deaths, I have a confession. There are many things of which I am ashamed, but there is one that frequently wakens me in the night, and which comes back as a perpetual pang. It is all the deeper for being so superficial. My parents visited me in Oxford for my twenty-first birthday. I was, I thought, in my element, with very clever friends and an even cleverer girlfriend. When they arrived in the room I had booked, I introduced my very clever friends to my mother and my father. Later on, my mother cried because I had never before called her 'Mother'. She was my mum.

Exodus 33:21–3

And the LORD said, Behold, there is a place by me, and thou
shalt stand upon a rock: And it shall come to pass, while my
glory passeth by, that I will put thee in a clift of the rock, and will
cover thee with my hand while I pass by: And I will take away
mine hand, and thou shalt see my back parts: but my face
shall not be seen.

For a long time, I used to go to bed late at night. Reading over
my notes about the Nelson case had been instructive, but I had
one self-imposed stricture. I had spoken to contemporary
theologians and read all the material that was readily available;
I had gone through the documented accounts in Church reports.
I had read a lot of Kierkegaard again, and a lot of Nietzsche,
and tried to find an intellectual atmosphere in which I could
approach this question with as little prejudice as possible. One
thing I had not done was to avail myself of a service close at
hand. At the time, I was Literary Editor of *Scotland on Sunday*, so
had certain privileges regarding our archive and our library. I
had, most years, sat in the library going through what our sister
paper, the *Scotsman*, had reviewed one hundred years ago as a
bagatelle piece to put out over Christmas. I knew there were
things there that would not be on the digitised system where
I had read reports and obituaries and tirades and pleadings

special and otherwise. What I had not done, deliberately, was see his face.

I had an aversion to, as well as a sour selfishness about, seeing him. At school, we had 'done' *Macbeth* and I still remember remembering the line 'there's no art / To find the mind's construction in the face'. My English teacher, Alec Beaton, who saw in me a passion I did not yet feel and to whom I owe more than I can ever express, gave me *Hamlet* to read over the holidays. I had the option of it or *Great Expectations*, and chose the shorter. Then, at school, we had to watch *Hamlet* in the 1980 BBC version when we came to 'do' Hamlet. 'Doing', by the way, is reading the play aloud in class, and biting your lip whenever a question is raised about the text and your answer is sneered at because 'you're reading too much into this' by your fellow pupils in the top stream. Not that I harbour grudges. It had – yet again – Derek Jacobi in the lead role. He was utterly unlike the Hamlet in my head. Not that that was a bad thing, and a teenager being exposed to alternatives to their own self-involved thoughts is no bad thing at all. But having cast 'my' Hamlet, I shrinked my nose at this version. He didn't even have glasses – for some reason I always thought of Hamlet with glasses. I wear glasses. With Nelson, I allowed an unhealthy idea to take hold: that once I saw him, I would scry his true nature – his eyes would reveal it. Or his choice of jacket.

The Nelson in my head was at least at some level seductive. The ministers I had known – Tom Donald and James Watson and the Douglas Dupree whom I met once I went to Oxford and flirted with his Deep South Anglicanism (he was a man once described as having a voice like honey being poured into your navel) – had a glamour about them that was in part devilish in the only good sense of that word there might be. Tom's arched and arch eyebrows, his murine teeth; Jim's sneaky fag curled inside his palm and foursquare rigidity; Douglas's quarterback physique jumpered down in a humble hunch and a smell as if a more vulgar man had just walked down the corridor wearing too much cologne: they were men who imposed but also beguiled, who were charming and potentially dangerous, or judgemental, or choleric. It didn't do to mess with them. They were, after all, God's mortal ambassadors. Nelson, I thought, would have a widow's peak and an anchor or balbo style of beard, or even, at a push, an extended goatee. He would cut a dash, and leave a scar of charm or a static of danger lingering in the air around him. He would be somehow stricken and striving. There would be the unsaid and the pronounced, tight-lipped goodness and a willingness to break the rules for goodness in his startlingly blue eyes.

Basically, I managed to merge Sherlock Holmes and my own dad. Make of that, Freudians, what you will. Dad was at the time, and still is, all those things: he is strong where I am insubstantial, he is attractive where I am shilpit, his eyes are piercing where mine are presbyopic, he is honest where I have been found wanting, many, many times, though not usually by him. But this is not about us. It is about the first photograph of James Nelson that I saw. He looked like a moderately well-off pork butcher.

The first picture was of a man in a poacher's jacket, a jaunty, vaguely Tyrolean hat, minus feathers or fish-flies, a tweed suit, a tweedy tie, and puffs of blond or grey hair. He was striding down a country lane, hands in pockets, foot forward as if towards the future. The overcoat has a tint of tartan lining, the buttoned suit hints at a waistcoat. His eyes are invisible in such an old dot-matrix print, but his lips are upturned. Whether they are smiling, smirking or doing whatever the photographer asked is unreadable. Once the casket is open it cannot be shut. He is there, in another photograph, hand in hand with his new wife in exactly the same suit, and his hair is even more somewhere between blond and grey. In the pictures published in the *Scotsman* on 2 May 1994, his hair is clearly dark, with greyish badger strikes down the sides. In this I can see his eyes, and they are bagged. He looks tired, and one eye seems to be lazy or boss, just an eighth of an inch off.

There are others where he is shy, or shifty, where he is demure and downbeat, where he looks broken but not aggrieved, where he looks sad but still proud. There is one where he looks dashing – no, he looks happy. He looks absolutely happy. There are none where he looks like a murderer, but then what does a murderer look like?

I know that I am terrifically vain, and can spend parts of hours looking at photographs, drawings and paintings of myself. Applying the same strictures to those images as I do to the black-and-white pixels of Nelson, I find I do not recognise the person I am scrutinising. Except Nelson is always wearing a similar outfit: a douce suit and a starched collar and tie. He is almost wilfully unflash, despite what people would say about his previous life. His father, on the other hand, looks exactly as I imagined him. His glasses take up most of his face; he is never pictured either unfrowning or smiling. But at the same time he is old, and grieving. He ought to be allowed to be unhappy. In one picture he is sitting in a Fair Isle sweater, and has his thumb in his mouth. He might be biting his lip. He might be sucking his thumb. He could be pensive. He could be stopping himself speaking.

It's the quiet hint of a smile which Nelson sports that – what is the verb? Troubles? Haunts? Perplexes? Daunts? – infuriates me. It is illegible. He can look like a lost boy in one frame and like a sniggerer in the next. *He looks like he has got away with something*. But when I look them back over, he looks like he can never forget something. In the pictures where he made a public statement, he seems more than sincere, he seems positively anguished. *He looks on trial*. But then, of course, he is.

Poring over the stills, I realise that they are still. They are perpetual and unchanging. But my interest is in his change, if he did after all. The photographs are not light writing. They are fixed things of ink, which one cannot walk around or contemplate. They are not statues. They are glimpses, not visions. The more I look at them, the less I understand them. Except one. On 2 May 1984, the *Scotsman* published an article by James Johnston, headed 'Disputed selections defended'. It shows both James Nelson and his curious doppelgänger: Mr Iain Macdonald. Both were convicted criminals. But Macdonald was an embezzler, not a murderer. In the pictures, Nelson looks outwards, almost defiantly. Macdonald has his head hung. Nelson looks at the camera, and Macdonald seems to look at the floor. Of the two, Macdonald looks the more careworn and troubled.

Nobody seemed particularly to care about Mr Macdonald's fitness to be ordained. Was it because his crime was deemed the lesser? In some ways, it could be considered greater. Was not Judas Iscariot the treasurer of the apostles, the one who took care of the money and took from it and took remuneration for betrayal? There were no interviews with or articles by Mr Macdonald. Yet his name is linked with Nelson's in the Church's own reports. Article 2.4 is 'The Candidature of Mr Iain Alexander Macdonald'. Far more detail is given of his crimes: he had embezzled £118,000, the equivalent of over £600,000 in today's money; and even more detail is given of the 'intensive pastoral care' which he had been given and the fact that after he confessed he had also resigned from his Church offices. It seems like a model of repentance, and the picture seems to convey the same story.

The reports to the Assembly make mention of the fact that Mr Macdonald posted his application from Penninghame House Open Prison on 2 February 1981. Many years later, I gave an after-dinner speech in the same place. Penninghame House was no longer Penninghame House Open Prison. It ran courses on macrobiotic cooking and had a style somewhere, to my eyes, between bijou and chi-chi. Others may think differently. The owners evidently did. There was no sense at all that this had ever been a place of incarceration. It had changed. The dinner, as I recall, was rather nice, though whether or not it was also macrobiotic I am not in a position to say.

There is a famous paradox in Greek philosophy called the Ship of Theseus. If every plank of the ship commanded by Theseus is replaced during its voyage, to what extent is it the same ship when it arrives at its destination? We don't really worry nowadays if the 6.20 from Edinburgh to London is the same set of carriages as before, as long as it leaves around 6.20 (it rarely does). The 6.20 is defined by its leaving at 6.20. Penninghame House is a prison only if there are prisoners there. Iain Macdonald is not a swindler but a minister. James Nelson is not a matricide but a man of God. Things, we think, can change.

I spent far too long today looking at an oil portrait of myself. It was done by Andrea D'Avalos, and I sat listening to the soundtrack from *The Godfather* as he painted me. I do not look substantially different from the paints placed down over twenty years ago. It is, I've joked to friends, the anti-Dorian Gray. I don't change, and neither does it. I still even have the red paisley tie I was wearing when the image was made. I do have more grey hair now than then, and my hands often startle me when I type: I had not thought myself so much wrinkled. When it was first done, I thought I looked solemn and respectful, like a future bishop reading Athanasius, head bowed low in conviction, eyes invisible behind glasses. Sometimes now I think I look like a convict having heard the verdict.

The Gospel According to
St John 19:5

Then came Jesus forth, wearing the crown of thorns, and the purple robe. And Pilate *saith unto them, Behold the man!*

THE SECOND SERMON

The Gospel According to
St Mark 4:11–13

*And he said unto them, Unto you it is given to know the
mystery of the kingdom of God: but unto them that are
without, all these things are done in parables: That
seeing they may see, and not perceive; and hearing they
may hear, and not understand; lest at any time they
should be converted, and their sins should be forgiven
them. And he said unto them, Know ye not this
parable? and how then will you know all parables?*

There is a serious and significant essay by Shadd Maruna of
Queen's University Belfast, Louise Wilson of the University of
Sheffield and Kathryn Curran of King's College London, entitled,
'Why God Is Often Found Behind Bars: Prison Conversions and
the Crisis of Self-Narrative'. It is one of the very few papers to
discuss the topic.

> The jail cell conversion from 'sinner to saint' or from
> non-believer to true believer is a well-known, indeed
> almost clichéd character arch in feel-good fiction, history
> and media accounts. Yet this dramatic example of a

140

'quantum change' – a sudden identity transformation
qualitatively different from the more common, incremental
changes in human development . . . has relatively little
systematic development in the social science literature . . .

I would raise an eyebrow at a few words there. 'Often' is one, and
later I shall think more about it. 'Quantum' is another: the prisoner
is not a kind of Schrödinger's soul, trapped between sinnerdom
and sainthood before God peeks in the box. 'Arch' is the third. I
think, given the aesthetic references, they mean 'arc'. 'Arc' itself
is a kind of Freudian slip. In one sense, there is the echo of the
First Epistle of Peter, the second chapter, beginning at Verse 6:

Wherefore also it is contained in the scripture, Behold, I
lay in Sion a chief corner stone, elect, precious: and he
that believeth on him shall not be confounded. Unto you
therefore which believe *he* is precious: but unto them
which be disobedient, the stone which the builders
disallowed, the same is made the head of the corner, And
a stone of stumbling and a rock of offence, *even to them*,
which stumble at the word . . .

The idea of the arch held together by its capstone, the finally
placed crux, is paramount. If Gothic architecture was the Word
made Stone, then its reliance on clever balance was what every
cathedral aspired to in its spires and its gargoyles. But the arc is
also the ark, the Ark of Noah and the Ark of the Covenant as well.
It is where things are safe and secure, preserved and protected. It
is also the place that is finally absent and empty, void and
avoided, such as when Titus destroyed the Temple in Jerusalem
and found the Holy of Holies, said to contain the Ark, to be a

141

receptacle for nothingness. The 'sinner/saint' is more than an enigma; the 'saint/sinner' is a paradigm. The idea of such a moral paradox is also an ethical triumph. If the arc from sinner to saint can be the arch of a Church, it can also be the Ark in which every moral injunction and nothing at all resides.

Convert: from the Latin prefix *con-*, meaning 'thoroughly', or 'with', or 'around', and the verb *vertere*, meaning 'to turn'. It seems simple, and yet is radically complex. At the most literal level it might mean just to turn one's back on something; to set oneself, metaphorically, against the past. But it can also mean to transform completely, like base metals changed alchemically to gold. It shades into different meanings whether you think of it as active – I converted – or passive – I was converted. It can be thought of as a fundamental alteration, or a reorientation, as a choice or as an inevitability. It is also intrinsic to Christianity in a way it is not to other religions. Not one of the first Christians began as a Christian.

Judaism began as an ethnicity and became a philosophy. Israelites followed the God of Israel, and were different from Canaanites, Moabites, Edomites and the poor old Amalekites. But even at the beginning the idea of a 'genetic' Jewishness was problematic: after all, Moses married a non-Jewish woman, Zipporah, daughter of the Kenite shepherd and priest of Midian, Jethro. They had sons who flicker at the edges of the stories, Gershom and Eliezer, and grandsons even more shadowy, Shebuel and Rehabiah. Shebuel had no sons, according to the First Book of Chronicles, but Rehabiah's 'were very many' and not one of them named. There was a tradition of the *ger*, sometimes translated as 'proselyte' and sometimes as 'foreigner' and sometimes as 'resident alien': a non-Jewish person who observed Jewish law and who could, much later, 'become' Jewish. The *ger* was significant in the moral cosmos: in Leviticus 19:34, Moses says to the people, 'But the stranger that dwelleth with you shall be unto you as one born among you, and thou shalt love him as thyself; for ye were strangers in the land of Egypt: I am the LORD your God,' just after the LORD has been issuing directives about beards, not cursing the deaf and the inadvisability of making one's daughter a harlot. As noted previously, it was only in the second century AD, after the destruction of the Temple in Jerusalem, that Rabbinical Judaism started to codify the rules of who might and who might not be considered Jewish. In the absence of territory came a new form of ethnicity.

Can one convert to Islam? Mechanically, of course one can. It merely involves reciting the *shahada*: 'There is no god but God. Muhammad is the messenger of God.' But on a more technical level, this is not a conversion, but a return, a reversion. In the *hadith*, the collected sayings of the Prophet outwith the Qur'an itself, it is stated that 'no child is born but upon *fitrah* [a term 'meaning "innate goodness and submission to Allah"']. It is his parents who make him a Jew, a Christian or a Zoroastrian.' In Sura 7 – 'The Heights' – ayat 172–3, Muhammad reminds the readers and hearers that Allah said to all the future descendants of Adam, 'When your Lord took from the children of Adam – from their loins – their descendants and made them testify of themselves, he said to them "Am I not your Lord?" They said "Yes, we have testified" – lest on the Day of Resurrection you should say "Indeed we were of this unaware."' To become a Muslim means admitting you always were a Muslim.

Theologically, the *'Ahl al-Kitāb*, the 'people of the book', or non-Islamic monotheists, were accorded a certain degree of respect in the Qur'an, and *jizya*, the tax on non-Muslims, was a means of acknowledging without condoning. But what works for the iman might not work for the vizier. Islam found itself in the position of it being an economic benefit to have non-Muslim subjects paying the tax, even if their religious return would be preferred.

The Church of the Latter Day Saints, also known as the Mormons, take part of Islamic theology one stage further. If Allah had made all possible humanity attest to his Oneness before they became actual, the Mormons retrospectively baptise the dead. This has a biblical precedent – First Corinthians 15:29, 'Else what shall they do which are baptised for the dead, if the dead rise not at all? why are they then baptised for the dead?' – and the practice has been in place since 1840. It became controversial when it was revealed that some sections of the Church of the Latter Day Saints had been retroactively baptising victims of the Holocaust – if one were to adhere to their beliefs, Anne Frank is now a Mormon, whether she likes it or not. The idea of non-consensual conversion does jib the brain a bit.

A Christian, by contrast, is still something you become rather than something you are, always were or will be. Setting aside Jesus (who, it can be supposed, became a Christian as well as Christ when he was baptised) and the apostles, we can ask: who is the first Christian convert? I would like it to be the unnamed Ethiopian eunuch who had charge of all the treasures of Queen Candace, and who appears in Acts of the Apostles, Chapter 8. The Spirit sends Philip to Gaza and he comes across the eunuch reading the Book of Isaiah. He does not understand the meaning of the passage, and Philip enlightens him. 'See, *here is* water; what doth hinder me to be baptised?' he asks. 'And Philip said, If thou believest with all thine heart, thou mayest. And he answered and said, I believe that Jesus Christ is the Son of God.' Several rules in the Torah would have prevented the acceptance of the

Ethiopian eunuch – his being a eunuch for one. The idea of the first convert being a person otherwise rejected is bewitching, although, reading it again, I do worry that he is also wealthy, or at least, as we are told, he has the charge of all her treasure.

It also seems significant that this conversion story comes just before *the* conversion story, where Saul will become St Paul on the Road to Damascus. A gentile is converted before the apostle to the gentiles is formed. The first convert was probably neither Matthias, who does become an apostle, nor poor Joseph called Barsabas, who was surnamed Justus, the person who is passed over when the apostles are appointing a successor to Judas Iscariot, since they were both 'witness with us of his resurrection' according to St Peter. I would exclude the two unfortunate embezzlers, Ananias and Sapphira, since their conversion evidently did not improve their moral behaviour. I would even rule out St Stephen, the first martyr. We do not know if he personally knew Jesus – Pseudo-Hippolytus (the pupil of Irenaeus, the pupil of Polycarp, the pupil of Paul) lists him as one of the seventy or seventy-two disciples sent out in the tenth chapter of Luke's Gospel, in a text discovered in 1854 and of dubious authenticity. But Stephen does, at the point of his martyrdom, say, 'Behold, I see the heavens opened, and the Son of man standing on the right hand of God.' Late in the day, perhaps, but nevertheless visible. Likewise, we do not know the name of the 'certain man lame from his mother's womb' who is healed in Acts of the Apostles, Chapter 3, and then praises Jesus. Nor do we know the names of the Parthians and Medes and Elamites and dwellers in Mesopotamia and in Judea, and Cappadocia, in Pontus, and Asia, Phrygia and Pamphylia, in Egypt and in the parts of Libya around Cyrene, the strangers of Rome, Jews and proselytes, Cretes and Arabians who miraculously spoke to each other at Pentecost, when the promised Spirit descended. One of them must have been the first 'convert' who had no personal experience of Jesus. That they must be forever anonymous is pleasing in its own way. But the named one is Saul of Tarsus.

Saul does 'see' Jesus, even though, having 'made havock of the church', and 'yet breathing out threatenings and slaughter against the disciples of the Lord', he has been blinded first. Or had he? A light shone around him, but it is only later we are told that he was 'three days without sight', although he did have to be 'led by the hand'. His companions were 'speechless, hearing a voice, but seeing no man'. The vision Saul/Paul sees/does not see is laconic. 'Why persecutest thou me?' The conversion is prompted by an accusation. But Saul does not know who is speaking to him. The vision states who He is, and warns, '*it is* hard for thee to kick against the pricks'. The agenbite of inwit, the sting of conscience, the screech of chalk on a moral blackboard: Paul is told that it will be much easier all round to concede. To give up. This is conversion as the foregone accepted. But it has to be accepted even if foregone. It is a with-turning as much as a turning-away-from.

The most famous conversion outside of the biblical sources must be that of the Emperor Constantine, which made Christianity the official religion of the Roman Empire rather than a barely tolerated sect. Before the Battle of the Milvian Bridge, where Constantine defeated his final rival in AD 312, he supposedly saw a vision of the cross, and read the phrase above it '*en toutō níka*', usually rendered in Latin as '*in hoc signo vinces*': 'by this sign [or "symbol"] you shall triumph'. The intervention does not seem to have wholly persuaded the Emperor, who was baptised only on his deathbed. (That said, he did stop the gladiatorial games and his mother, Helena, spent a great deal of time collecting relics of the new state religion, including finding the cross itself. This has always bemused me. Surely the Romans would just reutilise crosses when they were crucifying people? What made this one so special it was retired from service? Even more curiously: who else might have been crucified on it?) Constantine is an early example of a problem Islam shared with Christianity: how can you tell if a conversion is genuine or expedient? When, after the pogroms of 1391 and the Alhambra Decree of 1492, Spain and Portugal required their subjects to be Christian, a great deal of pernicious intellectual energy went into deciding whether the so-called *conversos* – mainly Jewish but also Muslim believers who had converted to Christianity, or their descendants – were actual converts. Being forced to break dietary laws was always a good trick. Paella, in its combination of pork and shellfish, both forbidden in the Torah, was a dish that proved you were Christian – unless, like the Inquisition itself, you theorised how you could sin without sinning. (The Inquisition, incidentally, burned a large number of Bibles, since the texts would allow Jews to know how still to be Jewish. They did not see the irony.) Being forced to be something you were not was not seen as a betrayal: the Hebrew term is *anusim*, 'the coerced'. Moses Maimonides, the influential twelfth-century Jewish thinker, dealt with the status of the *anusim*. 'But their children and grand-children . . . are like children taken captive by the gentiles . . . Therefore efforts should be made to bring them back in repent-ance.' The sign of truthfulness was not adhering to a particular law, ritual or custom, but contrition.

St Paul is later freed from prison by angelic interventions, which, one would think, amply proves his contrite change of heart. The duty of Christians towards those in prison is clear, if infrequently implemented. In Matthew's Gospel, towards the very end, we get a statement of what a Christian might do, rather than what one is: 'For I was an hungred, and ye gave me meat: I was thirsty, and ye gave me drink: I was a stranger, and ye took me in: Naked, and ye clothed me: I was sick, and ye visited me: I was in prison, and ye came unto me.' Jesus himself had been detained by authorities. So too would be St Peter, although unlike Jesus, and like Paul, he would be divinely liberated. Prison might not be an oubliette for the godless, but, rather, the necessary dungeon into which He reaches.

The Maruna, Wilson and Curran paper examines four types of prison conversion. First, they look at those who convert for 'social identity'. Prison, I assume, is a lonely place. It must be lonely not just in the ostracism of the inmates, but also in their estrangement from themselves. Doubly condemned as 'the God Squad' or 'the Bible Bashers', those inside with a 'marginalisation within a marginalisation' find a kind of security in faith. One of their interviewees says, 'I don't feel like a prisoner any more, I feel like I'm set free.' Another says, 'The Bible says I am a new person in Christ Jesus. Whatever God says I am, I am.' They are enfolded, and join the fold.

Second, there are those who convert for 'creating a purpose for imprisonment'. These are those who 'continue to believe that the world is a benevolent place and they are good people'. One interviewee says, 'I got twelve years . . . there must be a reason. God must want me in here.' Another says, 'I genuinely believe that at that point God started to step in and speak to me and say "Now, look, come on, I'm actually going to show you something you've never considered while you're in here and that's where I'm going to bring you to when you walk out that door."' Their past was not a disgrace, it was an overture. The prison is 'a mission field', a concept strongly aligned with the third category.

To the third: the convict who believes in their moral superiority. To quote the paper: 'Several interviewees discussed God's "call" for them to preach. The prisoner begins to view himself as an instrument through which God works for the benefit of others. This position of power and influence that the inmate now assumes contrasts sharply with the common social position of prisoners as disenfranchised and powerless individuals.' These anonymous interviews are among the most fascinating and disturbing. 'I ran scared from the presence of the Lord and I did it for a long time . . . God is doing everything in me and through me.' 'My identity today is knowing I am a man of God and knowing that He has called me to preach and teach the Word so I look at myself as a minister of God and that is my strength.' 'Sometimes I feel as though He says do this or do that and sometimes I feel as though he says right just go on with what you normally do.'

Finally, there is the most obvious reason for conversion: that it is conversion. 'You know, life can make you feel like I did which was totally worthless . . . And that everything you do is wrong, and I suppose one of the things Christianity says to you is that your sins can be forgiven.' 'I haven't done anything that hasn't been done before because I'm redeemable as a person, as a human being.' 'You know my faith tells me that everyone is a sinner, but everyone can be forgiven to the same extent and there's no kind of levels of forgiveness.' The authors of the paper note that this form is particularly common among those who have committed the most serious of crimes, especially murder. 'Self-narrative' is the key structure here. Conversion is a way by which the past might be rewritten.

I had naively thought that Nelson and Macdonald had been altered by their crimes, and drawn to faith in the aftermath. But both had always already and anyway been professed

Christians. The story would be so much simpler if God, as he did with St Paul and St Peter, set the prisoner free in terms of both iron bars and thinking.

Reading about Iain Macdonald, I realised something. Section 2.4.3 in the Assembly Reports states: 'He had given service as an Elder and as a Lay Reader, to his congregation and to his Presbytery, and was well known in his community. After his confession, he resigned from his offices in the Church.' He was a Christian before he committed his crime, and was a Christian afterwards. The same holds true for James Nelson. In the articles which brought his name to prominence, it is said that 'there is a strength of faith behind Jim Nelson. It did not come in a sudden conversion.' Nelson himself then adds and elaborates: 'In fact I had to say to myself, I've been going to church, operating on a façade. What does that make me? I'm talking about a tremendous need in my own situation – we're talking about love of brother. Whether it was my conscience pricking me or not, I said to myself "What are you going to do about it?" . . . I don't see it as a Road to Damascus experience.' That he uses the word 'pricking' seems both subliminal and measured.

Nelson did not convert in prison, but he did find a calling. It was nothing to do with murder or with his 'self-narrative' as a murderer. He recollected that 'the prison chaplain in Saughton, the Rev. Tom Downie, preached a sermon on the Bengali floods of 1970 in which thousands were killed'. At the time, by his own admission, Nelson 'couldn't have given two hoots. It was just another tragedy.' This would have been a mere matter of months after he committed the crime for which he was imprisoned. But the sermon niggled him sufficiently that he spoke further with his minister, took a correspondence course and found that 'the more I could invest, the more I could discern'. He was blunt about some aspects: 'Ordination made it more difficult for Jim Nelson in prison rather than easier. "You are viewed suspiciously. It doesn't get you remission."' The paper on prison conversions touches only lightly on this angle: that by seeming to convert, one might be seen to be a different person. Conversion could be tactical still.

Our culture generally has a deep suspicion of converts. What might the indubitable sign of a genuine conversion be? This may seem like a question raised by a less religious age sceptical of conversion, yet the Calvinist Churches in the seventeenth and eighteenth centuries probably devoted more energy to detecting 'false' conversions than they did to evangelising their beliefs. Tracts such as *The Parable of the Ten Virgins* by Thomas Shepard or Matthew Mead's *The Almost Christian Discovered; or, The False Professor Tried and Cast* or Jonathan Edwards's *A Treatise Concerning Religious Affections* attempted to discern the difference between conversion and capitulation – or, indeed, a willed but erroneous belief.

Let us indulge in a little thought experiment. Take, for example, Brandy Ledford.

Born in 1969 in Denver, Colorado, she and her dance drill team went on to win the 1980 world championship. She has been in various TV series and movies: *Demolition Man, Stargate SG-1* and *Stargate Atlantis, Andromeda, Baywatch, Irresistible Impulse, The Outer Limits, A Woman's Rage*. Her IMDb biography describes her as 'a devout lover of Jesus and a completely UN-fundamentalist Christian'. It mentions, coyly, that she 'took a turn at modelling . . . while prevailing quite successfully in that field she wanted something more fulfilling'. She was in fact a soft-core porn model, and one of the first sex videos leaked on the Internet featured her and a member of a heavy metal band. She must have been one of the first people to experience a very new kind of old humiliation. Or take another, this time a male individual. Born in 1912, he was relatively dilatory at school until he read about the possibility of space exploration. This galvanised him tremendously and he excelled in his studies, eventually working with the government of the day in the development of rockets. At the end of the war he took the opportunity to work elsewhere, and eventually was given that country's highest scientific order. A keen and outspoken proponent of extrasolar exploration, he had a conversion experience in 1956 after attending an Evangelical Church, which he had presumed would be a 'country club as I'd been led to expect'. He became increasingly mystical, saying that 'through science man strives to learn more of the mysteries of creation. Through religion he seeks to know the Creator.' He had a private interview with Martin Luther King. He was Wehrner von Braun, the Nazi developer of the V2. Now, which of these, if either, or both, might you consider a convert of true heart? It is easy to dismiss one as having toiled for the Devil and sought to balance the moral balance sheets, the other as a lost soul who, having trafficked on her looks, finds a constant 'boyfriend' (her words) in the Second Aspect of the Trinity. Think on it: seeking out the marks and authentications of conversion is remarkably like being a witch-finder.

But there is one conversion story which I cannot doubt. I can doubt St Paul at points – deep-cover Tetrarchy agent, converter of revolution to codification? I can doubt Constantine's conversion for gain or to reduce pain. I can doubt Wesley and Bunyan, I can doubt every 'wretch like me' who 'now can see'; but I cannot doubt George Price. His story is told in an exceptional biography by Oren Harman, *The Price of Altruism*, and features in one of the documentaries of Adam Curtis, *All Watched Over by Machines of Loving Grace*, as ingenious as the conceit of a metaphysical poem, unrelated ideas and images revealing their occult connections.

Price was born in New York in 1922. Having graduated, and completed a doctorate, at the University of Chicago in chemistry, he went on to teach at Harvard and the University of Minnesota, and was a consultant at Bell Laboratories and IBM. An awkward, wilfully eccentric and unclubbable figure, he had lost his father at the age of four, and his mother (a former actress) had had to take in lodgers during the Depression. He took as his personal motto a phrase he wrote for an article in *THINK*: 'Many of the most imaginative and important inventions have been made by outsiders not employed in the field concerned, who have followed their own schedules and worked according to their own plan.' Contemporaries recall him as being both smug and juvenile, with a fixing stare despite weak eyes. He was an atheist who nevertheless married a Catholic, was prone to anti-Semitic outbursts and was divorced after eight years. Given he would say to his wife things like 'Better our daughters be prostitutes than nuns', this seems unsurprising.

He moved to London in 1967 to work with the evolutionary biologists W. D. Hamilton and John Maynard Smith. Although Price made significant advances in several fields, he is best known for his work that led to the Price Equation, concerning frequency of changes in a gene over time. What that innocuous-sounding description actually implied was radical. Price had found a way to explain altruism in evolutionary terms. The question of why an organism would commit an unselfish act – even one leading to its own destruction – in a universe ruled by survival of the fittest had been a vexation to biologists from Charles Darwin onwards. Price provided the answer: altruism correlates to how closely you are related to whoever you sacrifice yourself for. It was Price's work that would lead Richard Dawkins to name his most famous book *The Selfish Gene.*

You might expect with such a résumé that Price would retire and deploy his formidable intellect on other interests: he had written on game theory and its implications for the Cold War, for example, and had published two papers debunking attempts to prove extra-sensory perception. Instead he became a Christian, and an uncompromising one at that. In his own words, 'I am the hardware and the Gospel is the software.' So, given the injunction in the Gospel According to Saint Luke 6:29, that to 'him that taketh away thy cloke forbid not *to take thy* coat also', Price would give away his clothing to the homeless and mendicant of north London. Living in squats and sleeping in his office, he attempted to become the embodied contradiction of his own theory: a creature of utterly selfless kindness. In 1975 he committed suicide, and the mourners at his grave in St Pancras comprised Hamilton and Keynes and five alcoholic tramps.

There is an extremism in Price which is both pitiable and admirable. It would be possible to see his conversion as merely symptomatic of the mental illnesses and depression that had previously afflicted him. It might have been possible to argue him away from his hyper-literal obedience to the Gospels. But we cannot doubt that he had the courage of his convictions. Conversion did not make him happy, or bring him peace of mind, or free him from his past. The only immortality he gained was the named equation.

The Torah records two instances of something similar to and deeper than conversion. In Genesis 17, Abram, who is now ninety-nine years old, is called to walk with the Lord. 'Neither shall thy name any more be called Abram, but thy name shall be Abraham.' The story of Jacob, Abraham's grandson, is told in

Genesis 32: 'And he said unto him, What *is* thy name? And he said, Jacob. And he said, Thy name shall be called no more Jacob, but Israel: for as a prince hast thou power with God and with men, and hast prevailed.' In the New Testament we are never told why Saul becomes Paul, but we are told that Simon is renamed Peter in Matthew's Gospel: 'And I say also unto thee, That thou art Peter, and upon this rock I will build my church; and the gates of hell shall not prevail against it.' It's a pun – a rare example of Jesus making a joke – on the Greek *petros*, meaning 'rock', or rather 'pebble', a stone you would kick aside on a track. In each of these name-changing stories, the individual struggles with faith before being altered. Saul was persecuting the Church, and Simon had just been upbraided as one of 'ye of little faith', though he did avoid the various wrong answers he had heard to Jesus' question: 'Whom do men say that I the Son of man am?' (Peter, for once, gets it right: his career as an apostle is mostly characterised by his being a bit dumb about things.) Abram has just been told a promise to him so ludicrous – that his elderly wife will be the mother of generations – that he scornfully laughs; Jacob has just fought the entire night with God himself.

None of them elect to change their names. Their nature is changed and their name imposed upon them. It would have been easy and cowardly for Nelson and Macdonald to change their names, to become ministers under assumed names; but they knew that the only entity that can truly do that is God. If they were to be men of faith, they had to be so under their given names. But to become an ordained minister is a different kind of anonymity altogether. They wanted to change their title – no longer mister, no longer Prisoner 24601 – to the Reverend.

The Second Epistle of John 1:8

Look to yourselves, that we lose not those things which
we have wrought, but that we receive a full reward.

The Hebridean storyteller Ian Stephen has a witty and wise yarn about a ship's cook on a Lewis vessel. Sometimes drunkenly, sometimes not – the story varies in each telling – he goes above board with a washing-up bowl full of dirty water, and cowps the contents overboard. At the last minute he realises that all the ship's cutlery was still in the bowl, and is now at the bottom of the briny. When it comes to dinner, the crew seat themselves in front of plates and ashets and pots, bemused until the captain asks where the cutlery is. 'Well,' replies the cook, 'is a thing lost if you know where it is?'

I have often thought of that story when pondering the phrase 'to lose one's faith'. The word 'lost' derives from the Proto-Indo-European *leu-*, meaning 'to separate', 'untie', 'divide' or 'loosen'. In Old English it acquires the sense of 'to perish' or 'be destroyed'. The past participle of the Old English *leosan* is *loren*, a trace of which remains in words like 'lovelorn' or 'forlorn'. I think that for a time I was faithlorn.

The first time, though, that I lost my faith it was because I had flung it from me, as definitively as the ship's cook emptied the bowl into the deep. No schoolboy is mature enough to read

Nietzsche. In a kind of self-aggrandising petulance, I too declared God Dead, and found a vainglorious heroism in the idea of being a being that created meaning in a meaningless, yawning void of a universe. My meanings were fairly simplistic and shoogly, all told. It was an atheism where the *a-* meant less than the *-theism*; at times it was actually a milquetoast Manicheanism, a rage at the Nobodaddy father and a glorification of rebellious sons of light. My preening sixth-form self scorned the stupidity of believers. Hadn't their own God told them they were sheep? We were goats: pugnacious, omnivorous, hardy, with eyes you only elsewhere see in squids and knees that would not bend. I grew up. Actually, I grew down. I was lulled as a student into an Anglican liturgy far from the sparse and spartan faith in which I had been raised. Knowing the difference between a chasuble and a soutane, knowing the Collect for the Day, knowing when to kneel and when to stand was more important than understanding why one did any of it. There is a repetition in Anglicanism which is beautifully beguiling. It is like a precise and ornate clock that ticks and tocks sedately, when I had been used to an alarm clock. The God of Shocks could be stilled by the simple act of doing a thing again and again.

I lost my faith the second time when my girlfriend at university left me. My attachment to the Anglican Church, it seemed, was provisional on my being attached to an Anglican family, despite the fact that she herself was— Since so much time has passed I could not say if she was an agnostic, an atheist or as uninterested as possible. Jehovah, to her, was not as fascinating as Plato. Once, I had upbraided a friend who had left the Church because he now had a girlfriend, and snidely said that one's faith did not reside in one's boxer shorts. Mine did, too, it transpired. This was the atheism of apathy and atrophy. I couldn't be bothered

157

with the Church, or much else. Like an unexercised muscle, my faith shrivelled. So did I.

I crept back to church out of loneliness alone. I didn't believe, but I could make a passable impersonation of it. Except that I couldn't. Visiting my parents at Easter, I found myself struck by a trembling in my legs when I had to stand up to sing the hymns; I would fidget and falter; I felt a gauze glaze me. I had to leave the church and blamed the pollen from the daffodils. Even at my wedding, I twitched as if I had St Vitus' Dance. It was the only saintliness I might acquire. It seemed as if I were being struck down for my lukewarm, Laodicean and unfaithful belief; and yet wasn't this the very intervention that my teenage self had yearned for, an unequivocal electrification as the Hand of the Lord was placed upon me? Those were my best days, when I shook with fear.

So the third loss was the period of hiddenness. I carefully took my faith and put it in a box, tied it around with twine and placed it in a psychic attic, and bolted fast the door. Atheism was, in many ways, just easier. It was uncontentious not to believe. It was mandatory in places. My first atheism had been, I thought, sophisticated and philosophical; this was acquiescent and bathetic. It had an imponderable air of beige. At the time I wrote several articles I now regret, in their flip, condescending, curled-lip tone.

What changed? I went back to live in a village rather than the city. I went to church in the way one went to the school fair or the coffee morning. A part of me rationalised it, with a 'fake it till you make it' charlatanism. But then I read G. K. Chesterton. It was just another quick review, and yet something about his ebullient embrace of paradox, his wholesome antagonism to the norm was unexpectedly joyous. He did not discount the horrors we and he faced, but instead observed that beneath the skin, the skull is always smiling. While I had acclaimed and lauded an intransigent modernism opposed to everything Chesterton stood for, I couldn't shake off the sense that he had warned against the likes of Hitler and Hirohito while my beloved Ezra Pound, Wyndham Lewis, Céline, Knut Hamsun and Filippo Marinetti had shamefully marched in step.

Chesterton never said it, but a phrase began to niggle in my brain: *credo quia absurdum*. If it is a lie, as he observed, it is a lie so preposterous no one would make it up. My minister sagely counselled me that engaging with faith as a kind of intellectual contrarianism is a perilous path. It is. Yet I wish to be the me that believes more than I wish to be the me that mocked belief.

To hard truths and stubborn confessions. In countless ways I still do not believe, and not through want of trying (I always liked the retort of describing oneself as a practising Christian, hoping one day actually to master it, as if faith were the F# diminished seventh arpeggio). But. In my early twenties I had a dream. I was in the ruins of Melrose Abbey, near where I grew up, though I was dreaming in a bed in Oxford. Melrose has always had eldritch associations for me, especially so as at the time I was reading the Venerable Bede's *Historia Ecclesiastica Gentis Anglorum*, which recounts the story of a monk, Drycthelm, who had a dream-vision of hell. He would afterwards stand in the River Tweed, in shivering, sleety weather, and rebuke his fellow monks that he had seen colder places. There is a circular window in the remnants of the south transept in Melrose Abbey; in the dream it was late autumn or early winter and night. A full moon was low and large and mournful, and I watched it fit perfectly into the window. At that point I understood everything. I understood what the Real Presence of Christ in the Eucharist really meant. I grasped the Hypostatic Union. The *felix culpa* was simplicity itself. The *point* of *everything* was *clear*. I woke up. I wrote on the papers next to my bedside table the phrase 'ALL IS LENS', and fell back to sleep. At dawn, I had a miasmic sense of what I had dreamt, but none of the specificity of the dream I had known while I was dreaming. Ever since, I have yearned for that moment of unconscious absolute certainty.

It was not an experience beyond language; it was an experience where language was entire. I overstood rather than understood. I didn't just know, I knewn. 'Think' and 'thank' were the same word. In the aftermath of the dream I have scrabbled around in the edges of language, like a child playing with Lego trying to build a cathedral. It seems as if language itself has banked for future use potentials yet unexplored. Did you know, for example, that English has a future passive perfect continuous, without really needing one? ('In twenty seconds' time I will have been being bored by this person for exactly quarter of an hour.') There is a poetry of prefixes and suffixes we are yet to understand: I can believe or disbelieve, but can I misbelieve? I might conceivably be an atheist or a theist, but who are the untheists, the abtheists, the retheists, the distheists, the antheists? Might one be an intheist, patterned on the example of 'valuable' and 'invaluable'? Might faith be like the meaning conjured from a phrasal verb, where 'to put him up' and 'to put up with him' are different, and the meaning cannot be derived from knowing the meaning of each of the individual words? If I cannot be faithful or faithless, can I be faithwracked? Or faithing? Or faithish? Or faithean? Or faithwards? Or faithry? Or faithick? Or faithilytic? The *-lytic* suffix derives from Greek, and it means 'to loose' or 'untie'. And in the beginning was the Word. And when you light a light you are visible to everyone, and not just those who wish you well.

Nelson had – quite obviously, even to those who had not eyes to hear or ears to see, as one vicar once said – lost people. He had made them lost. How did it prey on his conscience?

The Book of the Prophet Ezekiel 9:11

And, behold, the man clothed with linen, which had *the*
inkhorn by his side, reported the matter, saying, I have done
as thou hast commanded me.

I have a profound dislike of essentialist arguments, especially
when it comes to national characteristics, which is only equalled
by a fascination with those glitches of discrepancy that unveil
unnoticed differences. There are many differences between
Scotland and England, some irrelevant and fatuous, some perva-
sive and important. A critical one for this story is a certain kind
of story. In part this is the cultural background to decisions
made, both by the men who wished to become ministers of the
Church and by the Church in which they sought to become
ministers. In part, and not the least of the concerns, is that one
would directly cite one of the stories. The stories all involve
ministers.

If one wanted an index to measure the difference between
Scotland in 1916 and Scotland in 2016, an unusual but accurate
indicator would be the standings of two novels: Walter Scott's
The Tale of Old Mortality, and his friend, acolyte, rival and tattler
of posthumous tales James Hogg's *The Private Memoirs and*
Confessions of a Justified Sinner: Written by Himself: With a Detail of
Curious Traditionary Facts and Other Evidence by the Editor. The

former was published in 1816, as part of the pseudonymous 'Tales of My Landlord' series, and sparked a national debate about the representation of the Church of Scotland in the seventeenth century. The latter was published anonymously in 1824, having had the equivalent of a trailer put out in the influential *Blackwood's Magazine*. In 1916 Scott was still the school-prize-giving novelist of choice. Hogg was out of print, and those who could read him read him in a bowdlerised version, where his name was even taken off his own spine: he was just 'The Ettrick Shepherd'. *Confessions*, as I shall call it, is now a canonical text in Scottish literature. The novelist Ian Rankin and the late filmmaker Bill Douglas both aspired to create a cinematic version.

The reasons for Hogg's ascent are both obvious and oblique. In 1947, the French novelist André Gide wrote an introduction to a reissue of *Confessions*, praising its psychological complexity and seeing in it a precursor of modernist literature, such as his own *The Vatican Cellars*, an equally askance look at religion, belief and wickedness. 'How explain', he writes, 'that a work so singular and so enlightening, so especially fitted to arouse passionate interest in both those who are attracted by religious and moral questions, and, for quite other reasons, in psychologists and artists, and above all in surrealists who are so particularly drawn by the demoniac in every shape – how explain that such a work should have failed to become famous?' The critic Walter Allen referred to the book as 'the most convincing representation of the power of evil in our literature'. John Carey produced a fine edition and an introduction which, in characteristic style, picked out all the contradictions and complications in the book, with forensic precision.

It requires such gimlet eyes. The novel opens with the Editor's account of the story, then presents the account of the Sinner,

Robert Wringhim, then tries to substantiate the tale. Its structure makes it postmodern *avant la lettre*, and many readers have thrilled to its ambivalences and ambiguities, to its haziness and elisions. The Sinner is a weaker and maybe illegitimate son, his putative father being a radical preacher and his possible father a rake and debauchee. The Sinner is pious, sincere, unhappy, ungracious and haunted. He is the convict of his convictions. Not least of these is his analysis of Calvinism: if the Elect are predetermined to Grace, then nothing they do can influence that outcome. This is sound theology, except for the fact that he is persuaded to it by an elusive and evasive friend, who calls himself Gil-Martin. Gil-Martin might be Robert's fractured consciousness hallucinating his own double; he might be the Devil appearing as exactly the kind of hallucination he would expect. At Gil-Martin's prompting, Robert will – or perhaps Gil-Martin will – murder his slightly dissolute older brother George. Wringhim begins to doubt that the Elect are allowed to do anything – an awkward and weird premonition of the Satanist Aleister Crowley's belief that 'Do what thou wilt shall be the whole of the Law'. But the Editor also loses faith in his rational deductions about the case. The body of the Sinner, when they open his grave and find his coffin-lodged manuscript, is miraculously preserved. The righteous preacher is also the sly transgressor. The enlightened man is left in the dark about the facts before him. Each has his beliefs folded back on him; each is tempted to think the truth is out there. It is a dazzling, discomfiting book. When it was reprinted in the Blackie and Sons edition, the editors chose to omit entirely the Editor's narrative and represent it as *Private Memoirs and Confessions of a Fanatic*. The very few reviews the first edition received thought it merely extravagant and eccentric. The book in which the murderer always was the minister slipped still-born. I have spent too many hours wondering if Nelson ever read it.

Perhaps one of the reasons that *Confessions* was so egregiously overlooked was that Hogg had been gazumped. In 1822, John Gibson Lockhart, a notoriously acerbic reviewer, contributor to *Blackwood's Magazine* and the son-in-law of Sir Walter Scott, had published his own controversial novel about a man of faith: *Some Passages in the Life of Mr Adam Blair, Minister of the Gospel at Cross-Meikle*. Although Lockhart is now remembered as a major biographer, an occasionally fine poet and a waspish literatus, he had aspirations to be a serious novelist, and *Adam Blair* is the best of his four attempts. Lockhart and Hogg had a sometimes testy, sometimes companionable relationship, and Lockhart had penned caricatures of Hogg for *Blackwood's*. In a neat irony, Hogg included himself in *Confessions*, as a version of his stereotype as a rustic, guiding the Editor to the Sinner's grave, and the Editor bears more than a passing resemblance to Lockhart. (In another of the novel's doublings, while the Editor thinks the preservation miraculous, very alert readers of a topographic bent would realise that Hogg directs them to a specific place he knows very well in Ettrick, and one of the only peat bogs in the area, which would account for the body's incorruption.)

Adam Blair opens in a sentimentally melancholic vein, with the minister looking out of a window on cheerful scenes, and recollecting the deaths of his wife and children, with only one of his offspring still living. He rekindles an acquaintance with a woman now called Charlotte Campbell, who once had loved him and who had been a friend of his wife. She is a remarried divorcee, a woman who is more sinned against than sinning, but who certainly has weights in the latter's scales as well. She stays with Adam, and the idea that a widower and a remarried divorcee

165

were living together in a 1770s Scottish parish without the parishioners passing comment somewhat stretches credulity. What snaps it, however, is a scene in which Charlotte rescues Adam and his surviving daughter from a swollen river (this trope, oddly, will resurface), and as they shiver together in the aftermath, there is a kiss with more passion than expected. An emissary from her husband removes Charlotte to his home at Uigness, and, in a dwam, Adam follows her, 'his mind somewhat shaken by so many unwonted species of excitement'. He is passionately welcomed, stricken with remorse, succumbs to a fever and, when he awakens, hears a funereal pibroch on the bagpipes; while nursing him, Charlotte catches the same fever and perishes from it. The 'surprisingly honourable' Captain Campbell returns, and accepts Adam's confession and repentance, sufficiently so that he can return to his parish, prematurely white-haired.

If *Confessions* seeks to unsettle, *Adam Blair* yanks rather graspingly at the heartstrings. The *Edinburgh Review*, the great rival to *Blackwood's*, in a review rather pointedly headed 'Secondary Scottish Novels', says that such techniques 'will enable any one almost to draw tears who will condescend to employ them'. It is 'wallowing naked in the pathetic'. This is to an extent unfair – this kind of deliberately lachrymose literature had strong precedents, from Mackenzie's *The Man of Feeling* through Goethe's *The Sorrows of Young Werther*. The most stringent and outraged reviews, however, dealt with the book's immorality. Blair is described as having 'betrayed in his manner something of that abstraction of thought with which those who have ever had misery seared at the root of their heart are acquainted'. If Lockhart's intention was to show that beneath a solemn visage and ministerial robes there still throbbed intense passions, the response was: 'Dear Lord! Lockhart has shown that beneath a solemn visage and ministerial robes there are throbbing, intense passions!' Adam Blair was compared with the pornographic *The Amours of the Chevalier de Faublas* and *The Memoirs of the Duc de Lauzun* (referred to by Lockhart in a letter complaining about the reviews as 'another book unmentionable'). The *Scots Magazine*'s review from which the analogies come also described it as 'this most detestable volume . . . a miserable farrago of licentious badinage, couched in a vile methodistical lingo, equally alien to piety and taste, and which has no doubt been assumed as an artifice of concealment for the poison which lurks on every page'.

The *Edinburgh Review* was not so intemperate but did remark that the novel was 'mighty religious, too', though its 'devotional orthodoxies seem to tend, now and then, a little towards cant'. It may be, though, that the hysterical fulminations about an unconsummated affection are a feint from what makes *Adam Blair* more genuinely troubling: that it depicts a minister suffering from despairs and doubts. When contemplating what Blair has lost, Lockhart reaches a melodramatic pitch, the power of which, regrettably, is in its cumulative effect:

> There is an old thick grove of pines almost immediately
> behind the house; and after staring about him for a
> moment on the green, he leapt hastily over the little brook
> that skirts it, and plunged within the shade of the trees.
> The breeze was rustling the black bough high over his
> head, and whistled along the bare ground beneath him. He
> rushed he knew not whither, on and on, between those
> naked brown trunks, till he was in the heart of the wood;
> and there, at last, he tossed himself on his back among the
> withered fern leaves and mouldering fir-cones. Here
> everything accorded with the gloom of a sick and

shuddering soul, and he lay in a sort of savage stupor,
half-exulting, as the wind moaned and sighed through the
darkness about him, in the depth (as he thought, the
utmost depth) of abandonment and misery. Long-
restrained, long-vanquished passions took their turn to
storm within him – fierce thoughts chased each other
through his bosom – sullen dead despair came to banish or
to drown them – mournful gleams of tenderness melted
his spirit for a moment, and then made room again for the
strong graspings of horror. Doubt hung over him like
some long-laid spectre risen again from a roaring sea, to
freeze and to torture – Faith, like a stooping angel, blew
the shadow aside, but the unsubstantial vapour grew
together again into form, and stood within sight a phantom
that would not be dismissed . . . Now boiling with
passions, now calm as the dead, fearing, hoping, doubting,
believing, lamenting, praying and cursing – yes, cursing all
in succession – Oh! Who can tell in one brief hour what
ages of agony may roll over one bruised human spirit!

One brief hour. Or five minutes.

This may strike us as histrionic, but it accurately coincides
with many Calvinist narratives of dejection and subjection. It
also bears comparison with George Wringhim's epiphany on
Arthur's Seat in Edinburgh after seeing the early-morning 'wee
ghost of a rainbow' in the haar:

He seated himself on the pinnacle of the rocky precipice,
a little within the top of the hill to the westward, and, with
a light and buoyant heart, viewed the beauties of the
morning, and inhaled its salubrious breeze. 'Here,' thought

he, 'I can converse with nature without disturbance, and without being intruded on by any appalling or obnoxious visitor.' The idea of his brother's dark and malevolent looks coming at that moment across his mind, he turned his eyes instinctively to the right, to the point where that unwelcome guest was wont to make his appearance. Gracious Heaven! What an apparition was there presented to his view! He saw, delineated in the cloud, the shoulders, arms, and features of a human being of the most dreadful aspect. The face was the face of his brother, but dilated to twenty times the natural size. Its dark eyes gleamed on him through the mist, while every furrow of its hideous brow frowned deep as the ravines on the brow of the hill. George started, and his hair stood up in bristles as he gazed on this horrible monster. He saw every feature and every line of the face distinctly as it gazed on him with an intensity that was hardly brookable.

Between them, *Adam Blair* and *Confessions* instigate a distinct and distinctively Scottish strain of novels, concerning the imperilled faith of ministers and dark nights of the soul in men of faith.

Was it a dark night or a glorious dawn that drew James Nelson towards a life of faith? Was it despair or relief? It is not a question I want to ask but – was he tortured?

The Book of the Prophet
Jeremiah 36:18

Then Baruch answered them, He pronounced all these words unto me with his mouth, and I wrote them with ink in the book.

If we were being terribly precise about this eddy of literary history, the next works would be J. M. Barrie's *The Little Minister* in 1891, John Buchan's *Witch Wood* in 1927 and *Farewell Miss Julie Logan* in 1932, again by Barrie. There is a text beforehand, though, which has many of the same characteristics and may originally have been part of the subgenre; Stevenson's *Strange Case of Dr Jekyll and Mr Hyde* of 1886. Or rather, the novella he wrote in 1885 and which his wife, Fanny, burnt, considering it 'a quire full of utter nonsense', as she wrote in a letter. Let us consider the facts. Stevenson had read Hogg's work some time before being awoken from 'dreaming a fine bogey tale', which he latterly claimed was the inspiration for the novella. Although in its various adaptations, a steaming vial of some unspeakable tincture causes the transformation, no such immediate trigger is ever given in Stevenson's text. It is a story full of imprecations: God bless me, Good God, I swear to God, O God, for God's sake, in God's name, thank God, God grant, God knows, before God, God alone knows, and so forth. At one crucial moment the lawyer Utterson, a friend of Jekyll's, says, 'God forgive us! God forgive us!' The idea of a good man turning bad is not so much a transformation but an anti-conversion (or is it? Utterson recollects that Jekyll was 'wild when he was young; a long while ago to be sure; but in the law of God there is no statute of limitation' – it may be a de-conversion, an un-transformation). When Jekyll is in a fit of becoming Hyde, the servants remember hearing their master's voice 'cry out upon the name of God; and who's in there instead of him, and why it stays there, is a thing that cries to Heaven'. In Jekyll's confession, he even admits that the 'scientific' endeavour was to separate the good and wicked parts of mankind, to discern the elect and the damned parts of a being and find a means by which they are 'housed in separate entities'. The names have been analysed beyond the level of the phoneme, yet to me they sound vaguely biblical – an angelic Jekiel, an Israelite king somewhere between Jehoram and Jehoahaz and Jehoiakim, and 'when the wicked rise, men hide themselves', 'thou mayest not hide thyself' and 'hide thy face from my sins'. Were I to speculate like Utterson – the Utter Son? – I might wonder if Fanny Stevenson had told her husband what she thought of the first draft as well as committing it in writing to a friend. With no evidence whatsoever, I assert that the original title of the book was the *Strange Case of the Rev. Jekyll and Mr Hyde*. In his confessions, Jekyll writes:

> It chanced that the direction of my scientific studies, which
> led wholly toward the mystic and the transcendental,
> re-acted and shed a strong light on this consciousness of
> the perennial war among my members. With every day,
> and from both sides of my intelligence, the moral and the
> intellectual, I thus drew steadily nearer to that truth, by

171

whose partial discovery I have been doomed to such a
dreadful shipwreck: that man is not truly one, but truly
two. I say two, because the state of my own knowledge
does not pass beyond that point. Others will follow, others
will outstrip me on the same lines; and I hazard the guess
that man will be ultimately known for a mere polity of
multifarious, incongruous, and independent denizens.

'Not truly one, but truly two': could there be any better
description of a convert?

Since we have to discuss *The Little Minister* subsequently – it
was a book Nelson quoted at a significant moment that comes
later in his/our story – let us delve into *Witch Wood*. The working
title for what Buchan thought was his best novel was *The Minister
of Woodilee*, and in his autobiography, *Memory Hold-the-Door*,
he said, 'I wrote of the Tweedside parish of my youth at the time
when the rigours of the new Calvinism were contending with
the ancient secret rites of Diana.' This conflict of paganism and
Christianity was one explored in his previous novel, the Greek-
set *The Dancing Floor*, but much of the strength of *Witch Wood*
comes from its heartfelt connection to Buchan's own native
heath. He had, moreover, been working on a biography of the
Marquis of Montrose, the Covenanter turned Royalist, and since
the novel is set during Montrose's lifetime, its authenticating
details are precise. It begins: 'Time, my grandfather used to say,
stood still in that glen of his.' Buchan immediately disavows the
very premise. On returning to the glen, the narrator remarks,
'No one could tell me when or why the kirk by the Crossbasket
march became a ruin, and its gravestones lay buried in weeds.
Most did not know it had even been a kirk.' But the narrative
disavows the disavowal. The Rev. David Sempill, newly appointed

to the parish in the seventeenth century, finds a place similarly in transition. It is a perpetual ruining.

Sempill is a moderate Presbyterian, equally ill at ease with the status quo as with revolution. He also has something of a conceit for himself, believing of the commentary that he is working on that 'Sempill on Isaiah would be quoted reverently like Luther on the Galatians or Calvin on the Romans'. Buchan, the son of a Free Church minister and later the King's Lord High Commissioner to the General Assembly, is being clandestine here. If Sempill were being as assiduous in his commentary as we are led to believe, he would have to be writing an exegesis on Chapter 2, Verse 8 fairly soon: 'Their land also is full of idols.' In the woods around his parish he discovers a 'draped altar' around which 'women half-naked' and 'men with strange headpieces like animals' dance 'widdershins, against the sun'. Worse, the celebrant of this 'infernal sacrament' is none other than one of his own elders, Ephraim Caird, a man whose devotion to the Covenant is more strenuous and rigorous than his own. (In this regard, *Witch Wood* is the prototype of *The Wicker Man*.) Sempill also, out of human charity and goodly Samaritan principles, shelters a survivor of Montrose's defeat by the Covenant forces at the Battle of Philiphaugh in 1645, a conflict where the Covenanting commander supposedly said 'the wark gangs merrily alang' as women, children and prisoners of war were massacred. Sempill's witch-hunt against the pagans turns into a witch-hunt against him for harbouring a renegade; at the same time, the plague breaks out (in a startling premonition of Camus' *La Peste*, where physical pestilence is an allegory for moral contamination). His sole supporter, the anachronistically cosmopolitan Katrine Yester, will die while trying to help him stave off the infection. Given his name means 'simple', Sempill proves both straightforward and naïve in negotiating the politics of the period. His test of faith is to be normal in abnormal times. He fails.

When J. M. Barrie was writing *Goodbye Miss Julie Logan*, which was a ghost story for the Christmas Eve edition of *The Times*, he confessed to an editor, 'The fact is I think I am dead.' He described the work as 'elusive I fear and perhaps mad'. In the form of a found diary, the reader is presented with a passage from the life of Adam Yestreen, a minister in the year 186–. There is a name to conjure with: Adam needs no glossing, but Yestreen is a Scots word meaning 'yesterday evening'. Snowed in during his first winter in the parish, Yestreen is increasingly isolated and anxious: 'It is the stillness that is so terrible. If only something would crack the stillness,' he confides. He has been told various stories of a 'spectrum', and thinks at times that his violin, which he has forsworn playing, is being played. He thinks he writes an entire diary entry only to discover that all he has written is 'God help me'. His solitude is broken by Julie Logan, whose dangerous allure might be sexuality – Yestreen has been warned that the purpose of a violin is to be played: what is the chief end of man? as the catechism puts it – or her Catholicism and Jacobitism, or her actuality as either ghost or hallucination. In all of these novels of spiritual angst, whether the protagonist is misty-eyed like Adam Blair, psychopathic like Robert Wringhim, awkwardly brave like David Sempill or self-deprecatingly innocent like Adam Yestreen, the crisis of the soul is mirrored in anxieties about the body. The psychiatrist R. D. Laing, who wrote *The Divided Self* and argued that madness is a sane response to an insane society, would be the perfect diagnostician of these works, where the repression of the natural causes the emergence of the supernatural and where clothing conceals more than nakedness.

Cucullus non facit monachum, as Feste says in *Twelfth Night*: the cowl does not make the monk.

This series of tropes reaches the twenty-first century in James Robertson's *The Testament of Gideon Mack*. Gideon, unlike his ancestors, does not believe; the ministry is a vocation in the sense of a profession rather than a calling. He has what the critic James Wood describes as an 'atheism, only a semi-tone from faith . . . like a musical dissonance, the more acute for its proximity'. This does not prevent Gideon having his own encounter with a rather benevolent and riddling darkness. As with *Adam Blair* and *Goodbye Miss Julie Logan*, a river is the emblem of an unchanged changeability; as with *Witch Wood* and *Adam Blair*, the woods are sanctuary and unsanctified. Robertson's humanism, indeed humane-ism, is more in keeping with Walter Scott than with the more fractious James Hogg, but it does highlight the seriousness of Scottish fiction about ministers. Contrast this with English novelists and their depictions: Edward Ferrars in *Sense and Sensibility* (who is usually not even depicted as a cleric when it comes to film); Henry Tilney in *Northanger Abbey*; Philip Elton in *Emma*, about whom, the characters agree, 'there is a littleness', and the self-satisfied William Collins; Edmund Bertram in *Mansfield Park* ('a clergyman is nothing,' Mary Crawford remarks in that novel); the satirical Rev. Stiggins in *The Pickwick Papers*; the 'oily exudations' of the Rev. Chadband in *Bleak House*; the 'wretchedly paid' Frank Milvey in *Our Mutual Friend*; the conniving Obadiah Slope in *Barchester Towers*; G. K. Chesterton's serene and offhandy Father Brown: there is no dark night of the soul here. But one is coming. It is coming close.

The Book of Job 15:22

He believeth not that he shall return out of darkness,
and he is waited for of the sword.

What it did was it whelmed. I was walking home to the cottage where I lived, at around ten o'clock at night. It was a walk I had walked many times, and I knew the intricacies of the road, its camber and its tilt, its potholes and abrupt screes. The hedgerows were wreathed in dying cleavers, or catchweed, or sticky willow, like a Miss Havisham dress cobwebbed across the entangled, fruitless hawthorn. As my feet fell upon the beginnings of crisp frost, my resentment grew: returning to a home than was unhomely, where no fire was kindled and nothing but the ghastly presence of my own company and memories awaited. Being sad in the silent beech woods, when even the rooks had stilled their cawing, is never a good idea.

I had been thinking about evil. I was asking myself if I had ever known evil. Malice, unkindness, selfishness, pride, vindictiveness: I could accuse myself of all of them. Snideness, brutality, putting down, despising, cruelly diminishing: I could also remember times when I had experienced them, as well as having inflicted them. But actual evil? Wickedness? True and utter badness? I went through the Decalogue instead, a kind of self-indulgent spiritual masochism. No other god, guilty. Graven

176

image, guilty. Take the Lord's name in vain, guilty. Sabbath, very guilty. Honour Mum and Dad? Beta plus, or a low 2:1. Kill? As yet unguilty. Adultery, conscience clear. Steal, less so. False witness – or rather lying – guilty. Coveting – practically a hobby. I revelled in my sense of sin, and that is what, I think, made its eye open and its sickness stir.

But these are just, in both senses, rules, and what gathered itself out of the darkness was not interested in rules. It began with the tingly feeling of being followed, that itchy sense when you suspect something but dare not turn around and prove it. It was a whitrick in the corner of my eye, something fleet and unfocused. I walked more quickly. I breathed more quickly. I had often been startled on this road – a barn owl noiselessly gliding across my path; a hare, as still and arched as a bow, loosing the arrow of itself across the field; the strange sensation of a line of spider's silk brushing across my face despite the distance between the trees seeming unfeasible. I had seen the Perseids flicker across the sky, and once one illuminated the whole landscape as if a distress flare had been set off, turning night into a parody of day. I had even, once, seen lightning strike metres ahead of me. It was there before its noise, with a petrichor smell and umber palinopsia. Guiltily, I had rather wished to be at its point of contact. It felt queerly second-best not to have been hit by it. These things can be surprising, or astonishing, or stagger-ing. But they were not fearful.

Walking more swiftly because you believe there is some malevolent thing behind you makes you walk more swiftly, which encourages the belief that there is some malevolent thing behind you. I could mark out the stageposts ahead: the oak tree, the houses, the school, the bottle bank, the turn-off. I began to hurry to them. That seemed to please it. There was something canine in its delight. When panicked, I have always recited lists to myself. Plays of Shakespeare in the order of the First Folio. Monsters in *Doctor Who* in order of appearance. Favourite symphonies as a countdown: Glass 10, Beethoven 9, Mahler 8, Shostakovich 7, Nielsen 6, Sibelius 5, Bruckner 4, Schumann 3, Ives 2, Prokofiev 1. Whistle, whistle. Still it loomed. I have often thought back to that night, and to what happened or didn't. I can rationalise it in any number of ways, but a core of the irrational remains. The sense of something unspeakable behind me and the sensation of unremitting pursuit are there whenever I cancel out the obvious explanations. It is difficult to articulate what it felt like. The sky became welkin and the earth chthonic. The air was stifling and stale despite the chill, and the lights dimmed everywhere, from windows to stars. The wind held its breath. The brook was static. I could smell every dead thing beneath the soil and my mouth tasted of copper. Whatever it was, it was the opposite of pallid. I started to run. My dad always says that I run from the knees down, a kind of scuttling hurry more than a run, but this time I actually used my thighs as well. Both my feet were off the ground at the same time at times.

Running made little difference. If anything, it was encouraged. If there is a manner in which to be gleeful without happiness or kindness, it had it. At points it felt as if I had dived into a pool, a sudden immersion into a different element, unbreathable and encompassing at the same time, but whereas water feels clean, this felt grimy. I checked off the staging posts: school, bottle bank, turn-off. It was contagious and claggy. I wish I had turned around, if only to confirm that this was nothing more than panic and melancholia. Not facing up to it was the worst of it.

I skidded round the turn-off up the track to the cottage, not caring to dance between puddles, not bothered about sheep-shit on my shoes, fumbling for keys as I ran. The mortice clicked. I ran into the bathroom and locked the door. I sat between the laundry basket and the shower, trying to explain everything away as quickly as possible. Then the worst happened. It felt as if two hands were placed around the cottage, and that they were twisting it like a Rubik's Cube, seeking an ingress, a switch, a weak nook to unwinkle. It looked for purchase and did not wish to bargain. It, if it was, was uncompromising. I crept out and found one of my copies of the Bible, and, as I had once been advised, started to recite Psalm 51: 'Have mercy upon me, O God, according to thy lovingkindness: according unto the multitude of thy tender mercies blot out my transgressions. Wash me thoroughly from my iniquity, and cleanse me from my sin. For I acknowledge my transgressions: and my sin *is* ever before me.' The wind started up again, and the keening of the sparrowhawks cut across the quiet. When, I do not know. I do not know how often I read that psalm before the – whatever – became bored and left me alone again.

A major strand throughout theology insists on belittling evil. St Augustine wrote:

> And in the universe, even that which is called evil, when it
> is regulated and put in its own place, only enhances our
> admiration of the good; for we enjoy and value the good
> more when we compare it with the evil. For the Almighty
> God, who, as even the heathen acknowledge, has supreme
> power over all things, being Himself supremely good,
> would never permit the existence of anything evil among
> His works, if He were not so omnipotent and good that
> He can bring good even out of evil. For what is that which
> we call evil but the absence of good?

179

St Thomas Aquinas, while disagreeing with St Augustine, invokes the same idea.

> It must be said that every evil in some way has a cause. For evil is the absence of the good, which is natural and due to a thing. But that anything fail from its natural and due disposition can come only from some cause drawing it out of its proper disposition. For a heavy thing is not moved upwards except by some impelling force; nor does an agent fail in its action except from some impediment.

There is a form of theology and philosophy which insists on the excusability of sin. Nelson himself would at times resort or retreat to this. It was delinquency or misbehaviour; it was an error or an aberration; it was a failing or a falling. But what if there was an act not just evil in itself, but *Evil* itself behind it: an inhuman but impactful force, just as impossible in its own way as perfect Goodness? What if Nelson had encountered that thing which does not have horns but certainly has hooves, unrelenting, remorseless, repetitive hooves? What if he did not make it safely home?

Although James Nelson undoubtedly committed an act of evil, I do not think he was evil. That does not stop me thinking that evil itself exists, and is real. It is not incarnated in Hitler, or Genghis Khan, or Caligula. But it is there, surreptitious and silent, pitiable in its way and predatory. The thing from the woods was angry and resentful. It might not have been my flickering faith that drew it close, but fellow-feeling.

Joel 2:31

The sun shall be turned into darkness, and the moon into blood,
before the great and terrible day of the LORD come.

There is an unaccounted day. Nelson has killed his mother on the evening of 30 October, clumsily hidden the body, washed, packed and put money into his wallet. He presumably has had to deal with the clothes he was wearing, which would have been splattered with blood. What does he do with the brick and the truncheon? Unknown. The dog is whimpering beneath the sofa. He leaves. He later told Stewart Lamont that he stood outside Forsyth's department store, looking at 'smart, up-market menswear he knew he could not buy'. He then went to Central Station, but 'couldn't settle'. He will give himself up to police back at the family home on the morning of 1 November.

The part of me that yearns for a deerstalker hat and the ability to play the violin is niggled by this. I begin to think he is innocent after all. Someone else committed the murder and, as the good and damaged son, he is covering up the true story. It makes a kind of sense. He never apologises – well, he isn't actually responsible for the crime. It might be somebody close: the choleric father? *Cherchez la femme* – they turn up together, to get her, and she snaps? A secret lover, who would be a member of the congregation of cold-eyed hypocrites? Remember the words

181

he used about her – and yet he takes the fall. As we all are taken by the Fall. It is utter abnegation and true kenosis, it is being a substitute for sin. It's also not true. There are the lies we tell ourselves and the lies I am telling you.

There is nothing known about what he did on 31 October, but one thing is certain. It was Halloween. It is inconceivable that, growing up in Central Scotland in the 1950s, Nelson would have been unacquainted with the poetry of Robert Burns. Burns's 'Halloween' is actually a charming poem about rustic customs, mostly to do with forthcoming romantic fortunes. Nelson's relationship with the unnamed woman which has caused his mother's outburst and his frenzy is not, in all likelihood, on a very sure foundation now. But Burns does footnote his title with the explanation that Halloween 'Is thought to be a night when Witches, Devils, and other mischief-making beings are all abroad on their baneful, midnight errands; particularly those aërial people, the Faeries, are said, on that night, to hold a grand Anniversary'; and that perennial of the Scottish classroom, 'Tam o' Shanter', will dramatically depict the Witches' Sabbath and its demonic master.

Did he check into a hotel, or wander Glasgow's ill-lit and smoggy streets? Did he eat anything, or could he not face eating?

Another detail. He has his car, a 'big Austin Princess'. His penchant for flash cars has been considered evidence of his moral failings and spendthrift attitude. There is much more tangible evidence of his moral failings now. Does he sleep in his car? Does he drive around in it? Why, if he has his car, does he end up wandering around Central Station? Does he contemplate taking a train? Does he sit in the bars that throng the streets outside it? Does he drink to steady his nerves or blot his memory, if he drinks at all?

The American fashion for trick-or-treating has not yet crossed the Atlantic. But there are still moderately ghoulish customs. My parents remember dressing up as ghosts or raggedy chimney sweeps or just with their clothes all put on backwards. It is a practice called 'guising' in the south of Scotland, and 'galoshans' in the west. They would carry 'tumshie lanterns', turnips hollowed out and with carved expressions. There was no 'trick' part. Going door to door, each child had to sing a song, or tell a joke, in return for toffee apples, or monkey-nuts, or 'claggan' (a kind of bonfire-toffee). They might also be given money: the anarchist Stuart Christie recollected getting twelve shillings and sixpence in the 1950s, worth about £70 today. It is hardly comparable with the Mexican Day of the Dead, but it is still unsettling in its own way.

Did Nelson go to the house of his lady friend? Were there knocks at the door? Were there unquiet spirits? There was a waning gibbous moon that night.

Nelson later confessed that the way his conscience manifested itself was the repeated phrase 'Why are you running away?'

Nelson handed himself in on All Saints' Day, when the Church of Scotland remembers all those who have died in the faith, especially Christians who have died a violent death.

The Book of the Prophet
Jeremiah 6:11

Therefore I am full of the fury of the LORD; I am weary with holding in: I will pour it out upon the children abroad, and upon the assembly of young men together: for even the husband with the wife shall be taken, the aged with him that is full of days.

Although the decision in the General Assembly ought to have been taken purely on legal and theological grounds, no one was under any illusions but that it was also a profoundly emotive case. The faction around William Morris certainly had strong arguments based on natural justice, Church precedent and certain biblical passages, especially sections in the Epistle of Paul to Titus and the First Epistle of Paul to Timothy. The Titus passage specifically deals with the moral character of preachers. They should be 'blameless, the husband of one wife, having faithful children not accused of riot or unruly', and should not be 'selfwilled, not soon angry, not given to wine, no striker, not given to filthy lucre'. The idea of the minister as moral paragon runs deep, though the passage itself had already been analysed a great deal in terms of, say, the ordination of women. For that matter, it does not say if the minister has children that they should be of good standing; it rather implies paternity is a precondition. Nevertheless, there was a long-standing tradition of reading Paul's injunctions as specific to a particular time and place, not as immutable instructions (Paul is remarkably precise in the First Epistle to the Corinthians in his demarcation of the difference between what he speaks 'by permission' and what 'by commandment', even saying, 'Now concerning virgins I have no commandment of the Lord: yet I give my judgement'). The passage in First Timothy is similarly complex, requiring a teacher to display 'charity out of a pure heart, and *of* a good conscience, and *of* faith unfeigned' and telling them not to 'give heed to fables and endless genealogies' (which always rather surprised me given the endless genealogies in the Bible itself). The real stumbling block for those opposed to Nelson's ordination comes in a discussion of the law being good, where it is said, 'It is not made for the righteous man, but for the lawless and the disobedient, for the ungodly and for sinners, for unholy and profane, for murderers of fathers and murderers of mothers, for manslayers, for whoremongers, for them that defile themselves with mankind, for menstealers, for liars, for perjured persons, and if there is any other thing contrary to sound doctrine.' Although this does not specify intrafamilial murder, it is a reference to the murder of mothers; and Paul goes on to align himself, in the past, with these very perpetrators of misdeeds. They also had insinuation. Other candidates had been turned down by the Kirk: how could they be certain they were making the right decision in this case? And how sincere was his calling? And did he even know himself?

'And he changed his prison garments,' as it says in Jeremiah.

The group committed to Nelson's rejection by the presbytery being overturned had their theological arguments as well, which we shall look at anon. But they also understood that this was an issue where people had to be swayed as much as convinced. The

Rev. James Whyte and others organised a petition to the Assembly, signed by sixty ministers, in support of Nelson's application. This, of course, garnered due attention in the press. There was also another factor. Nelson was now married.

Georgina Roden had been studying for a doctorate on the Book of Jeremiah when she met Nelson, a fellow student. They married in the October of the year before the Assembly's debate, and five weeks before the *Glasgow Herald* scoop. In an interview with the *Evening News* – a brave thing to undertake – she said, 'Five weeks of calm, that's all we had,' tagged with a journalistic 'muses wistfully'. In the interview Georgina talks about meeting Nelson socially and then going to dinners and parties with him. She 'knew there was something about his past'. She was evidently an astute and acute person, noticing 'all his reminiscences were about the sixties, you would think that the seventies had never happened to listen to Jim. I decided either he'd had a nervous breakdown or been in hospital, maybe prison'. In the *Glasgow Herald* article, a slightly different story emerges. When Nelson tells her, anxiously, over coffee, 'At first I didn't react because I suspected when he said there were gaps in his life. It was either this, or he was working for the Government in a secret capacity.' At this point in the interview, Nelson laughs and says, 'I was!' – another example of the almost inappropriate humour he could display, however truthful the statement is.

The journalist, Sheila McNamara, probes deeper into Georgina's reaction to Nelson's revelation. 'But you forget,' she replies, 'I'd known him a long time before he told me. I already had my image of him in my mind. I judged him by what I knew of him, not by his past. I know my own mind and I'm a good judge of character.' The article then rather snidely notes, 'She's 26. The age at which we're all good judges of character.' In reading all these yellowing clippings, my biggest surprise was the low-level sexism of this piece above all. Georgina Nelson is 'a forthright, open and very likeable girl', with 'nothing remotely scholarly about her' and 'not even from a church background'. In terms of Nelson's application, Georgina says that she is 'not ambitious. Never was. If Jim gets a church he'll obviously need help and a wife who is on hand, not a millstone round his neck.'

The photographs of Georgina Nelson show a pretty, if somewhat severe, young woman. The more tabloid *Evening News* has her in a mohair-looking sweater and with flowers – yellow Welsh poppies, I'd venture – in front of her, and a caught-moment smile. In the *Glasgow Herald* photograph, while Nelson sits on the chair arm of the armchair with a hint of a grin, she looks forward, almost daring faint disputations with the faith of belief. In another, she is wearing a pretty William Morris-ish smock, with a more austere dark page-boy collar and a cardigan, holding Nelson's hand. She looks like she is in love. I remember that look. She is certainly sharp. Of the letters berating Nelson, she wryly observes that it is 'funny that the supporters sign their names but the poison-pen writers never do', adding, 'I think a lot of folk are bitter because of something which happened to them at some point in it surfaces when something like this comes in the news.' She confesses that after reading the letters she would 'pace up an [*sic*] down here in a terrible state. I had to be restrained from writing back. Jim stopped me, he's a much calmer person. He said we'd got to expect that kind of thing. But I used to get angry and very upset.' In the *Glasgow Herald* interview we again get a strange disjuncture. In that Nelson says that he is still 'in danger of adopting an authoritarian position' – that characteristic he constantly tasks his father with – 'But I have mini-explosions rather than bottle things up. I tell people what I think of them.

But I don't have more violence in me than anyone else.' It is a position to which Georgina acceded. 'I think human beings are capable of inspiring acts of unselfishness and sacrifice, and appalling acts of depravity and cruelty, and that the elements of both are inside every one of us.'

What is paramount is her conviction. 'He's sure he'll win through. He's a great optimist. There have been times when I wanted to chuck it all in, but he never has. And at the end of the day, good will come from all this. He'll be a good minister. People may point him out at first as the man who murdered his mother, but through time they'll remember him as the minister who visited them when they were sick, or helped them in trouble.' He seems at times to be her own personal flail to castigate the doubters: 'If facing this situation makes people face their Christian commitment then it's a good thing.' In the 1983 *Evening News* interview she cleared up one thing which has troubled me since reading it – the venomous and anonymous note that said Nelson was being 'hogwatched'. 'Whatever that means,' she says – and I have never found a single reference to this phenomenon, outside of some minor Canadian non-fiction and literature opposing pork farms and many groups dedicated to the preservation of the hedgehog. I did wonder if there were some strange connection with the Gadarene Swine and the Old Testament prohibition on pork, but even that stretches it. Bad handwriting? Might it be 'dogwatched'? As with so much, it is simply baffling. Whoever knew what 'hogwatched' meant is probably long dead. The Nelson case, in its own way, was leaving people speechless.

'I'm the kind who makes up her own mind and sticks to it, regardless of what anybody says.' It is a decidedly firm and self-confident assertion. She rebukes Nelson's father, saying, 'All this conman business of his father's – it's just a personality clash, like in every family. Jim's dad is austere and authoritarian. Jim is more flamboyant.' 'Flamboyant' is not the word I would use to describe any picture I have seen of him, but it connects to certain asides about his profligate spending and fancy-car habits as a youth. In yet another irony, the same page has an interview with some of the women discussing the Motherhood of God.

The article in the *Evening News* ends in an especially sententious and sentimental vein. 'Whether flamboyance will prove an asset to his future hopes remains to be seen. But one thing will. His wife. Georgina Nelson.' It was not to be the case. The couple separated and divorced in 1997. Georgina Nelson, who still uses her married name, now lives in Bathgate, where she grew up, working as a hospital chaplain. I wrote to her to request an interview, which she graciously declined, while putting no impediment on my thinking about what this whole case meant. I reproduce in part here her epistle.

> Jim and I parted company twenty years ago, and my recall
> of the details of that difficult and controversial time round
> about the 1984 assembly is not great, except that the debate
> was earnest and heartfelt, and touched upon the great
> themes of repentance, forgiveness, and the meaning of
> grace. I cannot be of much help to you in this area – and I
> am not prepared to talk about Jim's personal life. I wish
> you well in your project, but I hope you will understand
> when I say that I have no wish to reflect too much on what
> is past. I recall Jim with affection and with sadness,
> because . . . for all the support that he received from
> people who truly believed in the possibility of new
> beginnings, his past was always with him. It always cast a

shadow . . . it affected the way that people viewed him;
affected his own sense of self, in the end, I think. All this
was inevitable, of course. It is not so easy to shed the
weight of the past, and it is arguable that we should not
expect or wish to do so. We acknowledge the free grace
and forgiveness of God, and yet, is it right that we then
walk away without sorrow or regret? Not a very Church of
Scotland notion . . . but I think that we do penance for the
rest of our lives. I don't think there is very much else I can
say, now, all these years later.

It is a model of theological and personal sensitivity. All I can say
is that I would have been honoured to meet her, and did not
wish to discuss their personal lives. Nelson for me is a keyhole
through which I can see issues and ideas that have troubled and
intrigued me for decades. But she is entitled, as we all are, to her
privacy. He was conspicuously less private once he and Georgina
separated.

The most curious thing is that when I have spoken to people
who attended that Assembly, one thing is always mentioned: that
if she could forgive him, who knew him best, then surely the
Church should too? Surely her magnanimity ought to be
reflected in the Kirk itself? Georgina Nelson's testimony
probably persuaded more individuals than any of the arguments,
any of the insinuations, any of the whispering campaigns and
stentorian crusades. For the record, I think she was right.

The Lamentations of Jeremiah 4:13–4

For the sins of her prophets, and *the iniquities of her priests, that have shed the blood of the just in the midst of her, They have wandered* as *blind* men *in the streets, they have polluted themselves with blood, so that men could not touch their garments.*

One of the intriguing things about the case of James Nelson is that it is a story which, at some level, is the wrong way round. The thought came to me when I was suffering from insomnia, and so wide awake at 3.00 a.m., the canonical hour of lauds. I was not praying, but was binge-watching a series of documentaries I had recorded from CBS, or CBS Reality Plus more likely, with the not at all salacious title *Killer Clergy*. The voiceover for each episode intoned, 'What drives a man of the cloth, one of the most trusted people in the community, to commit the ultimate sin?' The producers are evidently not awfully au fait with the Bible itself – there is an ultimate sin, as we shall later discuss, but it is not murder. Nor for that matter were some of the dramatisations of these homicidal ecclesiastics' homilies strictly speaking from the Bible: there was usually a canter through the opening of the Book of Job, or a piece from Revelation, or the Temptation in the Wilderness – anything, basically, which could include the actor saying 'Satan' or 'the Devil' in suitably sonorous tones. But at other times, the recreation of the sermon seemed to have lines that I could not remember or find in any Bible I possessed: 'And the woman will not be caught in death?' *Killer Clergy* is not the epitome of the art of documentary television. Most episodes – I watched a lot, though it would break a commandment to say I watched every second of each one – would open with a reconstruction of what the violent vicar in question claimed was the sequence of events. Doubts would be introduced. Talking heads, who were sometimes individuals involved in the case and sometimes crime writers I had never heard of, would pontificate. There was copious use of fake blood splattering the camera lens, and inset moments taken from 911 calls, crime scene photographs or police video recordings. In almost every episode, the actor playing the predatory priest was strikingly better looking than the grainy photographs or flickering videotape of the actual individual. Stock footage of slightly sinister-looking churches, grotesque statues of diminutive cherubs holding grave-flowers, a particularly emaciated and agonised Christ on the Cross and the full moon crossing the sky would be used as backdrops to the repetitive voice-over. The same snippets of imagined scenes were replayed about four times, to coincide with advert breaks. The music alternated between heavy metal and minor-key organ pieces or massed choirs. The writers had been remarkably ecumenical in finding fiendish divines from every strain of Christian denomination, I have to say. Every episode had a shot where the actor would look to camera, and it would move in and out of focus as they variously cackled, grimaced and seethed, backlit with the light of a demonic halo. They are unremittingly described as 'charismatic'.

Whatever its technical and aesthetic shortcomings, it was grimly compelling, and not just because I watched it in the watches of the night. I left with one significant thought and an

Ovaltine, to try to sleep until terce, prime having passed by a while back. The crimes of these men were, for the most part, either peculation from parishioners or Church funds, or spousal murder, usually to get a divorce while avoiding their faith's misgivings about that state, and usually with adultery or sexual harassment having already commenced. In one case – almost inevitably, it was the Catholic priest, given the programme's lowest-common-denominator approach – it was the revelation that he had plied young men with drink and sexually abused them. As always, sexual abuse on American schlock-umentaries is depicted as stroking someone's hair and leering. These were, as it were, the superficial causes, the secondary reasons for a point-blank gun, a two-by-four plank, sleeping pills mixed in a drink or arson. The real reason, always, is at the edge of things. Each man feared that their prominence and power, their standing and status, would be jeopardised if the tawdry and illegal acts came to light. They had evidently lost their moral compass, or smashed it to smithereens on a hillside, leaving it for bemused passers-by to stumble over and ponder years later. It was not loss of faith they exhibited. It was fear of loss of face. They were profoundly unmetaphysical crimes, and I went to bed to have a morning of uneasy dreams. Nelson was their antithesis: not good to bad, but bad to good. He did not seem sanctimonious. He did not want the prestige of being a minister, he wanted its anonymity, I decided. In one interview, he said of his hopes: 'not to be recognised in the bakery'. The dog collar becomes the Ring of Gyges: he is wearing a curious invisibility despite it being so recognisable.

I awoke, as I sometimes do, with another thought in my head. The man of the cloth being the man with the cloth stained in blood is an old trope. Historically, it is easy to read about the

Renaissance, the Dark Ages, the Enlightenment, the Industrial Revolution – any period you wish – and find the monster holding the monstrance. The archetype for it is Matthew Lewis's 1796 novel, *The Monk*, one of the most important texts in the development of the Gothic novel. It was, according to the poet Samuel Taylor Coleridge, 'the offspring of no common genius' which blends 'all that is awfully true in religion with all that is most ridiculously absurd in superstition'. He goes on, with the prudish and prurient simmering together, to state that 'if a parent saw [it] in the hands of a son or daughter, he might reasonably turn pale'. Mothers being pale already, one assumes.

The Monk is, in a high degree, utter hokum. The plot involves the eponymous monk, Ambrosio, to whom many people are attracted because of his sincere and eloquent faith, and because, since he was found outside a monastery in a basket, he is supposedly an orphan and a miracle. His faith is tested when a fellow monk, Rosario, who adores him, is revealed to be not just a woman, Matilda, in drag, but the model of his favourite painting of the Virgin Mary. After she saves him when he is bitten by a snake – all students here may write in capital letters SYMBOLISM – by sucking the poison from him, they become lovers. But once he has had Matilda, he has also had enough of her, and sets his sights on the virtuous Antonia. In order to rape her, he has to murder her mother, Elvira, in one of the more entangled subplots, all the while now knowing that Matilda is a witch and an instrument of the Adversary. When the autos-da-fé turn up, the noble noble who is our putative hero manages to bring Ambrosio before the Inquisition, and, in a last throw of the dice, he decides to sell his soul to Satan. Satan reveals that Elvira was his true mother – so he is a matricide – and that would make Antonia his sister, meaning he has committed incest.

It does not end well for Ambrosio, whose good soul was all the Devil ever wanted.

The moral outrage surrounding *The Monk* – the *European Magazine* denounced it for 'plagiarism, immorality and wild extravagance', the critic James Mathias claimed it could be indicted for blasphemy – did not suppress its popularity. It was the eighteenth century's equivalent of a slasher-flick: determinedly horrible, morally void and not stooped but steeped in vulgarity to its opponents. Lewis himself was 'a reckless defiler of the public mind; a profligate, he cared not how many were to be undone when he drew back the curtain of his profligacy; he had infected his reason with the insolent belief that the power to corrupt made the right, and that conscience might be laughed, so long as he could evade law. *The Monk* was an eloquent evil; but the man who compounded it knew in his soul that he was compounding poison for the multitude, and in that knowledge he sent it into the world.' But there is a moral system to *The Monk*, and not the one against which the outraged raged. Matricide again was a topic so taboo as to be lip-stopped; but so was incest. Incest in fiction is a difficult topic. If one agrees with the anthropologist Claude Lévi-Strauss, exogamy is the beginning of civilisation, and endogamy is the sanctioned taboo that must be overcome for families to turn into tribes: Oedipus is the tragic failure, Hiawatha the noble deviant who marries Minnehaha, even though she is not of his folk. Those who persist in endogamy or incest are the opponents of progress. *The Monk* locates incest – and therefore the enemies of civilisation – in a Catholic, Christian and aristocratic society, and British readers – Protestant, rational and democratic – thrilled to the horrors of a decadent and dying society while watching Europe in turmoil under the Terror and Napoleon. The anxiety continues. In E. Annie

Proulx's *The Shipping News*, incest is a symptom of the rural: what you do when there is nothing else to do and nowhere you might go. In *A Song of Ice and Fire* by George R. R. Martin, it is the spoiled elite, with the Lannisters indulging in sibling-incest, and also that elite's dark double, the Crasters, in the penniless wilderness, where the father gives his sons over to be killed and rapes his daughters. Incest, in every iteration of its cultural emergence, is a sign of who reviles progress.

The killer as priest, the priest as killer. There was only one place in plain sight where I thought there would be clues, and it seemed screamingly obvious. Anthony E. Pratt was born in 1903, and, leaving school at the age of fifteen, became a pianist on cruise ships and in pukka hotels. His poor eyesight meant he was not called up during the Second World War, and instead worked in a munitions factory. The tiresome nature of the work allowed him to come up with the board game which earned him enough money to leave his postwar job in the civil service – he bought a confectioner's and tobacconist's which he ran with his wife – and secured him a living for the rest of his life. The game was called Murder at Tudor Close and is better known as Cluedo. Dr Black has been murdered. Miss Scarlett, Professor Plum, Colonel Mustard, Mrs Peacock, Mrs White and the Rev. Green are staying in the house, where a candlestick, a dagger, a length of rope, a revolver, a spanner and a lead pipe are to hand, among the eleven rooms. There are 66 solutions where the Rev. Green, with one of the items in one of the rooms, will be the murderer. Cluedo's feel was taken from the so-called Golden Age of Crime: surely in that voluminous oeuvre there would be a version of the minister-turned-murderer, a metonym for what some feared Nelson might be?

The answer is: no. One of life's great pleasures is to have a rotten cold and a stack of fraying paperbacks, to stay swaddled in bed all day with Lemsip and a *grande dame* of crime fiction. It was a friend of my parents during my childhood who introduced me to the joys of Agatha Christie – as she said, the best thing is you often forget who actually did it, and can read it again as if new – and since then a not-so-guilty pleasure has been Christie especially, but also Ngaio Marsh, Margery Allingham, Dorothy Sayers, Gladys Mitchell, Michael Innes, Georges Simenon and Edmund Crispin. Christie first and foremost, but all of them to an extent, were rule-breakers and experimenters. Despite the so-called Rules of Crime drawn up by the Anglican, then Catholic priest and crime writer Ronald Knox, his personal Decalogue – the criminal must be introduced early but the reader may not have access to their thoughts; no supernatural entities; no more than one secret passage; no unknown poisons or scientific improbabilities; no Chinamen; no accident or intuition; the detective cannot be the murderer; the detective must reveal all clues that were discovered; the sidekick must not conceal information and ought to be a little dimmer than the reader; and no twins or doubles unless firmly established – was regularly flouted by Christie. Even if I cannot remember the name of the character who is the murderer, I can remember her structural devices. Everyone did it. The victim did it. The narrator did it. The detective did it. The sequence was always arbitrary. The murder was expected and even advertised. She was, as the French novelist Frédéric Beigbeder has written, a surrealist crime writer. In all her clever variations on the crime novel's themes, she never has an ordained individual as the murderer, and nor do her peers. There is occasionally a vicar *manqué*, a ne'er-do-well who is disguised as a vicar; but then impersonating a clergyman is not a criminal offence in the way impersonating a police officer is.

Reading around the Golden Age, it seemed more and more obvious that *then* a murderous priest was a step far too far, an unwritten taboo which even the ordained Ronald Knox overlooked.

Between emptying my nose and stumbling in a dressing gown to take another book off the shelf, another question came to me. If the priest as murderer was silently *verboten* in the Golden Age, what about matricides? This necessitated more than one trip to the library, and the answer was similarly unexpected. Matricides were as absent as killer clergy. There is one sort-of exception: Christie's *Ordeal by Innocence*, her own favourite novel. It does not feature her regular detectives, Miss Marple or Hercule Poirot, or even her intermittent sleuths Parker Pyne or Tommy and Tuppence Beresford. Instead, it opens with a scientist, Dr Arthur Calgary, who, after a road-accident concussion and a trip to the Antarctic, has returned to both his wits and the Northern Hemisphere. (I confess, I think just one of the two reasons for his not coming forward beforehand would have been sufficient.) He has important information about a case. Although Jacko Argyle has died in prison in the time Calgary has been away, the latter has proof positive that the crime for which Jacko was imprisoned – the murder of his mother – could not have been committed by him, for Calgary was the alibi who could never be traced at the time (knocked-noggin, penguin-watching, and all that). Calgary arrives at the Argyle household to prove the innocence of the late, unlamented Jacko, and is surprised that nobody is that keen on his news. The reason is obvious: if the delinquent Jacko didn't kill their mother, then another member of the household must have done. The father with the new belle? His new belle, who was once his secretary? The flighty daughter who claims she was at

– wait for it – *Waiting for Godot*? The eldest daughter, who has 'a large bun at the back of her neck; a style which at the moment happened to be fashionable although that was not her reason for wearing it so'? Her crippled husband? (The book has a great many terms for physical and mental disability that make me shudder a little to read nowadays.) The car-salesman brother thinking of lighting off for a new career in the Arab States? Jacko's rather common secret wife, who works in the cinema and blurts out that it's 'Just the sort of thing you do see on the pictures, and of course you say to yourself that sort of thing's all nonsense, it wouldn't happen in real life. And now there it is! It does happen!'? The Scandinavian kindergarten teacher who warns them all against each other? Well, I shan't give it away, but will say that the matricide is not a matricide. The late Mrs Argyle was the adoptive mother of the children, and her inability to have children herself has turned into a domineering attitude over the children she has plucked from destitution to affluence. But the shadow of matricide is everywhere in the novel, even at the outset when Calgary learns that their residence, Sunny Point, is known by the locals by its older name of Viper's Point. Christie glosses this with typical misdirection, with a quote from *King Lear*: 'How sharper than a serpent's tooth'. But the viper is also the dream of Clytemnestra, doomed to be killed by one of her own children. Whoever dealt the fatal blow, every child has harboured hatred towards their parents and siblings. It is an *Oresteia* with French windows.

How strange a change, that between the 1920s and the verge of the 2020s, the idea of the priest as monster and the monstrous priest as being so inconceivable as to be invisible should have altered so drastically. How unsurprising a similarity, that in the same period the taboo on matricide should be unaltered. Before endogamy and exogamy, before ordination, priesthood, paganism and shamanism, there is the pure fact that everyone starts to live inside another human being.

Nelson was a Gothic figure, but not in the obvious manner. He seemed to like women, with one notable exception. He was a mirror image of our images of murderous priests. He did not have children. Yet he said that were he to be so blessed, he would have to one day have a conversation with his child about what he had done.

Ezra 7:10

For Ezra had prepared his heart to seek the law of the LORD,
and to do it, and to teach in Israel statutes and judgements.

With 'impeccable theology', at a press conference Nelson out-lined his position on those who questioned the propriety of his being ordained. 'I'd suggest to them that following the invest-ment and endorsement of the Church, if they felt it was not fit and proper, then they were not merely counting my personal past (and present) but were limiting God's omnipotence – and implying His forgiveness is limited.' The Rev. Ronald Blakey, the secretary of the Church's committee of education for the ministry, affirmed that 'if sin is a reality, then so too is repentance'.

Newspapers reprinted long sections of the Assembly's notes on 'Matters Arising' in the cases of Nelson and Macdonald.

> If it is thought that there are no circumstances in which
> persons with a past criminal conviction can ever come to
> have a genuine vocation to serve in the ministry of the
> Church, then indeed it would be wrong even to receive
> applications from them. Such a view, however, would
> assume a human ability to determine what the Spirit of
> God will or will not do within a person's life, and this
> would be unwarranted. It would appear wiser, and indeed

humbler, not to try to set limits on Divine operations. If
limits are not set, there follows, however, an acceptance of
the possibility that such vocations could exist.

This is modal and careful: it is not yet about the specific cases, it
is about the general principles by which they might be judged. It
is also essential to realise that, unlike in the Roman Catholic
Church, the ministers are not themselves forgiving: only God
can do that, and His ways are inscrutable.

The report goes on:

> The Christian Gospel has much to say about repentance,
> conversion, and forgiveness: about the possibility of people
> being renewed within: about making a new start in life.
> The forgiveness of God which responds to human
> penitence is a total forgiveness, without conditions, and
> containing within it the element of 'forgetting those things
> which are behind'. The man with a past criminal
> conviction can not only be forgiven but can make a new
> start. That start could involve a call to the ministry
> of the Church.

There was no real rebuttal to the argument that the Church
could not delimit God's power to forgive, so the opposition
concentrated instead on the sincerity of conviction and whether
the ministry was the only way in which the candidates could
fulfil their desire for service. These were more contentious
issues. The Assembly noted that it could be argued that there
were more appropriate spheres of Christian service, but further
noted that this again would be 'an assertion, albeit in a different
form, that a call to the ministry was an impossibility'. It would

then depend very much on the candidates' own qualities, and it was raised during the Assembly that 'the applicants themselves in the personal statements submitted with their applications, were deeply conscious that a vocation to the ministry would be extremely unlikely for them', adding, 'They were the first, though not the last, to ask whether or not their service should not take some other form.' The Rev. James Whyte used a particular analogy in the debate: to suggest that despite the 'inner conviction' of the candidates, their previous actions disbarred them from the ministry would be to suggest that in the Parable of the Prodigal Son, only the elder brother who stayed dutifully at home and who petulantly resents the forgiveness bestowed on the younger brother would be eligible for the ministry. By raising the spectre of resentment, Whyte effectively characterised the opposition as the kind of flinty-hearted and morally censorious ministers who had caricatured the Church of Scotland. It made them look suspicious of 'the genuine sense of vocation' that 'existed in two forgiven men'.

The Assembly heard that 'the likelihood of future controversy was not seen as something to deflect the Committee to a Repudiation of the Selection procedure recommendation'. This is ecclesiastical legalese for insisting that despite the abstract ideas which foregrounded the debate, the actual decision concerned two particular individuals. One of the anxieties, or malicious whisperings, posited what would happen next: a double murderer? A rapist? A child molester? A child murderer? By insisting on the case-by-case consideration, this line of attack was stymied. The committee, as it said, 'would have wished for more joy in the Church about its unusual candidates than has sometimes been evident, but is confident that a difficult decision whether or not to allow two men to set out on the road to the ministry, was not taken lightly or irresponsibly, and was a right decision on the basis of the particular persons who presented themselves and on the information submitted'.

The remainder of the document takes great pains to establish that all proper procedures were carried out, and that there was no 'conspiracy' to put the candidates forward (especially at the same time as one another). The committee maintained that it was not in a position to 'impose secrecy either upon a Presbytery or a University', or indeed a person. It does deal with the 'puzzlement' of rejected candidates 'who felt their need for forgiveness was not so great', but reiterates its position on judgement on an individual basis, and not in comparison with other candidates.

Once again, Nelson's queer and awkward sense of humour nearly derailed things, especially when it came to the sincerity of both his repentance and his vocation. In his interview with the *Glasgow Herald* he said, 'If the jury had known the whole situation they might have said "go home – sin no more".' This seemed a radical underestimation of the severity of his crime. It even could be read as minimising his very need for forgiveness. Had he publicly repented? Was public repentance even necessary when it came to the most private things of the heart? He also said, 'It's nobody's business to condemn from the outside. The State requires retribution and reparation. It's linked to the idea of a debt to society. If you've paid it, it's paid. You've settled the bill as far as the secular public is concerned' – then, astonishingly – 'Those who want to play Shylock, that's their affair.' At the press conference he said, 'I should have thought that being a convicted murderer would have placed me in a unique position to advise on the pitfalls of life.' 'Pitfall' almost makes what he did sound accidental. On being asked if he thought he was capable of murdering again, he replied that it was inconceivable that the same set of circumstances would occur again, and, anyway, 'I'm a wee bit older, I'm a wee bit wiser.' This is hardly the kind of Damascene volte-face for which many would have hoped.

What was remarkable was that outside of New College, the media was generally very supportive, with the more critical comments left to the letters pages. In a contemplative piece to accompany the interviews in the *Glasgow Herald*, Stewart Lamont wisely stated that 'public opinion is not the determining factor' in the case, adding, moreover, that 'those who judge the matter without knowing the person, confining themselves to the wider issues of morals and wisdom are in danger of judging (and trying in his absence) someone of whom they have no knowledge. Their opinion is therefore only one worthy of mild interest.' Lamont, having known Nelson for several years, can instead give the *ad hominem* defence. He marshals the biblical precedents for the morally lapsed – even murderers – to find favour in the eyes of the Lord, and sets this against the metaphysical quandary: 'We cannot affirm an all-powerful ever-loving God and limit His forgiveness, although His churches may not show the same inexhaustible charity.' He proclaims, profoundly, the 'gospel of second chances', while admitting that what the Church has done is 'a gamble'. 'Normally base motives are associated with a gamble, but if this one comes off, they will deserve the rewards of righteousness.' I find myself slightly uncomfortable with that last sentence, as if the promotion of Nelson was also a solipsistic way to advertise their own virtuousness. Nelson, again, invisibles himself. He is the ghost of his own story. Stewart Lamont would change his mind on some matters in the future as well.

In the *Evening News*, Rennie McOwan's article was even more outspoken. Under the headline 'Isn't this what the Church is all about?', it begins: 'The plain fact about the James Nelson case coming before the General Assembly of the Church of Scotland is that it shouldn't be there at all. To have a debate on something that is of the very essence of what the Church is all about is rather like discussing whether football clubs should sign footballers or accountants be able to add up.' While castigating the unco guid who equate respectability with goodness, the article gives a particularly pointed defence of Nelson:

'It is saddening to have a situation whereby a person can kill someone in a rush of blood' – again, this seems slightly belittling of the actual offence – 'and repent for a lifetime . . . whereas others can grind the faces of the poor, make domestic life a living hell for other people and in private and in public display all the other dark aspects of human living, pride, envy, anger, temper, injustice, selfishness, false witness, lack of charity, bad social consciences, and ability to make public noises about humanity and an inability to love one's neighbour as oneself.'

It is the kind of piece we used to call a marmalade-choker: an article which sets out to provoke as much as possible. It both supports and excoriates the Church. 'The Assembly can debate home rule, or dog licences, more aid for the Third World, unemployment, the missions, the gender of God, drug traffic and calls to Government about nuclear weapons until the cows come home, but to little public avail. Everyone else can do that and some other bodies much more effectively.' I am a little bemused about which bodies would debate the role of missionaries or the Motherhood of God better than the Church itself. But the passage does insist that the Church is not an extension of liberal (or even illiberal) social policy, nor is it a lobby group. It has a higher calling. In another confusing passage, McOwan states that reformation – becoming a new person through Christianity, even if it happens in prison – 'should be accepted as a normal course of events – if somewhat sparse – by prison chaplains and family ministers, otherwise their role degenerates into simply helping former prisoners find accommodation, providing cash-aid, tea and buns, and where possible, a job. All very necessary, but it need not be done by ministers.' Need not perhaps; but to visit and help prisoners is a key biblical injunction. There may be others who can assist in rehabilitation, but for Christians it is commanded, not chosen. At certain points, the article is breezily dismissive. 'The problem of possible insincerity is there,' we are told, 'but that can be coped with.' How? No answer. 'The crunch issue is not whether persons, or committees, or presbyteries, were correctly informed at particular stages. That is important, and if there has been error here (and that criticism has been refuted) it can be dealt with by administrative assurances.' Again, it *was* a crunch issue, and the Church had rightly defended the different forms of oversight and supervision, the relationship between the concentric circles of congregation, session, minister, presbytery and Assembly committee which has been so integral to its identity as a Church. When I sat through the debate on ministers in civil partnerships, one point was deemed to fall under the Barrier Act of 1697. A young clergyman asked if said Act could be displayed on the large digital screen, to slight smiling sighs from the Church's legal counsel, who pointed out it would certainly occupy more than one slide. But it was hugely informative and important: it set out precisely how the Assembly was compelled to consult presbyteries if they were to make a ruling that would innovate in worship, doctrine, discipline or governance. It was invoked during the debate on female ministers (who were approved the following year); then for a proposed union with the Scottish Episcopal Church (which failed) and for the right of a parish to call, if so wished, a minister in a same-sex partnership (which was passed). It was not invoked in the cases of Nelson and Macdonald. It was not, therefore, a change in how services were conducted, what the Church believed, how it should punish infraction and determine fault, or how the Church itself managed its own affairs. It was both above and below such concerns. I rather like that the *Evening News* article – accompanied by a photograph in which, beneath the words *In Principio Erat Verbum*, Nelson looks like a cheeky poacher and Georgina stands behind his shoulder with a half-smile and intense focus – had two subheadings to break up the text. Nowadays they might have been 'Murderer' and 'Salvation' or 'Controversy' and 'Divinity'; here they are 'Structures' and 'Dimension'. It might have been the *New Scientist* at a glance.

As any pub bore will tell you, wrongly, opposing ideologies resemble each other, because politics, ken, is like a circle. Although there are many differences of doctrine between the Calvinist Church of Scotland and the Jesuits, there are similarities. Both prize intellectual subtlety and view intelligence as a means towards God, not an impediment to be overcome. The Church of Scotland excelled itself in 1984. At the core of the theological contention over Nelson was not a positive, but a double negative. The Kirk was not saying, You are definitively a fit and proper person to be the shepherd to a flock. It was saying, We can't say that you're not. They could not say that Nelson was not forgiven; they could not say that he had not experienced a profound change and had a true calling; they could not say that he was not one of the Elect, however surprising and disturbing that might be. They voted. By 622 votes to 425 it was agreed that James Nelson might be ordained, and serve as a minister.

THE THIRD SERMON

The Epistle of Paul the Apostle
to the Ephesians 4:1

*I therefore, the prisoner of the Lord, beseech you that ye
walk worthy of the vocation wherewith ye are called.*

What unsettles you more – the idea that a person is fixed in their
wickedness, and no amount of therapy or prayer, intervention or
deprivation, unspared rod or outreached hand can change their
inalterable wickedness; or that someone you deemed wicked
might actually change, might be redeemed or rehabilitated,
restored or restarted, made new or made over? Whether we are
secular or religious, there is an understanding that the purpose of
prison is to punish, to protect and to reform. In an ideal world,
anyone leaving prison is more equipped for their future: they
should be better – morally, emotionally, psychologically, physically – than when they went in. We know, both the secular and the
religious, that we do not live in an ideal world. I sometimes think
that the difference is the religious are unsurprised by this.

We know the world is unideal and have the facts to prove it.
In 2015, just over a quarter of prisoners released from UK prisons
had reoffended within a year of release. Thirty-eight per cent of
juvenile offenders would commit another crime within a year of

release. From some prisons in the USA, there is a coin-toss chance that you will be detained again. Recidivism is the shadow that hung over the potential Rev. Nelson.

Yet in a purely technical sense, recidivism was a logical impossibility for Nelson. He had no other mothers to murder. But matricide is not a crime distinct from murder, and the concern must have been that having once shown a loss of control so grievous as to take a life, that choler might re-emerge with equally desperate results. Which is worse? Premeditated, cold and calculating murder, or murder in a rage, a passion? Which is more likely to be purged, which more likely to be repeated? Such judgements are all necessarily inductive: past events are no indicators of future actions, current demeanour no guide to future alteration. In terms of the likelihood of reoffending, many might have thought Macdonald the riskier (had not Judas Iscariot himself been skimming the finances? Hadn't Peter miraculously killed a couple because of financial impropriety? The Bible's denunciations of the love of money – for example, the Epistle of James 5:1 begins: 'Go to now, *ye* rich men, weep and howl for your miseries that shall come upon *you*' – are far more rhetorically inflamed than its stance against murder).

There is a Greek myth – a parable might be a better denomination – about the god Momus, the spirit of mockery and sarcasm. When Athena, Poseidon and Hephaestus competed about who was the best artist they respectively produced a house, a bull and a man. Momus supposedly criticised Poseidon for not putting the bull's horns below its eyes so it could see where it would gore, and Athena for not fixing wheels on the house so it could be moved. In Lucian of Samosata's *Hermotimus* we get the critique of Hephaestus. Men should have windows in their chest so that the innermost secret workings of the heart might be revealed.

Laurence Sterne, in *The Life and Opinions of Tristram Shandy*, alludes to this story:

> If the fixture of *Momus*'s glass, in the human breast, according to the proposed emendation of that arch-critick, had taken place,—first, This foolish consequence would certainly have followed,—That the very wisest and the very gravest of us all, in one coin or other, must have paid window-money every day of our lives. And, secondly, That had the said glass been there set up, nothing more would have been wanting, in order to have taken a man's character, but to have taken a chair and gone softly, as you would to a dioptrical beehive, and look'd in—view'd the soul stark naked;—observ'd all her motions,—her machinations;—traced all her maggots from their first engendering to their crawling forth;—watched her loose in her frisks, her gambols, her capricios; and after some notice of her more solemn deportment, consequent upon such frisks, &c.—then taken your pen and ink and set down nothing but what you had seen, and could have sworn to:—But this is an advantage not to be had by the biographer in this planet . . .

Momus is a trickster god, a spirit of the contrary and the 'best-not-to-wish-for' attitude. Had Hephaestus taken his advice, one thing would have disappeared: trust. Trust is a precious and precarious virtue, particularly because it can be easily abused. The annals of recidivism are full of trusting souls disabused of their trusting nature. The worst offenders used that trust as a glimmering fly-fishing bait – a stonefly nymph or a Parmachene Belle – cast on murky waters. Those who thought they were fishers of men turned out to be gullible prey.

Probably the most significant novel written by the late Norman Mailer is his Pulitzer Prize-winning *The Executioner's Song*. Mailer, in thrillingly and extravagantly verbose fashion, investigated the case of Gary Gilmore, the first person to be executed in the United States since the re-establishment of capital punishment in 1976. Gilmore was a double-murderer, and part of the case's fascination is that he lobbied to have his punishment enacted sooner rather than later. The appeals and stays of execution were a form of 'cruel and unusual punishment', delaying the despicably inevitable, especially after Gilmore had already attempted suicide. Mailer said in an interview with Michael Lennon, his official biographer, reprinted in *Conversations with Norman Mailer*, that the book's crux was that 'we have profound choices to make in life, and one of them may be the deep and terrible choice most of us avoid between dying now and "saving one's soul"'. Gilmore strived for, ambiguously, a 'good death'. The only meaningful choice is the choice of when to die. The only meaningful freedom is the freedom not to be. It is not a novel about redemption or transformation, but a book about the glinting knife-edge of what happens when the only possible existence is non-existence. Gilmore eventually had at least one actualised choice: he was killed by firing squad in 1977. One can see what attracted Mailer to this almost romantic story of dignity, death and detainment. He had head-butted Gore Vidal after an unfavourable review (leading to one of Vidal's best quips – 'words fail Norman again'). In 1960 he had stabbed the second of his six wives twice with a penknife. He was pugnacious, egotistic and quick-tempered, but also guilt-ridden, self-loathing and melancholic. *The Executioner's Song* is him gazing into the abyss and seeing if he would dare, like Gilmore, to leap.

Even before *The Executioner's Song* was published in 1979, Mailer had been contacted by a reader, someone who had heard of his research into the penitential system. At the age of twenty-one, Jack Abbott had been sentenced to prison in Utah for forgery. His sentence was increased when he fatally stabbed another inmate; it was increased again after he escaped and robbed a bank. Abbott wrote to Mailer to claim that Gilmore's account of prison life was not the whole truth, and offered to provide him with authentic details about his time behind bars. In 1981, a book was assembled from Abbott's letters to Mailer, entitled *In the Belly of the Beast*. It was a searing account of being a 'state-raised convict' whose teenage experiences of incarceration had set him on a route towards solitary confinement, paranoia and psychosis. As he writes, 'We have no legal rights *as prisoners*, only as citizens. The only "rights" we have are those left to their "discretion." So we assert our rights the only way we can. It is a compromise, and in the end I greatly fear we as prisoners will lose—but the loss will be society's loss. We are only a few steps removed from society. After us, comes you.' *Après moi, le deluge.* Mailer lent his name to Abbott's appeal for parole. After all, the robbery and escape were attempts to elude an unbearable system; the shivving was a direct consequence of him being in prison, to which he had been sent for nothing more than bounced cheques. *In the Belly of the Beast* proved that Abbott was an eloquent and insightful individual, who was self-aware about how the system had systematically dehumanised him. 'Mr Abbott has the makings of a powerful and important American writer,' Mailer told the Utah Board of Corrections. Everything about Abbott must have appealed to Mailer: writer, fighter, unimpressible, unbelieving. He wrote in the introduction to *In the Belly of the Beast*, 'Not only the worst of the young are sent to prison, but the best—that is, the proudest, the bravest, the most daring, the most enterprising, and the most undefeated of the poor. They are drawn to crime as a positive experience—because it is more exciting, more meaningful, more mysterious, more transcendental, more religious than any other experience they have known.'

On 19 July 1981, a laudatory review of *In the Belly of the Beast* appeared in the pages of the *New York Times*. It is unlikely that Abbott saw it. The *Nation* referred to him as 'a stunning writer and a tenacious thinker'; the *Soho News* compared the author to the dissident writer and gulag inmate Aleksandr Solzhenitsyn, and called the work 'awesome, brilliant, perversely ingenuous'. 'Ingenuous' is a weasel word here, implying both innocence and ingenuity. Abbott did not read the review because he was on the run, six weeks after being released from prison, five weeks after appearing with Mailer on *Good Morning America* alongside British comic actor Dudley Moore. The night before the review was published, he had stabbed a waiter to death. Their argument had been about access to lavatories. Abbott was apprehended in Louisiana, working on an oilfield. He was later reimprisoned, and after writing a sequel, *My Return*, which received mediocre reviews, managed to hang himself in his cell in 2002. Mailer, later, said it was 'another episode in my life in which I can find nothing to cheer about and nothing to take pride in'. The acerbic critic Michiko Kakutani wrote a skeweringly brilliant piece on the whole business. 'It was', she said, 'the wishful impulse to see Mr. Abbott's life as a story not just of crime and punishment, but of crime and punishment and redemption; and it was the fervently held belief that talent somehow redeems, that art confers respectability, that the act of writing can somehow transform a violent man into a philosopher of violence.' The *Michigan Law Review* began its critique: 'A society with a better understanding of prisons would never have incarcerated Jack Abbott, and certainly would never have released him.' The moral: 'Do not confine whom you would not destroy.'

The poet Percy Shelley had written of authors in his *Defence of Poetry*, 'Their errors have been weighed and found to have been dust in the balance; if their sins "were as scarlet, they are now white as snow"; they have been washed in the blood of the mediator and redeemer, Time.' The citing of living poets was exactly the problem with Abbott, and was even more so with an even more terrible creature: Jack Unterweger, the Austrian author and serial killer. Time may even clean the consciences of those who assisted in his release.

There was a time when Unterweger was the epitome of re-habilitation by culture. His memoir about his internment, *Fegefeuer, oder die Reise ins Zuchthaus* (*Purgatory, or the Journey into Prison*), had become a standard school text. His children's stories, *Wenn Kinder Liebe leben* (*When Children Live Love*), had been broadcast on state radio. Two future recipients of the Nobel Prize for Literature, Günter Grass and Elfriede Jelinek, supported Unterweger's plea for parole. He became that rarest of things, a literary superstar, photographed in a number of poses: sporting 1920s gladrags, nude with his prison tattoos and in tawdry Vegas cowboy suits, always with a strangely innocent look. Many of those who knew him commented on his 'baby-face' looks and air of vulnerability. In 1976, Unterweger had been imprisoned for the murder of Margaret Schäfer, although he already had a string of convictions for burglary and fraud. In 1975 he had also been convicted of sexual attacks on four women. Latterly, Unterweger would claim that the murder of Margaret Schäfer had been triggered by her resemblance to his mother, who had abandoned him and left him with (in the words of his autobiography) his violent, alcoholic grandfather. He never knew his father, supposedly an American GI. 'I guess I started to hate her', he said of his absent mother, 'and when I encountered this girl, years later, at a time when I was living at rock bottom, something about her – the way she looked and talked – reminded me of my mother. We got into an argument and I hit her once, and then everything seemed to go blank. Later I realised I'd killed her.' It's a pleasingly psychological explanation, and completely ignores the fact that he had already brutally assaulted several women.

'Insofar as personal development is evident in literature, Jack Unterweger has fully realised it.' This was the testament of a lecturer in criminal psychology when Unterweger appealed for release in 1990. 'In working on this book,' Unterweger said, 'I wrote three different drafts. By the time I got to the third draft, I no longer recognised the person I was writing about as being myself. Through the process of self-analysis through writing, I was freed from the pressure of my childhood, mother, etc.' There were vested interests in believing that Unterweger was transformed. One journalist wrote, 'We know the rehabilitation success of our prisons is not overwhelming. I don't say that to be critical; I mean only that the example of Jack Unterweger as a successfully rehabilitated offender would be a significant and opportune result. Otherwise one must doubt the earnestness of the state's dedication to rehabilitation.'

After his release, and on a journalistic assignment to California to write about the lives of sex-workers, Unterweger berated the attitude he had faced in the aftermath of freedom: the opinion of the nebulous 'they' was 'once a murderer, always a murderer'. At some level this is simply true: as the Greek tragic playwright Agathon, in one of the few lines of his work to have survived, wrote, 'Not even God can change the past.' (We'll see.) What

217

Unterweger was really saying was 'once a murderer, only a murderer'. Only he wasn't. Once he was released Unterweger, the poster boy for rehabilitation and a darling of the chattering classes, killed eleven more women: two in Czechoslovakia, six in Austria, and three in California where, of course, he had been sent to write about the lives of sex-workers, given his expertise. The crimes were so similar it is hard to think of Unterweger as a criminal genius. The women were strangled with their own bras or tights, they were usually left in woods partially concealed by leaves, they were sexually brutalised using branches or a metal rod. While the habitués of the Viennese coffee shops could thrill at his transgressive literary genius, the Viennese police were trying to interpret a very predictable monster.

When he was sentenced for his crimes in 1994, Unterweger committed suicide in his cell. He had attempted suicide on one of his first arrests. He used the same knot for his noose as he had on the women he killed: a kind of sick homage to his own violence, especially since the knots he used could be tightened and loosened at will – but not by him. He recorded his thoughts onto audio cassettes, the contents of which have never been released. The real irony was afterwards. Unterweger was very knowledgeable about Austrian law. Since the court's ruling had not been confirmed and reviewed, Unterweger's lawyers argued successfully that he had died an innocent man. The FBI described him as a 'uniquely high-functioning psychopath'. That 'uniquely' troubles me. It implies that he was somehow exceptional and somehow unpredictable. He was neither. He was, if anything, unreadable. Was Nelson legible? Am I prepared to be his reader?

Abbott and Unterweger are obvious versions of our collective fear that there are perpetually evil people in the world. That both their causes were advanced by the literary community makes for especially uncomfortable thinking: are our stories about characters like Sydney Carton in *A Tale of Two Cities* or Silas Marner in Eliot's eponymous novel, which attempt to show moral growth, nothing more than stories?

Unterweger and Abbott are, in their own way, clear-cut cases, where even their suicides are not evidence of repentance. Ambiguous cases can be even more unsettling. Two years after Unterweger published *Purgatory*, and a year after Nelson's appeal to the General Assembly was upheld, Derek and Nancy Haysom were stabbed to death in their home outside Lynchburg, Virginia. She suffered six wounds; he thirty-seven; newspapers claimed the number 666 was daubed in blood in the house. Their daughter, Elizabeth, an aspiring short-story writer, and her boyfriend, Jens Söring, the son of a West German diplomat, went on the run after the double funeral. After travelling to Brussels and Bangkok, they rented a flat on Baker Street in London – the home of the fictitious Sherlock Holmes – and were arrested by a store detective in Marks and Spencer's on cheque fraud charges. Both confessed to the murders. After extradition, Haysom testified that Söring had committed the murders and she was an accessory; he withdrew his confession and claimed she was the murderer and that he had confessed because he thought his father's job would guarantee him a degree of immunity. Söring maintains his innocence, and has appealed ten times for early release, never successfully. Lizzie Haysom is due for mandatory release in 2032.

The 'baby-faced' Söring had been in a rock band and wanted to be a filmmaker. He also espoused a rather naïve, hippyish Buddhism. But once extradited, he claimed to have converted to Christianity in prison. Since then he has written five books about penal reform and Christianity, most notably *The Convict Christ* (2006) and *The Church of the Second Chance* (2008). Söring is evidently an intelligent individual – he was both an Echols and a Jefferson scholar at the University of Virginia – and reading his treatises is a doubly uncomfortable experience. In part the books are difficult reading because Söring is quite simply right about both the iniquities of the penal system and the Church's teachings about prisoners. But they are also problematic in the uneasy sense of being self-justifications.

In Isaiah Chapter 42, it is said, 'I the LORD have called thee in righteousness, and will hold thine hand, and will keep thee, and give thee for a covenant of the people, for a light of the Gentiles; To open the blind eyes, to bring out the prisoners from the prison, *and* them that sit in darkness out of the prison house.' As mentioned earlier, the great ethical injunction in Chapter 25 of the Gospel of St Matthew explicitly commends Christians to visit prisoners: it does not specify wrongly accused prisoners, or the innocent falsely imprisoned. Many of Söring's readings are astute and precise. He points out that the very first miracle attributed to Jesus is the healing of the Gadarene demoniac, often seen as a triumph against supernatural forces. Yet the 'man with an unclean spirit' is also someone who has been repeatedly 'bound with fetters and chains'. For Söring, the 'man with an unclean spirit' is an archetype of the prisoner, although the Gospel states that 'neither could any *man* tame him', and all attempts to restrain him have been foiled. Nevertheless, this idea that the man from the country of the Gadarenes is a precursor of Christ's later engagement with and forgiveness of adulteresses, tax-collectors and the generally shunned is compelling.

While he discusses Peter and Paul, Joseph and Samson, Onesimus and Zacchaeus, Söring's central concern is the idea of Jesus as prisoner, as convict, as a literal 'dead man walking', sentenced to capital punishment (Söring himself both feared he might be condemned to the electric chair, and plea-bargained to ensure that Lizzie Haysom was spared it). In dealing with topics such as prisoner-on-prisoner sexual abuse, the rates of HIV/AIDS infection in American prisons, the sheer number of people, especially those who are young, male and not white, in custody, Söring makes a strong case not just for reform, but for root-and-branch reconceptualising. It might not be the 'prisonless society' envisioned by the government minister who released Unterweger, but it is a step towards a more considered and caring form of incarceration.

'Some readers of this book', he writes, 'may see my description of Jesus as a prisoner as self-serving, since I have been continuously incarcerated since 1986. To this charge I plead guilty. Christ did "not come to call the righteous, but sinners", so I believe he has a special interest in lowlifes like me and "had to be made like [me] in *every* way" to redeem me [Mark 2:17; Hebrews 2:17]. I selfishly claim Jesus as my older brother and Saviour.' I used to be troubled by the word 'selfishly' in that extract. Now it seems very in keeping with a kind of hubris that St Paul uses to provoke and prompt. The word now that sits uneasily is 'lowlifes'. Söring may have been laid low by his imprisonment, but he was anything other than a lowlife: his was a privileged background. That slight out-of-tuneness occurs time and again. Is the Via Dolorosa, or the Stations of the Cross, really a 'perp walk'? Is John the Baptist a 'jailbird'? Other phrases – 'crime bug', 'chow hall' – create a kind of imperson-ation of sassy insider knowledge. When he writes, 'Somewhere on the top tier I left behind my soap dish and my shampoo, my towel and my dignity – but not, thank goodness, my virginity', it jars with his advocacy of the rights of homosexual, transgender and raped prisoners. That 'thank goodness' is especially perjink.

Prison may be 'a hell on earth', according to Söring, but it is more of a hell for others than for him. He's a survivor, and survivors need to be sleekit.

In *The Church of the Second Chance*, Söring interviews prisoners, guards, lawyers, chaplains and victims. One thing becomes clearer reading it next to *The Convict Christ*. There is a sly accretion of excusability, even when dealing with the worst of crimes. In his interview with 'George G', the self-confessed rapist is allowed to say, 'Everyone I attacked was a complete stranger, because I thought anyone I knew already wouldn't love me. So I only attacked people I didn't know, because with them I could fantasise that they loved me. I would have sex with the victim' – ahem, no, you raped them – 'but I would never beat her or hurt her sadistically. I always kissed my victims' – good for you! – 'because it was part of my fantasy to be loved.' If this were an isolated example, one might not baulk: but almost everyone Söring interviews or describes has mitigating circumstances, prior victimhood or subconscious reasons for their crimes. His account of speaking with one inmate begins: 'Here's the bad news . . . [he] allegedly raped [a] fifteen-year-old and then killed both her and her mother.' It's as if everyone in prison is actually innocent.

None of my misgivings ought to detract from the genuine work Söring has done, in terms of both revealing the disastrous state of some prisons in the United States and stressing the duty of the religious to speak out about them. But the misgivings remain. In some ways, he harms his own argument by insisting on the prisoners being victims (of others, of upbringing, of neglect, of abuse) and not addressing the victims of their crimes, who are normally blameless, and who may often have had similarly difficult lives to lead. When the Rev. Nelson's sister spoke to the press, she was clear that they had had the same misfortunes to face; but one of them was a murderer and one was not.

Rereading Söring's work, two things began to seep into me. The first was his use of inverted commas, as if terms like 'justice' and 'prisoner', 'punks', 'her' and 'God' are to be held in tweezers and kept coldly watched and distant. The second was a bizarre note in the Acknowledgements to *The Convict Christ* where Söring thanks his 'research elves'. It's the patronising tone that jangles. For all that I admire his cleverness and perception, it made me realise he was not a man I would care to meet. Nevertheless, when he recounts a prisoner yearning simply to see the other side of the tree he can glimpse through his barred window, he makes the actuality of prison tangible, palpable, present.

He is also indubitably correct that Christ died a convict's death. He makes much of the fact that the 'first person in heaven' is one of the convicted thieves crucified alongside him. This has been a disputatious issue since the Crucifixion. In the Gospels of Matthew and Mark, we are told that two criminals were executed alongside him: in Matthew they are silently noticed; in Mark they both berate him – 'they that were crucified with him reviled him'. In the Gospel of Luke, however, one of the 'malefactors' says, 'If thou be Christ, save thyself and us,' while the other begs, 'Dost not thou fear God, seeing thou art in the same condemnation? And we indeed justly; for we receive the due rewards of our deeds: but this man hath done nothing amiss. And he said unto Jesus, Lord, remember me when thou comest into thy kingdom. And Jesus said unto him, Verily I say unto thee, To day shalt thou be with me in paradise.' John is silent in his Gospel about the thieves, but does include the words 'Woman behold thy son!' and 'Behold thy mother!' as he commends Mary into the care of an unnamed disciple. The penitent thief has been named in various traditions as Dismas, Demas, Titus, Rakh or Jobab. His status is one of the problems that Samuel Beckett's tramps or resistance fighters, Vladimir and Estragon, discuss in *Waiting for Godot*. 'One of the thieves was saved. (*Pause*.) It's a reasonable percentage.' When Vladimir goes over the story again, they become itinerant textual critics:

> 'One out of four. Of the other three, two don't mention
> any thieves at all and the third says that both of them
> abused him.' 'Who?' 'What?' 'What's all this about?
> Abused who?' 'The Saviour.' 'Why?' 'Because he wouldn't
> save them.' 'From hell?' 'Imbecile! From death.' 'I thought
> you said hell.' 'From death, from death.' 'Well what of it?
> 'Then the two of them must have been damned.' 'And why
> not?' 'But one of the four says that one of the two was
> saved.' 'Well? They don't agree and that's all there is to it.'
> 'But all four were there. And only one speaks of a thief
> being saved. Why believe him rather than the others?'
> 'Who believes him?' 'Everybody. It's the only version they
> know.' 'People are bloody ignorant apes.'

There is *a* solution to the stichomythic exchange proposed by Beckett. They both abused him initially and one repented. One asked not for release but for blessing. Söring, to my knowledge, still asks for release before blessing. Others, released, do not even ask for blessing.

When Jim Nelson was requesting to become a minister, one name came up everywhere: Jimmy Boyle. It was in the newspapers, it came from his father, it was the absolute simile for a repentant whom everyone seemed to distrust. Like Söring, Boyle denies the murder charge that took him into the prison system.

Boyle would be the first to admit that he was a man of violence. A gangster and debt-collector, he had graduated from petty theft to knife crime. He was first convicted for assault to severe injury by stabbing in 1963, when he already had fifteen previous convictions as a juvenile. He was found guilty of murder in 1967, and his sentence in HMP Barlinnie was extended after he assaulted the assistant governor. In 1973, Peter Whatmore, a psychiatrist, Ken Murray, a prison officer, Kay Campbell, a social activist, and Joyce Laing, an arts therapist and proponent of art brut, established the Barlinnie Special Unit, a dedicated service for the most uncontrollable and violent offenders which offered various therapeutic services, including arts and writing practice. In the words of the exhibition held in 2017 in the Kelvingrove Art Gallery, its vision was to create 'a way out of a dark place'. As one former prisoner said, it was a space where they were treated as humans and not animals.

James Boyle was the most prominent beneficiary of the Special Unit's services. In 1977 he published an autobiography, *A Sense of Freedom*, which was made into a film in 1981. It rather brilliantly cast the Scottish actor Fulton Mackay, who was better known for his depiction of the prison officer Mr Mackay alongside Ronnie Barker in the prison-set sitcom *Porridge. A Sense of Freedom* showed a far starker, more brutal and inhumane – many would say truer – version of what imprisonment actually entails.

I once visited Barlinnie. I had chaired an event with the then governor, Derek McKay, on narratives of rehabilitation and asked if I might come to the prison. It was an unnerving experience: as you travel to the Glasgow suburb where it is situated, the presence of the building looms over the area. The security measures mean

225

that even the innocent feel guilty. Derek showed me records of the Special Unit that he had found in a skip when he took over, and as we went through the names and signatures, he mentioned which of them were still in the prison at that moment. The purpose of the Special Unit was not, in a way, to turn people into model citizens in the outside world, but to make them less problematic inside the prison. But Boyle became the figurehead for its successes at rehabilitation. He went on to have a career as an artist and sculptor, and wrote a novel, *A Hero of the Underworld*, to which I gave a moderately unfavourable review. His real aesthetic success, however, was a play co-written with Tom McGrath, *The Hard Man*. McGrath was a significant figure in Scottish literature – he was one of the few people to whom Alexander Trocchi, the novelist, pornographer, heroin addict and pimp, sent his manifesto, *Sigma*, the 'Invisible Insurrection in a Million Minds'. McGrath's 1979 play, *The Innocent*, was an autobiographical work about the interrelation between counter-culture and drug abuse; he also produced a version of *Electra*.

The Hard Man blends vaudeville and Brechtian ideas of alienation to create a compelling study of hypocrisy. If Söring zeroed in on the gap between what the Bible says about prison and the actions of most Christians, Boyle and McGrath used crime and prison as a mirror on the iniquities and inequalities of the capitalist system. 'Johnny Byrne', the surrogate figure for Boyle, says, 'I was providing a social service . . . I'd been prepared to do business with them when you hadn't. While you were sitting back and pretending not to notice I had been there to care for their needs. My methods with defaulters were quick and to the point but they weren't any different from your precious world just a bit less hypocritical and undisguised. Let's face it the whole world is a money lending racket and if it takes a man's whole life to kill him with his debts it doesn't make it any the less an act of murder.' Byrne is both the opposite of the brutal assistant governor Commando and his imitation. This is reinforced by having his gangster sidekicks also play the prison officers: the brutalised becomes brutalisers, the dispossessors are self-dispossessed.

Inevitably, there was a media storm about it. Reflecting on the original run before its 2011 revival, the actor and director Peter Lichtenfels remembered that 'the tabloids were intent on making sure he' – Boyle – 'stayed in prison'. The play was accused of romanticising violence, and even excusing it. The final scene is a version of a dirty protest, where Byrne, smeared in his own excrement, challenges the prison officers to beat him in his utter abjection. It is neither glamorous nor excusable.

When Nelson was compared to Boyle, it was never in terms of successful rehabilitation, but with the sneer of impenitence. Both, it was assumed, had got one over on the creative and ecclesiastical powers. Boyle's subsequent work has never achieved the *succès d'estime*, or even the *succès de scandale*, of *The Hard Man*. But the gangster turned artist remained in the public eye, and, like Nelson, would be routinely scrutinised. The sentence does not end with release.

The French philosopher Michel Foucault wrote extensively about the 'birth of the prison' in *Surveiller et punir* (*Discipline and Punish*), published in 1975. Although his primary concern is the movement from bodily sequestration to spiritual improvement and from public execution to private reformation, he devotes a major section to the idea of the prison as Panopticon. The eighteenth-century British philosopher Jeremey Bentham had proposed the idea of a prison where the condemned believed that they were always being observed. Part of the genius of the idea is that, over time, the idea of utter surveillance replaces the actuality of continually being watched. It seems, in *Discipline and Punish*, as if the Panopticon is a technological innovation in terms of prison. Given it was written before our era of sousveillance – where every mobile phone can track your whereabouts, where the streets bristle with security cameras, where your history of web browsing might at any moment become public knowledge – it still seemed to me a piece of wrong thinking. If you were a peasant in sixteenth-century Scotland, you were under no illusions but that every act, every thought, every whim was not just seen, but recorded by an omniscient, unforgetting God. The Panopticon is basically a prosthetic God, an attempt to be as gods in a secular age. Being as gods has never ended well for humanity.

No functioning Panopticon now exists, except the one that exists everywhere and by our tacit consent. But for Abbott and Unterweger, Söring, Boyle and Nelson, its precursor, its prototype, was already in place: it does not require WiFi. It is every surreptitious glance, every twitched curtain, every malicious whisper. It is that infraction – legal, moral, theological – shall not go unnoticed by someone. It is me, walking past James Boyle's Edinburgh home and inwardly tutting at the sculpture in the garden, or reading into a Söring typographical error a questionable character. It is you, now, unaccountable judge of the story, unelected judge of the storyteller.

In Book II of Plato's *Republic* he imagines the opposite of sousveillance and surveillance, in the myth of the Ring of Gyges, which permitted invisibility. No person, Plato argues, could be moral if they might not be seen. Are our morals conditional on our being-in-sight? Why would someone not use being unseen to assist quietly and help in silence? Imagine creeping around, guileless and guilt-free, allowed to redress wrongs and prevent harms, comfort the needy and console the weak: is that so unthinkable?

Yes. As Kafka wrote in 'In the Penal Colony', 'Guilt is never to be doubted.' John Knox would agree. Our innermost sins are rarely outwards; our outward goodness is rarely matched in our hearts. We are broken things. 'Of the crooked timber of humanity', wrote Immanuel Kant, 'no straight thing may be made.' Hamlet, in a moment of uncharacteristic understatement, thought that all of Denmark was a prison. All the world's one; a place we endure and must persist in despite never having chosen to be here. All the self's a prison. I cannot change my astigmatism or eye colour, my shoe size or my memories, my predilections or allergies, and which of you by taking thought can add one cubit unto his stature? All the words are prisons. I cannot say a thing without the shades of its former meanings haunting it ('love', 'lore', 'lone', 'lobe', 'lose': each with history more than they can encompass). Other tongues have already dirtied every syllable, other teeth have clacked their sullied phonemes. We are hurled and whirled into world, words and forms we did not choose.

The Epistle of Paul the Apostle
to the Hebrews 7:12

*For the priesthood being changed, there is made of necessity
a change of the law also.*

Quo vadis? In the apocryphal Acts of Peter, the soon-to-be-saint
flees Rome to avoid his execution, and meets on the road his
friend, master and God. He asks, 'Where are you going?' *'Romam
eo iterum crucifigi'* is the response: 'I return to Rome to be
crucified again.' Shamed, Peter goes back, and is crucified upside
down, at his own request. It is one of the earliest aftermaths to
the biblical stories. The Bible itself does not state what happened
to Peter, or Paul, or John, or Mary Mother of Christ, or Mary
Magdalene, or Mary the wife of Cleophas, or Joseph, or Luke, or
Matthew, or Mark, or any of the shepherds, or the Magi who
became known as Caspar, Balthazar and Melchior, or the man
possessed by spirits in the Gadarene, or the centurion's daughter,
or the woman afflicted with a flux, or the Roman soldier who
thrust vinegar, or the one who said, 'Truly this was the Son of
God,' or Lazarus, or Pilate, or Caiaphas, or Gamaliel, or Joseph
of Arimathea, or Zacchaeus, or Eutychus, or the prophet Agabus,
or Silas, or Dorcas, or Lydia, or Barabbas. The Bible is very
good at end things – how it will be, how we shall be, how all

230

must be – and very slight on the *next* things. It is an eschatological text, full of prophecies that were written after the event and possibilities for the future from desperate peoples, displaced in time. In some ways, its utter disregard for story-telling is its imprimatur. But we still have a story to tell, and one that might not end well.

Mr Nelson had a calling but not a charge; a vocation but not a living; an acceptance but not a welcome. He was an aspirant minister but not a minister. He shimmered around his alteration. I remarked to an acquaintance that I was thinking about him, and she recollected working on BBC Radio Scotland when he had been allowed to be, but not been chosen to be, a minister. His father telephoned the programme, on air, and berated him, as a conman, a liar, a thug, a cheat. It would be a brave parish that went under the media scrutiny of having the first murderer as their spiritual leader. It would be a foolish parish that did not think this through beforehand.

Next to an advert in the *Scotsman* for those 'worried or confused by the new VAT tax' – a terrible pleonasm – 'on double glazing', Peter Macdonald cast an eye back on the General Assembly of 1984. It is a pensive and delicate series of observations. Describing the Church as the apex of the 'establishment', and commenting wryly on the 'lace-trimmed court dresses' and 'traditional frock-coats' of a phalanx of worthies, Macdonald wonders if 'these figures, so set in their formalities, are the real heirs of an itinerant carpenter turned preacher whose concern seemed so much more for the powerless than the powers-that-be'. With its concern for respectable piety and financial probity (having read through the entirety of the Report of the Trustees of the Church of Scotland Housing and Loan Fund for Retired Ministers and Widows of Ministers for that year, I can certainly attest to their scrupulous anxiety about money, down to the widow's mite as it were), the Kirk had become trapped in what Macdonald called 'suburban captivity'. The case of James Nelson had been an intervention into the cosy catastrophe of declining Church membership. He writes:

> Apart from being an unprecedented event, and therefore a historic one, the appeal by Mr Nelson to be allowed to continue his training for the ministry offered the revealing sight of those who pride themselves in being people of principle wrestling with principles. They acquitted themselves with dignity. Whether their decision – to allow him to proceed – was right, only time will tell. Mr Nelson's greatest difficulties are likely to come when he has to persuade, not the General Assembly, but the men and women of a congregation that he should be their minister – if he gets that far. For already there are signs that the 'Nelson Controversy' is not going to go away. To say that he has disturbed the Church is an under-statement – but a Church that is not ready to be disturbed, or to disturb others equally profoundly, is hardly worth the name. And if this case has persuaded some of those who felt outcast that there is space for them too, that may yet be a more important result than the future of one ministerial candidate.

Of course there were shriller voices. Under the headline 'Convicts issue may empty kirk', the *Scotsman* reported on the Rev. Robert Wotherspoon and the Rev. Gilbert Drummond, who were frank about their objections. 'This kirk session views with grave concern and utterly deplores the decision taken by the

Assembly to admit a convicted murderer and an embezzler to the ministry of the Church', wrote Drummond, adding, 'Any thought of peace and unity of the church being maintained is a delusion.' Wotherspoon noted that his congregation was 'deeply disturbed by what happened at the Assembly', while invoking the Barrier Act. But legal machinations and theological disputations aside, there was another method of refusing to sanction the Assembly's decision: the withholding of funds. Deeds of covenant – regular payments to the church by members of the congregation – might be cancelled. A similar threat was issued after the acceptance of ministers in civil partnerships, nearly thirty years later. The Church of Scotland has always had a policy of redistribution of funds – so richer parishes assist poorer ones – and some of the more affluent congregations have sometimes jibbed at this, wishing their contributions to be hypothecated to their concerns. Doctrinal controversies are often a façade for self-interest. With a certain sneering humility, they said, 'Only because of our real concern for the work of the Church and our care for those who would really suffer did we resolve, at this stage, not to withhold our congregational mission and service fund contributions.' Piety and probity in perfect accord, one might say. In a way, the article of 7 June shows that neither scrutiny nor scepticism would desist in the light of the decision. Wotherspoon's invocation of the Barrier Act was rejected, but he persisted in the media: 'If we carry on like this it seems to me church discipline is in chaos', he said, while clearly going against the manifest will and decision of the Assembly.

The reporting of the decision is not without its ambiguities. The Assembly debated for three hours over Nelson, and for thirty minutes over Macdonald. 'Only the television cameras were still – by order', said the *Scotsman*. It also said that the

Assembly 'gave its blessing', which it assuredly did not. It merely allowed due process to continue unhindered. Nobody there was in a position to give a blessing anyway. Nelson was described as 'pleading his own case in a calm voice' – as if a thunderous denunciation and intemperate ire would have been expected – 'that did not betray the extreme pressure he and others acknowledged he was under'. He 'denied seeking the limelight and regretted that he had laid himself open to a charge of disturbing the peace of the Church'. 'There was no escape for him' – the article continues – 'from publicity.' There was no escape either from God.

It had been 'nerve-wracking', he said, and he himself did not think that finding a parish would be unproblematic. But in terms of his critics, he said, 'They will have to think about their own interpretation of the Gospel. I do not claim to have a monopoly on the truth.' If a prospective minister himself does not think the truth they proclaim is completely and unwaveringly true, I wonder who can say that with impunity. It is a slip – perhaps not a Freudian slip, but a Petrine slip. A former Moderator, the Rev. James Matheson, summarised the impact of the decision, saying, 'Our decision today will make what our view of our own ministry is not only to ourselves but others – that we regard ourselves no more and no less than sinners saved by Christ.' Iain Macdonald was given the last word, asking that he and Nelson 'could be left free of publicity now to develop their ministries so that they could play their part in healing the divisions created'. This was going to be unlikely. Rereading the article, I feel especially sorry for Macdonald. He has already vanished. The headline ignores him completely, reading 'Kirk backs Nelson's right to preach'.

By April 1985, Nelson and Macdonald had completed their licentiates. The Rev. Blakey said of Nelson, 'He has had a very successful period and all the reports have been very favourable, and he has been found totally satisfactory in his year of service as a probationer.' Nelson was contacted by the papers at the same time, and said he was now 'optimistic' about finding a charge. But the kind of Petrine slip occurs again. 'Before his sentence, he said, each time he had reached an interview stage, he had been offered a job.' There is, perhaps, a difference between most jobs and one vocation. The man who had moved back in with his parents in impecunious circumstances and, no doubt, shame, and who had had to resit his exams, was also slightly braggartly about his career. At the same time, he has proof which is hard to dispute. Eighty members had joined the church in St Andrews where he was a probationer after the Assembly's decision and the surrounding media storm. 'Even in the dark days of winter', a later article in the *Scotsman* continues, 'when church heating had broken down and he had taken over the pulpit while both the minister and the associate minister had been ill, there had been no drop in attendance.' In another moment of blasé blurting, Nelson claims that although the presbyteries were 'split down the middle', in the congregations 'only 1%' had been in dissent. In the accompanying photograph, Nelson looks bewildered and more grey-haired and 'MacDonald' [*sic*] looks like an ITV newsreader announcing the 'and finally' story.

In the long term, Wotherspoon and Drummond were right, but for the wrong reasons: the kirks emptied anyway. Regular church attendance and membership dropped from 20 per cent of the population in 1983 to 7.5 per cent in 2016. The Church will need two hundred new ministers by 2020. These problems were understood even at the 1984 Assembly: Appendix E of the reports to the Board of Practice and Procedure admitted that 'the Church is seen to be middle-class, middle-aged, obsessed with finance and no longer relevant to daily life'. In the evidence amassed from the presbyteries, the culprits were manifold and sadly comic read thirty years later: 'discipline and authority appear to be in decline', 'greater car-ownership', 'TV [which] creates a sedentary, passive, non-participatory lifestyle', 'increased numbers of "working wives"', 'opening of swimming baths on Sundays', 'young people . . . often being prepared to work for specific causes, eg CND, environmental conservation, natural childbirth', schools teaching 'religious as opposed to Christian education', 'unseemly haste in closing churches'. This is nothing new. In his 1851 poem 'Dover Beach', Matthew Arnold heard the Sea of Faith's 'melancholy, long, withdrawing roar' leaving but the 'vast edges drear / And naked shingles of the world'. Almost despite the poem's plangent pessimism, the image of the tide hints it might one day turn and return. For me, it seems more like a glass of water being poured onto sand. No effort will refill the glass. The kirks emptied anyway, but Nelson's becoming a minister can hardly be said to have been the cause.

Zephaniah 1:7

*Hold thy peace at the presence of the Lord GOD: for the day
of the LORD is at hand: for the LORD hath prepared a sacrifice,
he hath bid his guests.*

Isaiah 6:6-7

*Then flew one of the seraphims unto me, having a live coal in his
hand, which he had taken with the tongs from off the altar: After
he laid it upon my mouth, and said, Lo, this hath touched thy lips;
and thine iniquity is taken away, and thy sin purged.*

It's a story that keeps on giving, as they say around the newsdesks.
The Assembly result was never the end, nor was it the beginning.
It was neither Alpha nor Omega. It meant that every step was
matched with a beady eye, every next stage a chance for the
recursion of an older story. On 11 June 1984, it was reported that
'Mr James Nelson, the convicted murderer who is seeking to
become a minister of the Church of Scotland, yesterday
conducted morning service at Ceres Church, in Fife, under the
eyes of a group of assessors from the Presbytery of St Andrews.'
It's a piece of journalism full of sly legerdemain. Just as texts
from the Bible are often wrenched out of context to justify
a spurious argument, Nelson's words were noted and recast.
The theme, apparently, was courage, and the text Isaiah 35:3,
'Strengthen ye the weak hands, and confirm the feeble knees.'
Given the median age of most congregations this might be wholly
appropriate – another account cites three parishioners aged 77,
59 and 62 – but the newspaper report says it 'could be seen as
referring to Mr Nelson's own difficulties in persuading the

presbytery to allow him to complete his training', going on to suggest that the subsequent verses in Isaiah directly reflect Nelson's experience. But they introduce a subtle ellipsis. The God that will 'come and save you' in the text 'will come *with* vengeance' as the report notes, but they omit '*even* God *with* a recompence'. The articles note that Nelson 'admitted to being very nervous' prior to what they archly call the 'ordeal'. The parishioners were all extremely favourable about the sermon, and it was observed that the Rev. Professor James Whyte, Nelson's supporter in the debate, was in attendance. He only commented that 'it was a fine service' and commended the numbers in attendance. The congregation was clearly swelled by some reporters. Nelson apparently said 'there is good and bad in everyone. Sometimes we are not ourselves, but God loves us whatever we do': without the context this is made to look self-justifying. Perhaps it was. It is disappointing we do not learn more about the service. A service is more than a sermon.

A typical Church of Scotland service will open with the Bible being carried in before the minister, a greeting, a hymn and then prayers of penitence, thanksgiving and the Lord's Prayer. Then there is a homily for children just before they are taken off for Sunday School, and then another hymn, usually specially for departing children. The lessons for the day are read, then the sermon is given. There is a hymn after the sermon, the offerings are taken – it was drummed into me it was an offering, not a mandatory 'collection' – and then prayers of intercession, a final hymn and the blessing. Did Nelson give an uplifting little parable to the children? What hymns did he choose? ('Just As I Am, without One Plea'? 'I Am Not Worthy, Holy Lord'? 'Make Me a Captive, Lord'? 'Not What These Hands Have Done'? 'God's Perfect Law Revives the Soul'?) Some of the door-stepped churchgoers' comments are primly anodyne: 'He is quite all right'; 'I don't see anything wrong'; 'It was a well-conducted service'; 'I would echo Professor Whyte's words.' On the other side of the country, Claremont Parish Church, East Kilbride, was hearing from Iain MacDonald. Typically, it received less attention, and Macdonald's name even acquired a capital letter it had thitherto lacked, as if he was rippling out of memory. His sermon seems to have been more attuned to the congregation's knowledge of the situation, taking as his text Ezekiel 36:26: 'A new heart also will I give you, and a new spirit will I put within you: and I will take away the stony heart out of your flesh, and I will give you an heart of flesh.' Their minister, the Rev. Keith Steven, told the reporters he hoped Mr Macdonald 'will be allowed to get on with his year at Claremont just like any other probationer assistant'. He added that Macdonald had been 'unfairly tagged along in the wake of the Nelson affair'. It is a strange twinning: men both parallel and dissimilar. But then the Bible is full of such doublings: Jacob and Esau; Moses and Aaron; Elijah and Elisha; Peter and Paul.

One of the truisms of journalism is that stories beget stories. Reporting on Nelson's sermon was a sure way to restoke the story. Duly complying, the Rev. Helen Johnstone wrote from The Manse in Balgray, Tealing, Dundee, to complain that in its reporting the *Scotsman* had misinformed readers about the ministry trials: 'It is not the sermon alone which will be assessed, but the entire conduct of public worship', and this in itself was but one of three tests. Nor were the candidates examined only on their knowledge of theology, they were also tested on Church law and procedure. No correction or clarification was deemed necessary to be published. The next day, however, the Rev. David Gynes from St Paul's Church, Livingston, fired a broadside at the broadsheet, asking, 'When will you and other newspapers cease to refer to Mr Nelson in every item which mentions him as a convicted murderer?' With due sarcasm he says that 'to be consistent every item you carry about a person in the news should list all their known peccadillos, so that I should perhaps sign this letter D. Gynes, recipient of two parking fines and one speeding fine, 1970, paid in full'. One might question whether there is a moral equivalence between murder and motoring offences. Getting into his stride, he also takes on Wotherspoon and Drummond, saying that their misgivings show the 'deplorable trend in our nation of accepting democracy and democratically made decisions only in so far as one personally agrees with them' – this! In 1984! Lo, there is a prophet in Zion! – and mordantly asking if Wotherspoon and Drummond intend to challenge the Assembly's decision to raise the annual stipend for ministers. The next day, a member of the laity, Iain McGregor of Portobello High Street, Edinburgh, fulminated under the subheading 'Not both ways' that 'Mr Nelson, under normal circumstances, was destined to be a jobless nonentity until the Kirk intervened.' Attacking David Gynes for his 'humanist assertion' about the Assembly vote, he cites the Acts of the Apostles 4:32. When I looked this up, I was rather surprised – not as surprised as in learning, when I distracted myself by wondering how many Bibles I actually had, that I appear to possess an admittedly excessive twenty-one Bibles in ten different translations, not including commentaries – that this is the verse about the Church's unity bestowed by the Holy Spirit, and also a fundamental verse in the idea of Christian Communism ('neither said any *of them* that ought of the things which he possessed was his own; but they had all things in common'). Rereading and rereading this fading photocopy of a letter, I cannot decide in the

243

slightest about what it means. When McGregor refers to 'Mr Gynes and his brethren' is this ingenuous or sarcastic? When he says that 'perhaps he should set an example', is he really advocating the institution of Christian Communism in West Lothian?

Nelson next is in the spotlight, or has it put upon him, when he applied for a vacant charge in Kirkmichael and Tomintoul, Speyside, and was invited to preach at Abernethy Church on 5 May 1985. The *Aberdeen Press and Journal* notified readers, describing him as 'The man with a conviction for murder whose move into the ministry has caused controversy within the Church of Scotland . . .' The reporter, John Duckers, was clearly doing some digging, discovering that while Nelson was on parole he had stayed in 'Roshearty' (another typographical slippage) in Pitsligo, Buchan, where it was not that he drove the church minibus, but rather that he 'worked as a minibus driver at the St Fergus gas terminal'. There seem to have been ongoing tensions at Hope Park in St Andrews, with one Thomas Savage telling the paper that Nelson's services were boycotted and church members had let it be known that Nelson 'would be refused admission to their homes'. It clearly caused a stooshie in Tomintoul. An anonymous member said, 'People who have been lying down, taking it easy have sat up. Everybody is speaking about it.' Nelson had by this stage fulfilled all the assessors' tests, but this was not covered in the national media. 'Very few', he said, had been 'hostile towards him' at Hope Park; hostility albeit being on something of a sliding scale.

Was it a genuine desire to testify or crafty media management that led Nelson to choose as his text in Abernethy – well, it's not known and nor is the text. His sermon was on 'repentance and the call to service' according to both reports, and was 'from St Mark' according to one of them, and involved Christ not being selective about his followers – 'children, tax-collectors and sinners'. Looking through the Gospel of St Mark, I would reckon it must have been 2:17: 'They that are whole have no need of the physician, but they that are sick: I came not to call the righteous, but sinners to repentance.' Just beforehand the Pharisees are mumbling that Christ consorts with 'publicans and sinners'. It is daring, even, to preach about Christ not being judgemental at a service which was occurring only so that he could be judged. The *Scotsman* clearly had its copy phoned in, as the most interesting thing it can find to say is that 'eight vacancy committee members travelled the 13 miles to the sixteenth-century church', the service was at noon, and Nelson arrived with his wife twenty minutes early.

The *Glasgow Herald* under the headline 'Murderer Preaches Repentance' said that he 'seemed relaxed'. His – almost tetchy? – response to being asked by a pork-pied pressman how his message had been received – 'You'd better ask the congregation that' – seems to be at odds with this. It also has a photograph of a bespectacled elderly lady, in a knitted hat and long coat, shaking hands with Nelson. He has a winning smile in it; is wearing an academic gown and hood and ever so slightly scruffy shoes. It's not the content of the photograph, but its existence that intrigues me. He has just preached before a congregation including people considering him as their possible minister, and someone is taking a photograph of him doing the traditional handshake at the end of the service. It argues that the people of Kirkmichael and Tomintoul had been decorous towards their guest. If the paper could have run a picture of him being shunned, I am sure they would have done so.

It seems they were just being polite, as in October of the same year, 'Convicted killer James Nelson' is applying to be the minister of Cockenzie Old Parish Church in East Lothian. The much shorter article follows a well-worn pattern. The crimes are reiterated. A representative of the vacancy committee acknowledges that there have been applications, but the committee has not yet met to discuss them. A local person gives a nugget of information – in this case, a Miss Chris Buchanan: 'I think they are probably applying for lots of churches.' That 'they' is important. What seems to have made Cockenzie more newsworthy is that the other applicant was none other than Iain Macdonald. Neither seems to have been offered the charge. It is beginning to look as if that is where the story peters out.

But then, an even smaller notice, in the *Scotsman* for 21 February 1986, barely a column-inch long and headed 'Ex-convict selected for Kirk post'. The entire article reads:

> The Rev. James Nelson has been selected as sole nominee for the joint Church of Scotland charge of Calderbank and Chapelhall in Lanarkshire. Mr Nelson was selected by an overwhelming majority of the vacancy committee and he will now preach as sole nominee a week on Sunday. Mr Nelson began studying for the ministry while serving a prison sentence for the murder of his mother. The interim Moderator, the Rev. James Dunne, said 'There was no dissension in the vacancy committee. The vast majority of the committee felt he was the best man for the job.'

Nelson chose as his text the Epistle to the Colossians 3:17: 'And Whatsoever ye do in word or deed, *do* all in the name of the Lord Jesus, giving thanks to God and the Father by him.' The sermon touched on forgiveness, with Nelson being reported to have said, 'There are times in each of our lives when the evil we don't want is the evil we do,' a paraphrase of what Paul says in Chapter 7 of the Epistle to the Romans. His wife accompanied him to both services. A parish has every right to reject the candidate put forward as sole nominee, and so it was duly put to the vote. He was selected as minister of Calderbank and Chapelhall by 283 votes to 76. There are two other items of interest in the reports. First, Nelson also quoted from a novel by J. M. Barrie, *The Little Minister*: 'The life of every man is a diary in he which he means to write one story and writes another.' The second is that the parishes of Chapelhall and Calderbank are twenty minutes' brisk walk from Barrachnie Road, Garrowhill, where the murder took place seventeen years beforehand.

The Gospel According to
St Luke 19:3

And he sought to see Jesus who he was; and could not for the press,
because he was little of stature.

The Little Minister was undoubtedly a strange work to reference.
J. M. Barrie's 1891 novel is sometimes held up as the paradigm
of the so-called Kailyard School – a work of lachrymose
romanticism, calculatedly mawkish. It is nostalgically narrated by
the dominie of Glen Quharity, and the eponymous minister –
the Rev. Gavin Dishart, 'a pocket edition of a man' who 'did
not bang the Bible with his fist as much as might have been
wished' – has just been installed, at the age of twenty-one, into
the vacant charge of Thrums. Thrums had already been the
setting for Barrie's *Auld Licht Idylls* of 1888 and *A Window in
Thrums* of 1889, linked short-story collections concerning his
mother's upbringing in Kirriemuir in Angus as part of the more
Calvinist-inclined Auld Licht faction. 'Thrums is the name I give
here to the handful of houses jumbled together in a cup', wrote
Barrie, 'until twenty years ago its every other room, earthen-
floored and showing the rafters overhead, had a handloom. In
those days the cup overflowed and left several houses on the top
of the hill, where their cold skeletons still stand. When viewed

from the cemetery where the traveller gets his first glimpse of the little town Thrums is but two church steeples and a dozen red stone patches.' Barrie at the time was working in Nottingham, and among his rejections was one from Frederick Greenwood of the *Saint James Gazette*, on the back of which was scribbled, 'But I liked that Scotch thing – any more of those?' As Barrie later reminisced, 'So I sent him a marriage, and he took it, and then I tried him with a funeral, and he took it, and it really did look like we had him. My mother was racking her brains by request for memories I might convert into articles.' Readers of *The Little Minister* had already encountered the Rev. Dishart scuttling and scudding between stories in the previous two collections. He took centre stage in the first Thrums novel, and the reclusive and damaged narrator becomes a character in his own right as well. It is a double fissure of Barrie himself: the prematurely aged and melancholic yarn-spinner; the naïve, otherworldly and childlike – even in stature – unexpected hero.

The quotation Nelson used comes from the first chapter. It continues: 'His humblest hour is when he compares the volume as it is with what he vowed to make it. But the biographer sees the last chapter while he is still at the first, and I have only to write over with ink what Gavin has written in pencil.' This crucially implies that biography is a kind of palimpsest; that the diarist writes into a future, and the biographer in it.

But there are further curiosities about Nelson's choice. Despite the reputation of the Kailyard School, it is a novel about lust, alcoholism, industrial unrest, child poverty, corruption, resentment at the police, old women forced into poorhouses and orphaned girls forced into marriage. It is not a unified community: 'We are not one family,' Barrie writes; 'to flit from Tanage Brae to Haggart's Road is to change one's friends.' It is no dwam of nostalgic utopia. Perhaps the critics who denounce Barrie have not actually read the book, but only seen the stage musical version, *Wild Grows the Heather* – I wish there were a causal link here, but it was the first musical in which my grandfather played the lead at Kelso Amateur Operatic Society.

Many of the very finest parts are the chorus-like set pieces of dialogue between the various villagers, with backgrounds ranging from United Presbyterian to outright atheist. They discuss, with all the pusillanimity and parochialism of small-town Scottish life, the choice and actions of the new minister. They are written in a subtle and innovative form of Scots dialect, varying from character to character, blending Scripture and slang with a timbre all its own. One of the worthies, Snecky, talks about how he preferred another candidate: 'I says to mysel', "Thou art the man."' But he says, 'Betsy wraxed up her head, and he wasna praying. He was combing his hair wi' his fingers on the sly.' Nelson chose, in other words, a novel concerned with the niceties and nonsenses of ecclesiastical prejudice in selecting a minister.

Gavin Dishart's nemesis, his signalled undoing, is Babbie, the Egyptian, or gypsy – a pagan force against his Calvinist probity with a quick line in backchat and awfully charming eyes. From the outset we are primed to expect tragedy. Gavin perorates more than delivers a stirring speech as he gives his life for a worthless man at the novel's ending. Yet again the scene takes place in a swollen river, with Gavin diving in to save the reprobate: so many of these Scottish novels about tested faith seem to have an engorged river in them (I freely admit I had tears in my eyes when, in the middle of the swollen flood, Gavin denounces his congregation with the words 'all the pound notes in the world would not dam this torrent for a moment'). And yet. The ace in Barrie's sleeve was a happy ending all along: Gavin is rescued – a substitute sacrifice is found, in true *deus ex machina* style – and Babbie and Gavin have a long and happy life together. It infuriated Robert Louis Stevenson. '*The Little Minister* ought to have ended badly', Stevenson raged in a letter to Barrie, 'we all know it did and we are infinitely grateful to you for the grace and good feeling with which you lied about it. If you had told the truth I for one would never have forgiven you. If you are going to make a book end badly, it must end badly from the beginning. You let yourself fall in love with, and fondle, and smile at your puppets.' Yes, Robert Louis Stevenson is absolutely right. But the sucker punch and hoodwink of a happy ending is a strangely delightful double bluff, and its final lines are bittersweet without being sentimental. The narrator tells us: 'Only one bitterness remains. When I found Gavin in the rain, when I was fighting my way through the flood, when I saw how the hearts of the people were turned against him . . . I cried to God, making promises to Him, if He would spare the lad . . . and He spared him; but these promises I have not kept.' Nevertheless, Nelson also chose a novel with an unexpectedly joyful denouement, albeit with a splinter of curious trust-breaking in its closing words. With his wife at his side, the propriety of citing a novel which turns on a minister's head being turned by an exotic woman probably went unnoticed. It should not have done. Nor, I presume, did anyone notice that when Dishart arrives at the start of *The Little Minister*, his only companion is his pious, self-denying mother, on whom he dotes, and for whom he has studied so fervently to lift them out of poverty. Dishart, before he is a minister, before he is a martyr, is a son. Did anyone in Nelson's congregation notice how awkward it is that this man of all men is quoting a book about filial piety?

The Little Minister is a far more complicated text than it seems. Gavin, the narrator realises, 'was watched from the rising of his congregation to their lying down, whose every movement was expected to be a text to Thrums'. In another of reality's upstaging of fiction, Barrie gifted to the original of Thrums, Kirriemuir, a cricket pavilion. For it to be built, the dells and nooks where Gavin is first bewitched by Babbie were filled in. Moreover, the pavilion boasted a *camera obscura*, a dark room in which a pinhole allows light through, rotates, bends and transforms it by mirrors, to play it out on a surface. Think of a nineteenth-century CCTV, a Panopticon, where every action, every meeting, every tear and every giggle might be being watched, unseen.

Many of Barrie's stage works deal with how lives might be lived differently, from the inversions of class in *The Admirable Crichton*, to the wilful play-acting in *Quality Street*. By far the most goose-flesh inducing is *Dear Brutus*, his 'Midsummer Fantasy' in which a group of people – a dissolute painter, a larcenous butler, various women who are married to the wrong man or not married at all – are allowed to see their alternate existences. It has, to my mind, Barrie's most heart-breaking line: in the fantasia, the childless couple have a child. As they prepare to return to 'reality', the child says, 'Daddy, daddy, don't go! I don't want to be a might-have-been!' Where *Dear Brutus* connects with *The Little Minister* is in the words of the former's mysterious Lob, an eccentric and eerie character who hosts a party in his country house and lures the others towards the woods: 'They say that in the wood you get what nearly everybody here is longing for – a second chance.'

'During last night's ceremony, Mr Nelson (42) answered in a quiet but firm voice the statutory questions put to him by the moderator. After the service he shook hands with the members of his congregation on the steps of the church.' It was 3 April 1984, and he was now the Rev. James Nelson. James Whyte was among those attending, his name transformed to White in the reports, like the Man in the Macintosh at Paddy Dignam's funeral in Joyce's *Ulysses* becoming M'Intosh in the newspaper notice of that event. There was a 'social' and the Rev. Nelson was presented with his pulpit robes. The photograph in the *Glasgow Herald* shows him beaming, but when you look at his hands curling around the sheaf of papers, the smile seems, if not forced, then formed. He has, I notice only now, no earlobes. But he is still referred to as 'The Rev. James Nelson, the convicted murderer'. Maybe that would pass. But for the time being, Nelson was forgiven; or, at least, accepted: by the Assembly, by the assessors, by the congregations of Chapelhall and Calderbank. The time is now, I think, to think about forgiveness.

THE FOURTH SERMON

First Epistle General of John 2:12

*I write unto you, little children, because your sins are
forgiven you for his name's sake.*

One of the off-the-cuff remarks Nelson made during the media
attention of 1984 was: 'I've forgiven myself.' Did he have the
right to forgive himself? According to some writers on forgiveness,
such as Jeffrie Murphy, an American professor of law and
philosophy, only the victim could truly forgive him, and in the
case of murder this is self-evidently a logical impossibility. The
best he might hope for is forgiveness-by-proxy.

It is a curious anomaly, despite the fact that everyone in the
course of their life will not only have been wronged, but will
have acted in such a way as to wrong another, that there is a
distinct paucity of philosophical and theological literature on the
nature of forgiveness. It seems to me that this is in part because
forgiveness tends to generate paradoxes that cut to the quick of
philosophy and get to the heart of theology. This sermon will
sketch the ways in which philosophers, theologians and literary
writers have engaged with the concept of forgiveness and the
often counterintuitive conclusions reached.

First, though, some notes towards a definition of forgiveness.

254

Forgiveness is not the same as exculpation, exoneration, extenuation, condonation, leniency, clemency, pity, pardon or compassion. It requires an active moral consciousness: if due, say, to Alzheimer's, I can no longer remember that you have harmed me, that does not amount to my forgiving you. Furthermore, we cannot say that forgiveness has occurred if the wounding party is, say, a psychopath who does not believe he has done anything wrong or requires forgiveness. Forgiveness is by nature contractual: it requires not only that the offended party forgives but that the offending party accepts being forgiven. I take it as read that we think of forgiveness as a moral virtue, in that we condemn those who are unable to forgive, thinking them hardhearted or vindictive. As, however, we turn from a consideration of forgiveness in a philosophical context to its religious significance, some of these definitions will be tested.

Looking at the Greek and Roman classics rather than the Judaic and Christian texts on forgiveness, one thing becomes immediately apparent. The pagans think surprisingly little about it. Achilles, in Book XVIII of the *Iliad*, curses 'gall': 'gall, which makes a man grow angry for all his great mind / that gall of anger that swarms like smoke inside of man's heart / and becomes a thing sweeter to him by far than dripping honey'. This captures the inferno of resentment and vengefulness that forgiveness seeks to obviate. But it is more than odd that nowhere does Achilles express any sense that the death of Patroclus at the hands of Hector – a direct result of his sulky withdrawal from combat – might mean that he requires to be forgiven. There are many reasons why we know that James Macpherson's eighteenth-century Ossian poems are in part a modern production based on original Gaelic fragments, but the ending of *Fingal* is significantly different from genuine classical epics. In *Fingal*, Fingal spares

Swaran on the battlefield. By contrast, the *Iliad* ends with Achilles killing Hector, the *Odyssey* with the murder of Penelope's suitors and the maids, and the *Aeneid* with Turnus being struck down by Aeneas. Much of the appeal of *Fingal* was this Christianised ending, offering a nobler conclusion than the classical model of vengeance.

Likewise, in *The Libation Bearers* and *The Kindly Ones*, Orestes never asks for forgiveness for the murder of his mother Clytemnestra: rather he argues that it was not a moral infraction at all, but an ethical response to her murder of his father Agamemnon. Similar scenarios occur in other Greek dramas. In Sophocles' *Philoctetes*, where arguments about the moral high ground are traded back and forth, at no point does either Neoptolemus or Odysseus ask to be forgiven for the attempts they have both made to deceive the wounded Philoctetes and steal his bow, which he had been given by Heracles. They threaten, cajole and reason, but never admit fault. Nor does Philoctetes say his return to the Greek army at Troy is conditional on a show of repentance from the Greeks for abandoning him on Lemnos. Ajax, in Sophocles' eponymous play, was intent on murdering Agamemnon and his brother in revenge for being slighted when they gave the armour of Achilles to Odysseus. Divine intervention means he slays the cattle and herdsmen of the Greek army instead. He too is overcome with shame – and he commits suicide rather than ask the gods or his fellow soldiers for forgiveness. In the problematic final third of the play, when the Greek leaders are torn between leaving Ajax's corpse for the scavengers or giving it a proper burial, Odysseus gains their clemency by arguing that one should respect even one's foes. At no point is it suggested that Agamemnon might forgive Ajax.

The plays of Euripides offer even more striking examples of

the shame and vengeance pendulum. *Hippolytus* ends with a scene which on the surface seems to be about forgiveness. Having been falsely accused of sleeping with his stepmother, Phaedra, the virginal Hippolytus is mortally injured when his father, Theseus, invokes a curse. Hippolytus does say that he 'sets his father free of any guilt for this murder'. But it has already been established that the goddess Artemis, who was favoured by Hippolytus over Aphrodite, has told Theseus he is acquitted of any charge through ignorance of the truth of the situation – specifically, that everything was caused by Aphrodite's anger at Hippolytus's being celibate. There is one potential act of forgiveness which is explicitly shunned: Artemis could forgive Aphrodite for the death of her favourite, but instead, after explaining that the gods cannot interfere in other gods' machinations, she will ensure she causes the death of a favourite of Aphrodite. Forgiveness is not forgiveness if there is no actual crime, and instead we have a deferred vengeance. *Medea* is very nearly a play about the antithesis of forgiveness. The foreign sorceress Medea has been betrayed by her husband Jason, whom she assisted in completing the quest that made his name. She plots a murderous revenge against Jason's new wife, Glauce, and her father, Creon. Not content with their deaths, she also kills her children by Jason, and deliberately leaves him alive to live in sorrow. Little pity is expressed for Medea either before her revenge, or afterwards. The one time she asks for forgiveness, it is in order to delay events long enough for her plot to be completed. No one admits to being wrong, or if they do – as Medea does – they revel in it. The stagecraft makes this even more monstrous: the machinery by which a god might normally descend, as Artemis does in *Hippolytus*, is used in reverse to show Medea, on her dragon chariot, an apotheosis of impenitence.

Characters in Euripides pray for pity, justice, revenge and the resilience to carry out their plans, but not for forgiveness.

Both Plato and Aristotle never give extended consideration to forgiveness, and herein lies one of the first paradoxes. In both the descriptions of the Platonic sage and the Aristotelian Megalopsychos ('Magnanimous Man'), the philosophers reach a description of the morally perfect individual who will neither require forgiveness (since all his actions are virtuous) nor need to forgive, as his virtue creates an ethical invulnerability that prevents him being harmed. As Plato has Socrates say in *The Apology*, 'Be sure that if you kill the sort of man I say I am, you will not harm me more than yourselves. Neither Meletus nor Anytus can harm me in any way; he could not harm me, for I do not think it is permitted that a better man be harmed by a worse; certainly he might kill me, or perhaps banish or disenfranchise me, which he and maybe others think to be great harm, but I do not think so.' In the *Nicomachean Ethics*, Aristotle contradictorily praises 'being angry at the right things and towards the right people, and also in the right way and for the right length of time' while claiming that the Megalopsychos is 'not prone to marvel since he finds nothing great nor to remember evils since it is not proper for the magnanimous person to nurse memories, especially not of evils, but to overlook them'. The reason neither Plato nor Aristotle devotes any time to the idea of either forgiving or being forgiven is that their perfectionist ethics aim at creating individuals of supreme equanimity, who cannot be emotionally or psychologically harmed by the actions of others. They have no interest in failure.

Given that Islamic theology draws inspiration from both the earlier Abrahamic religions and the philosophy of Aristotle, it is unsurprising that its thinking is a synthesis of the two where, if anything, the Stagirite has the edge over the Torah. It should be mentioned, however, that the five most beautiful names of Allah in the Qur'an all deal with forgiveness: al-Ghafoor, the most forgiving; al-Afuw, the releaser from the burden of punishment; al-Tawwab, the acceptor of repentance; al-Haleem, the clement; and Al-Rahman, the most merciful and compassionate. There are later texts, which, rather than presenting *hadith* from the life of the Prophet, analyse forgiveness from first principles. The Islamic position on *afw*, or excusing a fault, is that it is commendable for three reasons. It is merciful to forgo revenge, it brings honour to the forgiver (and should not be considered a sign of weakness), and it acts as an intercession as regards our own moral failings for which we might require *afw* from others. *Afw* is the accepting of a substitutionary punishment. According to Professor Mona Siddiqui, Islam teaches that while forgiveness is good, justice is better; and true forgiveness cannot happen if there is no justice. This is a position taken by many other philosophers. Forgoing revenge is not the same as pretending a fault never happened.

One exceptionally intriguing work is Abu L'-Ala al-Maari's *The Epistle of Forgiveness*. Al-Maari was a blind, vegetarian Syrian who studied in Tripoli, Baghdad and Antioch at the end of the tenth and the beginning of the eleventh century AD, and who has been described as a 'pessimistic freethinker': given that one of his statements divided humanity into two sorts, those with religion but no brains and those with brains but no religion, it seems a fair description. He also claimed we should forgo having children to prevent the hypothetical beings having to suffer by necessity when they were actualised, a stance similar to the aphorisms of the twentieth-century Romanian philosopher E. M. Cioran in *The Trouble with Being Born*. *The Epistle of Forgiveness* was supposedly written to counter accusations of al-Maari's irreligion. It has, with some justice, been compared with Dante's *Divine Comedy*, in that al-Maari is transported to Paradise, and converses with the spirits of the dead. (It takes its place alongside Drycthelm's vision in Bede, Cicero's *Dream of Scipio* and ibn-Shuhaid's voyage to the land of the djinns.) It seems to me, however, in its intellect and irony more readily comparable with the rambunctious medieval satirist Rabelais. The book is an act of forgiving as much as a discussion on forgiveness and other religious ideas, in that al-Maari's protagonist meets pre-Islamic Arab poets in Paradise, contrary to the orthodox position that belief in Allah is a precondition of entering Heaven. His depiction of Paradise is shockingly counterintuitive. It is a place primarily of perpetual metamorphosis and endemic amnesia. The poet who composed an elegy on his age is unrecognisable as a young man. Other poets cannot remember the verses attributed to them. Al-Maari puns that 'you are called man [*insan*] because you are forgetful [*nasi*]'. Instead of justice and recompense, we have a state of being forgiven characterised by radical transformation and elective oblivion. These are ideas that shall return. Al-Maari's own – rejected – epitaph is a paradoxical take on forgiveness and consistent with his riddling sense. He wanted it to state that his life was a wrong done by his father and not by himself. In 2013, a branch of al-Qaeda in Syria symbolically beheaded his statue. In some conservative Islamic circles, forgiveness was impossible to give to a non-Muslim, a *shirk*, or someone who repeatedly rejected Allah.

The classical schools of Stoicism and Epicureanism broadly follow the pattern of thinking already present: that forgiveness was either unnecessary or, in the absence of justice, weak. There is a notable parallel in Cicero's *De Amicitia* (*On Friendship*), where the question is raised over whether one could remain friends with a person who had, for example, betrayed the Republic. Cicero is confident that such an action would invalidate the friendship and morally compromise an individual attempting to forgive their friend. I emailed my first girlfriend, a formidably intelligent classicist, to ask if there were other references to forgiveness – Plotinus, perhaps? Lucretius? – I had missed and received a terse response saying, 'Forgiveness is not a concept for which I have any use.'

These ideas continue to reverberate in post-classical philosophy. Immanuel Kant proposed an ethical stance in *The Metaphysics of Morals*, with the characteristically natty phrase 'the duty of apathy'. In short – though little in Kant is – this is the idea that a moral judgement should be made without the influence of *Affecten* (affects) or *Leidenschaften* (passions). Affects are emotions like anger, quick to kindle and swift to subdue, while passions are like hatred, which seeks to go beyond our need to defend ourselves and rights. Imagine – Kant is usually best thought through in analogies – the difference between the yelp of touching an open flame inadvertently, and the restructuring of the self caused by repeatedly burning oneself to inure oneself to the pain of flame. The 'duty of apathy' is similar to the Stoic and Epicurean ideas of being 'without suffering', as indeed the Greek original means, but linked to a more complex view of the architecture of our emotions. While upholding the duty of apathy, Kant defines forgiveness in his *Lectures on Ethics* as 'the remission of compensation or payment'. Forgiveness for Kant is not a feeling, but an action, and the remission in question or the payment need not be either legalistic or pecuniary. To take Nelson as the example. His father did not forgive him, but what might his putative forgiveness have looked like? Through Kantian lenses, it might have involved resuming cordial relations – not cold-shouldering is a remission – or speaking with civility about his success. It would mean desisting in a pattern of behaviour for a greater moral good; it would 'consign his offence to oblivion, in regard to saying anything about it, and . . . display towards him the appearance of no longer recalling it', albeit that requires 'superhuman virtue'. That greater moral good is more ambiguous. Kant thinks of forgiveness as a 'duty of virtue' rather than a 'duty of right' in that it cannot be coerced. I can't be forced to forgive but I can be forced, and rightly so, from not slapping brats in a supermarket on a whim. By forgiving, we contribute towards our own moral evolution, and, in doing so, become an example that will make others wish to emulate us. There is a solipsism in this, which Kant squares by linking one's own steps towards moral perfection to a society's: the more I am magnetised, the more the iron filings around me twitch towards their destiny as apathetic philosophers. But he is not arguing for unlimited forgiveness. He states in the *Doctrine of Virtue* that 'meek toleration of wrongs' is not forgiveness. If forgiving abases our own self-respect, or encourages recidivism, it is not truly forgiveness. If we are to forgive without expecting restitution of some form – material, moral, metaphysical, mannerly – then we diminish our own self-respect; if we do so while knowing it is likely to happen again, then we are opening ourselves up to future infractions on our self, on our rights and on our haltering quest onwards to moral excellence.

Oh, Nietzsche. We had to come to you eventually and improperly. Nietzsche is to Euripides as Kant is to Sophocles: instead of putting conditions around forgiveness, why not throw it all to the winds, to the fires, to the dirt, to the deep? It is never easy to say what Nietzsche 'thinks' or 'says' or 'means', since the texts are so poetic, hyperbolic, sarcastic, declamatory, lyrical. On one level we could present Nietzsche's view of forgiveness as typical of the master and slave ethics in *On the Genealogy of Morals*. Like meekness, humility, obedience, diligence, celibacy or poverty, it is a necessity which is reframed as a choice in the slave's, the herd's, resentful subversion of the more powerful master-ethics. Nietzsche even refers to it as 'not-being-able-to-take-revenge'. Even the anger which an injured party might feel can be read as an admission of vulnerability – here Nietzsche departs from Kant, who thought of such angers as a necessary recognition of wrongdoing. But the fact that forgiving does imply a kind of agency means that elsewhere Nietzsche recuperates it as a feature of the *Übermensch*. In *Human, All Too Human*, aphorism 348 reads: 'It is far pleasanter to injure and afterwards beg for forgiveness than to be injured and grant forgiveness. He who does the former gives evidence of power and afterwards of kindness of character. The person injured, however, if he does not wish to be considered inhuman, must forgive; his enjoyment of the other's humiliation is insignificant on account of this constraint.' In *Beyond Good and Evil* he writes, 'Let us be careful in dealing with those who attach great importance to being credited with moral tact and subtlety in moral discernment! They never forgive us if they have once made a mistake BEFORE us (or even with REGARD to us) – they inevitably become our instinctive calumniators and detractors, even when they still remain our "friends". Blessed are the forgetful: for they "get the better" even of their blunders.' Nietzsche's fankle is caused by a key feature of forgiveness: that it cannot be compelled. As such it must be an act of will. Will is incompatible with slave-morality, and yet forgiveness seems to be an aspect of it. The quotation from *Human, All Too Human* is a means of weaponising the *echt*-polite phrase 'you really must forgive me'. It makes a

Catch-22: if the injured party does not forgive they are stony-hearted and morally etiolated; if they do the perpetrator is freed. Nietzsche takes Kant's idea of forgiveness as moral empowerment to the forgiver and renders it paradoxical. It is the psychology that Jacques Lacan would describe as the 'big Other': the response to 'If only I could' can rarely be 'Well, actually you can.' Politeness always trumps truth; morality always cedes to conformity. Lacan, in a nutshell, might be illustrated by the fact that few people ever answer 'yes' to the question 'Does my bum look big in this?'

Nietzsche has another strategy in rendering forgiveness problematic. One of the features of the *Übermensch* is the capacity to embrace the whirlpool of Eternal Return. Nietzsche describes it in *The Gay Science*: 'What, if some day or night a demon were to steal after you into your loneliest loneliness and say to you: "This life as you now live it and have lived it, you will have to live once more and innumerable times more" . . . Would you not throw yourself down and gnash your teeth and curse the demon who spoke thus? Or have you once experienced a tremendous moment when you would have answered him: "You are a god and never have I heard anything more divine."' The *Übermensch*'s embrace of *amor fati* – making destiny into choice like a transcendent variation of the slave-morality – is also an act of *self-forgiving*. It is the opposite of the phrase: 'If I could do it all again, I wouldn't.' The *Übermensch* accepts all the errors, infelicities, pains, mistakes, crimes, wrongs, sins committed and sins inflicted on them and willingly undergoes it all again. The *Übermensch*'s voluntary acceptance of Eternal Return is lauded in *Ecce Homo*, in the chapter 'Why I Am So Clever': 'My formula for human greatness is *amor fati*: that one wants to have nothing different, not forward, not backward, not in all eternity. Not merely to bear the necessary, still less to conceal it – all idealism is mendaciousness before the necessary – but to *love* it.' This conception of the *Übermensch* is in some ways strikingly Christ-like. Christ does make his destiny his choice – 'not my will, but thine' – and freely took on the shame of the Cross. Where they differ is that the crucifixion is the 'once and for all', while the *Übermensch* suffers again and again for his self. Self-forgiving might be the ultimate egotism, while the *amor fati* of the Cross is the ultimate self-emptying.

The major difference when we turn from the classics to the biblical sources is in the nature of who is doing the forgiving. There is no evidence for Zeus or Jupiter, Hera or Juno, Poseidon, Neptune, Minerva, Athena, Apollo, Artemis, Diana, Hermes, Mercury, Hestia, Vesta, Demeter, Ceres, Hephaestus, Vulcan, Dionysus or Bacchus – let alone Odin, Horus, Isis, Mithras, Ahura-Mazda, or Brahma, Vishnu or Shiva, let alone Kali, or Amaterasu-Ō-mi-kami, or Ogbunabali, or Tezcatlipoca, or Make-Make of Easter Island, or Baal – ever being entreated and implored to forgive their believers. Yet this is a consistent feature across the Old Testament: from Exodus 32:32 ('Yet now, if thou wilt forgive their sin; and if not, blot me, I pray thee, out of thy book which thou hast written'), to the Second Book of Chronicles 6:30 and 6:39 ('Then hear thou from heaven thy dwelling place, and forgive, and render unto every man according to all his ways, whose heart thou knowest; (for thou only knowest the hearts of the children of men:)' . . . 'Then hear thou from the heavens, *even* from thy dwelling place, their prayer and their supplications, and maintain their cause, and forgive thy people which have sinned against thee'), to the plangent Psalms, especially 19:12 ('Who can understand *his* errors? cleanse thou me from secret *faults*'), and the important verses in Jeremiah 31:34 ('And they shall teach no more every man his neighbour, and every man his brother, saying, Know the LORD: for they shall all know me, from the least of them unto the greatest of them, saith the LORD: for I will forgive them their iniquity, and I will remember their sin no more'), to Micah, whose praise at 7:18 reads: 'Who *is* a God like unto thee, that pardoneth iniquity, and passeth by the transgression of the remnant of his heritage? he retaineth not his anger for ever, because he delighteth *in* mercy.' To answer Micah – well, precious few deities being worshipped at the time. I will return to the Gospels later, but would at this point observe that there is a shift in the New Testament, whereby forgiving one another, not merely beseeching being forgiven, is held up as a moral exemplar, albeit a problematic one.

'He retaineth not his anger for ever.' Although he did not use these words, they are central to the most influential discussion of forgiveness in the aftermath of Pentecost. That said, it is somewhat surprising that this comes as late as 1726, with Bishop Butler's *Fifteen Sermons Preached at the Rolls Chapel.* Neither Augustine nor Aquinas, nor Luther nor Calvin devotes much time to the mechanics of forgiveness. We can understand why in the case of Calvin, as forgiving would be a work, and therefore a bargaining chip with God, who does not cut deals, and with Aquinas, since his God is so close to the Aristotelian Magnanimous Man – perfect in morality and therefore invulnerable – it is difficult to see why he would be hurt by our transgressions, rather than merely pitying us. Both Luther and Augustine are more fixated on their own need for forgiveness than on how forgiveness might operate in the world, between individuals.

Butler took a different tack. He concentrates on what forgiveness does to the forgiver primarily, rather than to the forgiven. In Butler's psychomachia, a sin causes grief and offence to the victim. Without forgiveness this natural resentment turns into implacable vengeance, thus causing the victim to sin. Forgiveness short-circuits the connection between abuse and revenge (it is notable that the classical myths where forgiveness might have been proffered or received tend to instead fixate on shame, justice and the incoherence of competing moral codes) and thereby breaks the circle of retaliation. As Butler writes:

> *Revenge* is a kind of wild justice, which the more man's nature runs to, the more law ought to weed it out: for as for the first wrong, it doth but offend the law, but the revenge of that wrong putteth the law out of office. Certainly, in taking revenge, a man is but even with his enemy; but in passing over it, he is superior; for it is a prince's part to pardon . . . This is certain, that a man that studieth revenge keeps his own wounds green which otherwise would heal and do well.

This neatly and nearly squares one of the problems with treating forgiveness as an Aristotelian virtue, a mean between extremes. If hard-heartedness is one extreme, what might be the other? Forgiving everything, a stance the philosopher Charles Griswold, in Kantian cant, has termed 'servility'? Butler formulates his theory so that by concentrating on the difference between healthy resentment and poisonous vengeance, one can forgive a person even while pursuing legal redress, and without pretending that a moral damage did not occur (a position cleverly satirised by W. H. Auden in *For the Time Being*, with the line 'I like commit-ting sins, God likes forgiving them, really the world is admirably arranged'). Butler's idea of resentment defined discussions of forgiveness during and after the Enlightenment, with the moral philosopher and sometime promoter of the dismal science of economics, Adam Smith, and the philosopher, sceptic and pub-backgammon expert, David Hume, for example, agreeing with him.

Butler preaches:

> Resentment is of two kinds: Hasty and sudden, or settled
> and deliberate. The former is called anger, and often
> passion; which, though a general word, is frequently
> appropriated and confined to the particular feeling, sudden
> anger, as distinct from deliberate resentment, malice, and
> revenge. In all these words is usually implied somewhat
> vicious: somewhat unreasonable as to the occasion of the
> passion, or immoderate as to the degree or duration of it.
> But that the natural passion itself is indifferent, St Paul
> has asserted in that precept, 'Be ye angry and sin not';
> [Ephes. iv. 26.] which, though it is by no means to be
> understood as an encouragement to indulge ourselves
> in anger, the sense being certainly this, 'Though ye be
> angry, sin not'; yet here is evidently a distinction made,
> between anger and sin, between the natural passion and
> sinful anger.

That surreptitious slide from 'Be' to 'Though' is one of the most beautiful pieces of writing I know – its caution and wry rebuke, its simple rewriting of the text to make it utterly different. Butler agrees, before his time, with Kant and Nietzsche. The recognition of a moral wrong, and the pain it causes us, is natural and not to be dismissed. Aristotle said that only a fool would not be aware of being harmed. The unthumping Butler agreed: 'No; it is resentment against vice and wickedness: it is one of the common bonds, by which society is held together; a fellow-feeling which each individual has in behalf of the whole species, as well as of himself.' Given how glorious his prose is, I shall indulge the reader with his eloquence.

> And this seems to be the whole of this passion which is, properly speaking, natural to mankind; namely, a resentment against injury and wickedness in general; and in a higher degree when towards ourselves, in proportion to the greater regard which men naturally have for themselves, than for others. From hence it appears, that it is not natural, but moral evil; it is not suffering, but injury, which raises that anger or resentment, which is of any continuance. The natural object of it is not one, who appears to the suffering person to have been only the innocent occasion of his pain or loss but one, who has been in a moral sense injurious either to ourselves or others. This is abundantly confirmed by observing, what it is which heightens or lessens resentment; namely, the same which aggravates or lessens the fault; friendship and former obligations, on one hand; or inadvertency, strong temptations, and mistake, on the other. All this is so much understood by mankind, how little soever it be reflected upon, that a person would be reckoned quite distracted, who should coolly resent a harm, which had not to himself the appearance of injury or wrong. Men do indeed resent what is occasioned through carelessness; but then they expect observance as their due, and so that carelessness is considered as faulty. It is likewise true, that they resent more strongly an injury done, than one which, though designed, was prevented, in cases where the guilt is perhaps the same. The reason however is, not that bare

269

pain or loss raises resentment, but, that it gives a new,
and, as I may speak, additional sense of the injury or
injustice. According to the natural course of the passions,
the degrees of resentment are in proportion, only to the
degree of design and celebration in the injurious person,
but in proportion to this, joined with the degree of the
evil designed or premeditated; since this likewise comes
in to make the injustice greater or less. And the evil or
harm will appear greater when they feel it, than when
they only reflect upon it: so, therefore, will the injury:
and consequently the resentment will be greater. The
natural object or occasion of settled resentment, then,
being injury, as distinct from pain or loss, it is easy
to see, that to prevent and to remedy such injury, and
the miseries arising from it, is the end for which this
passion was implanted in man. It is to be considered
as a weapon put into our hands by nature, against
injury, injustice and cruelty.

Resentment, for Butler, is both the moral awareness of wrong
done and the very virtue that, done badly, is a barrier against
forgiveness. It is a brake on vengefulness, anger, viciousness: it
is the internal court of our emotions. Resentment is what we must
feel and must forgo.

Malice or resentment towards any man hath plainly a
tendency to beget the same passion in him who is the
object of it, and this again increases it in the other. It is of
the very nature of this vice to propagate itself, not only by
way of example, which it does in common with other
vices, but in a peculiar way of its own; for resentment

itself, as well as what is done in consequence of it, is the object of resentment. Hence it comes to pass, that the first offence, even when so slight as presently to be dropt and forgotten, becomes the occasion of entering into a long intercourse of ill offices.

The word Nietzsche used to describe how slave-morality tried to undermine master-ethics was *ressentiment* – resentment: a peevish, snide virtue; a smug, impotent vice.

In the aftermath of my divorce – I remember signing the legal documents at Edinburgh's family court, and being struck that a mere day beforehand I had been signing copies of my previous books at a literary festival, and how remarkable it was that the same gesture could have such radically different meanings – I became something of a connoisseur of resentment. I knew there were deeds and thoughts, done and undone, that I would wish to be forgiven for, and knew equally well that my own capacity to forgive was a thin, ungracious thing. I nursed my hurts and savoured my grievances. The initial spur was an email from my soon-to-be-ex-wife, a few weeks before the papers would be signed, informing me that she was 'unexpectedly' in a new relationship. It wasn't so much the substance of the message, but that it had been sent at all: I did not feel I needed to know. It was, I argued to myself, a calculated flourish of triumphalism. If I were to use one word to describe resentment it would be 'pitchy'. Like pitch, it is viscous and amorphous; it does not just tarnish, but passes on tarnishment. It pitches, a kind of moral vertigo, a roiling *mal de mer* on dry land; or a form of sour and sharp tinnitus, a whine you cannot make vacate your skull. As soon as the resentment settled in, it spread. It was the start of the new academic year in Edinburgh, and everywhere there were newly struck young couples, strolling arm in arm in the autumnal light. If I, like Elijah or Elisha, could strike down at will, those streets would have been corpse-strewn. Worse than the bright young things – whom I viciously pitied, knowing that soon it would be tears and recriminations when their Freshers' Week flush of lust expired – were the fat couples, the ugly couples, the – be frank, be frank – stupid-looking couples with ill-considered tattoos and questionable clothing choices, lolling along. That they were allowed to love and to be loved was ludicrous and laughable. Why was I shuddering at a bus stop while they clasped together their clammy palms and linked their fingers, bedecked with cheap and gaudy, green-staining rings? It was something other than envy, something other than anger, something other than lust. The pride of it was that it was wounded, and the scab picked perpetually, since the pain was something to be proud of, a kind of nasty excellence. Resentment is a strange attractor, a means for grief to become flaw, and for other vices to be drawn towards it, for a crack of damage to welcome in an inundation of sin. The worst of them – the very engine of them – is self-pity. Self-pity has a corollary: since only I am morally evolved enough to recognise my own suffering, then finding fault in others is the default. (De-fault: the privative prefix again.) Resentment is like the drop of cochineal in the glass of water. Be it ever so small, it stains the whole. It is the curdled virtue.

The quotation 'to know all is to forgive all' is attributed to Mme de Stael, and it might seem as if an omnipotent God would necessarily also be an all-forgiving God. But there is a problem here. The phrase seems to imply that perfect knowledge would make every sin comprehensible. Yes, you stole my wallet, but I did not know then that your children were starving. If so, forgiveness is actually cancelled out, like algebraic terms on both sides of an equation. It is not forgiveness, but exculpation.

The most succinct account of forgiveness by a contemporary philosopher is Pamela Hieronymi's 'Articulating an Uncompromising Forgiveness', a paper that is all the better for admitting its own hesitancies. As with her work on the concept of blame, Hieronymi is aware that the common usage of terms can be slipshod, and that they come weighted with a great deal of historical baggage. Nevertheless, she attempts to create a feasible picture of the conditions and problems of forgiveness without begrudgement or coercion. She identifies three necessary features of uncompromising forgiveness: that the person forgiving not only believes but continues to believe that the wrong was serious; that they did not deserve to be wronged (does a child forgive the smack if he knows it was he who broke the crystal swan?); and that it could have been otherwise, that the wrongdoer had it in their power to act differently – the inverse of the Hopi animal-fable of the scorpion who is taken over the river on the back of a fox, and who, when it stings the fox and is reproached that they will both drown, answers, 'It is my nature.' The most important term in her title is 'articulate'. The forgiver has to be able not only to identify the wrong, but to give a cogent account for their reason for forgiving. They have to be self-aware as to why they are doing it. She queries the psychological mechanism that Butler proposed on the valid grounds that he depicts a change, a cessation of resentment in absolute terms. It is as if a shirt has been stained, and forgiveness is both the ethical detergent and deterrent; or as if resentment is a headache and forgiveness an analgesic. As she rightly points out, our emotional states don't come in single hues. They are not single notes that drown out all other sounds, but are more like chords. One can be both angry and loving, both compassionate and resentful at the same time; though despite her admirable belief in the emotional sophistication of humans, she admits this may be difficult. Moreover, she suggests that compassion – understanding though disagreeing with motivations, not wanting the wrongdoer to persist in regret, grieving that a person has displayed moral frailty or outright wickedness (Nietzsche, of course: 'I can forgive you for what you did to me, but how can I forgive you for what you did to yourself?') – might not be forgiveness at all, but a readiness to forgive. The 'revision' of the emotions, as she cleverly terms it, might not be subject to such reasonings. It might be that theology, rather than philosophy, is a harder and better guide to forgiving.

The best interrogation of the idea of forgiveness in modern times was developed in Jacques Derrida's *On Forgiveness*. With customary flair and elegance, Derrida observes a pair of major flaws in most discussions of the topic: conditionality and identity, which appear to be intertwined. To take the latter first: if someone, as, for example, Eric Lomax, the 'Railway Man', did, forgives an offender because they have evidence that the offender has seriously repented and changed, are they forgiving the offender, or granting forgiveness to the person whom the offender has become? This is tied to the former point: can any forgiveness be taken to be genuine if it comes with conditions, even Hieronymi's precisely articulated ones? I will forgive you if you do this or when you do that already seems to be a compromised position: it is neither freely offered, nor freely obtained. Derrida's essay reveals the intellectual naivety of anglophone writers like Jeffrie Murphy, the author of *Getting Even: Forgiveness and Its Limits* (even the title displays the conservatism and begrudging nature of his analysis). To Murphy, forgiveness is delimited by an 'if and only if' strand of thinking: he tries to taxonomise the preconditions whereby forgiveness might be offered or accepted. The difference with Derrida is striking. One of the paradoxical koans he offers is: 'Only the unforgivable is forgivable.' I take that to mean that any conditions (I will forgive if and only when) and any transference of person (I will forgive the you-in-the-now but never the you-in-the-past) would not constitute forgiveness. It would instead be either punitive or delusional. It is also profound about the correlation between forgiveness and agency. In my reading of the phrase, it also suggests that the only thing that can be forgiven is the act that it would be perfectly reasonable, even natural, for me not to forgive.

It is at this point that I want to return to the Gospels. It seems to me as if Derrida is closer to the Gospel narratives than the intervening thinkers. When Peter asks Jesus (in Matthew 18), 'Lord, how oft shall my brother sin against me, and I forgive him? till seven times?' Jesus replies, 'I say not unto thee, Until seven times: but, Until seventy times seven.' We can imagine a particularly literal-minded fundamentalist saying, 'Right, that's the four hundred and ninety-first time you've committed adultery! No forgiveness now!' Instead it is a standard formulation implying a limitless number. This goes radically against the Aristotelian notion that a virtue is a mean between excess and deficit. Forgiveness is not balanced between 'hard-heartedness' and 'servility' but is a continuous, ongoing requirement. One cannot be 'too forgiving' according to the Gospel narrative.

Forgiveness is central to the earthly mission of Jesus: it is, for example, part of the Lord's Prayer. But the different Gospels place different weights on it. The synoptic Gospels – Matthew, Mark and Luke – say most about the topic, but with significant differences between Luke and the other two. All three feature the story of the paralyzed man where Jesus upbraids the Pharisees

275

who accuse him of blasphemy. In Mark's version: 'Why doth this *man* thus speak blasphemies? who can forgive sins but God only?' To which Jesus replies, 'Whether it is easier to say to the sick of the palsy, *Thy* sins be forgiven thee; or to say, Arise, and take up thy bed, and walk?' This forges a psychic link between the idea of forgiveness and the idea of healing, in a manner which would please Bishop Butler. The focus has changed from a sinful humanity beseeching a perfect God for forgiveness to an ethical obligation for mutually sinful people to forgive each other: forgive us our trespasses as we forgive those who trespass against us. In John's Gospel – the most poetic and cosmological of the four – and the one which says least about the subject – this is stressed in the apostolic injunction: 'Whose soever sins ye remit, they are remitted unto them; *and* whose soever *sins* ye retain, they are retained.' John deals with forgiveness on only three occasions. The previous quotation is almost the first thing that Jesus says to the disciples after the Resurrection. In the first chapter of his Gospel, John the Baptist recognises Jesus as the Lamb of God, which taketh away the sin (singular!) of the world, and the eighth gives the story of the woman taken in adultery, which implicitly argues for forgiveness from the standpoint of humanity's mutual and ubiquitous moral imperfection.

Where Luke's Gospel differs is in creating a connection between forgiveness and contrition. Unlike Matthew and Mark, Luke consistently insists on repentance: in Chapter 17 he writes, 'Take heed to yourselves: If thy brother trespass against thee, rebuke him; and if he repent, forgive him.' This does not, however, compromise the overwhelming nature of the obligation. The next verse reads: 'And if he trespass against thee seven times in a day, and seven times in a day turn again to thee, saying, I repent; thou shalt forgive him.' The limitless nature of forgiveness is still central to this version of the Christian ethic, despite Luke's idea of the conditionality of repentance. There is in William Langland's *Piers Plowman* a clever analogy about contrition and forgiveness in a discussion about alms-giving. In the ninth passus of the C-text, a query is raised about false beggars and whether one ought to discriminate accordingly. No one, Piers is told, knows who deserves alms but God alone, so one should give to all and let those who receive them deceitfully take their own moral risk.

Other passages in Luke, however, make the link between contrition, repentance and forgiveness less clear-cut; and nothing was clear-cut about Nelson's being forgiven or being a forgiver. Richard Holloway, the former Bishop of Edinburgh, has written on the parable of the prodigal son in the context of forgiveness. He notes that the father rushes out to meet the returning son, before he knows whether or not the son has changed his ways. Although the reader knows that the younger son has repented (on account of his dire material circumstances), the father does not. Although the son intends to ask for forgiveness, there is nothing in the text to suggest that he would follow through on this intention. Holloway extrapolates from this that the act of forgiving might in fact engender contrition, rather than be withheld until there is evidence of it. This adds a layer of complexity to Butler's ideas about forgiveness. It is not just good for the offended party to forgive, but it enacts a moral benefit on the offending party. Given how frequently the parable of the prodigal son was raised during the debate on Nelson's fitness for ordination, this is crucial. The parable does not demand public contrition or repentance. In allowing that Nelson might be forgiven, it might make him penitent.

H. R. Mackintosh's *The Christian Experience of Forgiveness* (1927) attempts to reconcile the natural desire we have to see penitence with the 'timid and self-calculating love' that would withhold forgiveness until we have evidence of reformation. He defines penitence as 'truthfulness of mind', a genuine self-awareness of how unworthy of forgiveness we are. It is 'as lonely a business as dying', and 'contrition must be as solitary as sin'. Demands for public atonement are a kind of vengefulness, a means of moral humiliation. It is also perfectly possible to put on a seeming air of public contrition. It might even be argued that a public show of repentance, by its very self-regard, can appear duplicitous.

The synoptic Gospels all include a reference to one unforgivable sin – namely, 'blasphemy *against* the *Holy* Ghost'. Again, this is in the context of an almost universalist approach to forgiveness, where even blasphemy against the Son of Man can be forgiven. What is this uniquely unforgivable sin? Again, in *Piers Plowman*, in a series of similes on the nature of the Trinity (God the Father is a fist, the Son a pointing finger, and the Holy Spirit an open palm – but all three are one hand) the point is made that only stabbing the hand through the palm disables it entirely. Traditionally, the doctrinal answer as to the nature of the unforgivable sin is that it is the deliberate, obstinate rejection of forgiveness. This would seem to reassert the point made earlier that we cannot say forgiveness has occurred if the offending party does not believe they need to be forgiven.

How practicable is such an ethics of forgiveness? Can any human being live up to its requirements? It is, I would argue, supremely unpractical, and therein lies its moral genius, a stance the atheist philosopher Simon Critchley has admiringly called the 'infinitely demanding'. In *How To Stop Living and Start Worrying*, a primer of his ideas, he says in conversation with the novelist Tom McCarthy:

The self as recurrence, or as repetition, which is the way I
try to think about this in relationship to the experience of
conscience; not as a good conscience, but conscience as
an open wound, which you can't stop picking at – picking
at the scabs, making it bleed. It's something in a sense that
we are powerless over; we're compelled to repeat in that
way . . . what we're being taken back to is this state of
repetition, trauma and catastrophe that in a way forces
human beings to confront themselves and their
powerlessness and responsibility. If morality becomes a
question, as it is on BBC Radio 4, of nicely educated
people with shrill voices making choices between different
courses of action and being able to account for them, then
this is awful. I think the subject is a subject that can't
decide and has to decide, it's compelled to be responsible
but flees that responsibility.

The 'infinite demand' – perhaps best exemplified in the cancellation of the *lex talionis* ('an eye for an eye and a tooth for a
tooth') in Matthew 5 and Luke 6, where Jesus says, 'But I say
unto you, That ye resist not evil: but whosoever shall smite thee on
thy right cheek, turn to him the other also. And if any man will
sue thee at the law, and take away thy coat, let him have *thy*
cloke also. And whosoever shall compel thee to go a mile, go
with him twain' – confronts us with both a rigorous ethic and
the means to understand our failures within it. We are brought
into an understanding of our own frailty, which, by being
universal, creates a commonality between individuals. For a
while I obsessively compared the versions of the Beatitudes in
Luke and Matthew. (Perhaps if poor George Price had stuck with
Matthew, where the giving away of the cloak also is in the context

of legal suits, he might not have ended so sadly. But then, to take the more extreme option seems in keeping with him.) I suppose it twinges guilt in me because the Matthean version also had an explicit condemnation of divorce, which I parsed relentlessly at the time of my own. Justifying myself by arguing that she divorced me and not vice versa seems a shameful kind of ethical finger-crossing, the very kind of loop-hole ratiocination I affected to detest.

Perhaps the greatest paradox about forgiveness is how it relates to causality and temporality. What happens after forgiveness has occurred? Charles Griswold writes about the ideal of forgiveness as being 'knowingly to undo what had been done. The stubborn, sometimes infuriating metaphysical fact that the past cannot be changed would seem to leave us with a small range of options, all of which are modulations of forgetfulness, avoidance, rationalization or pragmatic acceptance.' There is a very Scottish phrase, 'I'll forgive, but I'll not forget', that I remember from one sermon as being held up as contrary to forgiveness. Yet it would seem, from a theological perspective, forgetting is exactly what forgiveness accomplishes.

The Epistle to the Hebrews 8 quotes the aforementioned verses from Jeremiah where God promises to forget sins after forgiving wickedness. The Psalmist asks that the sins of his youth are not remembered; in the penitential Psalm 51, David asks that his transgressions be blotted out. Again, in Isaiah 64:9, the prophet says, 'Be not wroth very sore, O LORD, neither remember iniquity for ever,' and at 43:25 God declares, 'I, *even* I, *am* he that blotteth out thy transgressions for mine own sake, and will not remember thy sins.' We might wonder how an omniscient deity has the capacity to forget.

The most radical solution to this enigma comes from the

German theologian Wolfhart Pannenberg. The American Professor of Divinity Frank Tupper describes his insight thus: 'Pannenberg's conception of retroactive continuity ultimately means that history flows fundamentally from the future into the past, that the future is not basically a product of the past.' Events in the future can therefore change events in the past. In terms of forgiveness, it is not 'as if' the offence has never happened: it is the case that the offence never happened. God's forgetting is the active undoing of the past from eternity. What Hannah Arendt called 'the predicament of irreversibility' might feasibly be solved through Pannenberg's paradoxical view of history. Emmanuel Levinas, the philosopher who greatly influenced Derrida, wrote of forgiveness that it 'acts upon the past, somehow repeats the event, purifying it'.

I think that the assertion I made twice earlier, that we cannot forgive someone who believes they have done no wrong, is actually wrong. Maybe we are commanded to forgive those who do not wish to be forgiven, and that very action can trigger the future reversal of time. This would side-step the problem for Calvinists of being instructed to forgive even if God himself is not going to forgive: rather than a variant on the notorious phrase of Arnaud Amalric, the Cistercian abbot who persecuted the Albigensians in the thirteenth century – 'Kill them all and let God sort them out' – we should 'Forgive them all and let God sort them out' – the act of forgiving the unforgivable instigates forgiveness. I confess I was rather pleased with the elegance of my thinking. Perhaps humanity was made to forgive even Satan.

Speaking with a friend in the ministry, I realised I was wrong. He pointed out that the Church of Scotland is closer to the original Hebrew in referring to 'debts' rather than 'transgressions' or 'sins'. When God forgets our sins, it means he cancels our debts.

281

The debt still exists but its repayment is not enforced. Ockham's Razor alone suggests this is a far less convoluted way of thinking about it than metaphysical time travel. It accords with Hieronymi's appreciation of the simultaneous nature of love and anger in forgiveness.

Forgiveness challenges assumptions about moral accounting and self-interest. In an age in which saying sorry has often replaced being sorry, forgiveness forces us to confront not just our preconceptions about morality and responsibility, but the very nature of identity and history. The etymology of the word, from the Old English *forgiefan*, not only means 'to grant', 'to allow' or 'to give', but 'to give in marriage': forgiveness, in its truest sense, is a binding reciprocal contract based on love. As Luther wrote, 'Where forgiveness of sins is, there is life and blessedness.'

The Gospel According to
St John 1:46

And Nathanael said unto him, Can there any good thing come out of Nazareth? Philip saith unto him, Come and see.

Who called Nelson? God called Nelson. What was the instrument of his calling? A majority of the congregation of the parishes of Chapelhall and Calderbank. And what like of a place is that?

It was ten thirty in the morning, in a misty and seemingly abandoned Airdrie, when I got off the train and decided to meander around the town centre until the bus to Calderbank arrived. There were numerous quirky shop names – Think Ink Tattoo Studio, Glamour Kutz, Captain Dugwash – and a lot of men holding pints of lager almost reverentially while a channel devoted to horse racing played in the background. There was a place called Yesterdays, describing itself as an 'Imbibing Emporium'. Airdrie Working Men's Club seemed to have been designed by an architect enamoured of the cuboid and little else. It sported a bizarre Inca-esque mural that looked as if nobody ever looked at it. There was a Jehovah's Witness Hall. I wondered how many of the flock who had opposed their new minister might have ended up here. Even buying a coffee would seem to invite questions about who I was, why I was here and when I was leaving, so I shivered up and down the streets till I could wait in the bus stop without looking like an obvious interloper. In retrospect, wearing the three-piece tweed suit was probably a bad idea. The bus, when it arrived, was an old boneshaker of a thing, and not knowing where I was going, I bought a day ticket and tried to rely on road signs to discern when I might be in Calderbank. Luckily, it hove into view fairly quickly, and I realised that I could easily have walked the distance, so sat on the bus for longer to make it look as if I knew what I was doing.

Calderbank Parish Church was a stolid nineteenth-century building, with an attached hall and broken beer bottles on the pavement outside. Across from it was the Railway Inn, where I thought I might buy lunch and listen in, and nearby to it a house I presumed must have been the manse. As a joint charge, one or other of the manses would have been sold. Had Nelson lived here? I could not tell. I had memorised a map of the area and knew that if I were to walk southeast, there should be a nature trail through some woodland towards Chapelhall. But the planners seemed to have liked curlicues of cul-de-sacs, so finding my egress made me look even more like a debt collector or paedophile. When I found the trail it was set within a row of pale and red-brick columns with crowns on them and rusted iron railings between, as if the site had once been the entrance to a Victorian factory, long demolished. One of the columns looked as if it had recently featured in a car accident. Inside, there was a choice: a hastily tarmacked stretch of paving or an obvious 'desire path' worn by frequent use. Given the post-industrial ambience of the place, and my strong suspicion that it was land reclaimed as pseudo-wild rather than a remnant of a once-wild, I took the moderately asphalted track. I reasoned that this was the kind of municipal project where well-meaning councils put in cycle paths. It terminated in a conglomeration of sheds, with an oil drum showing evidence of recent burning. A few cars, in various states of disrepair, were sort of parked, sort of abandoned. Two men came out of one of the corrugated buildings, and I hollered a breezy hello and turned on my heel back to the path more obviously trodden. Once on it, it revealed precious little evidence of frequent use: obligatory litter, once or twice plastic bags containing, I presumed but did not check, dog faeces hanging on branches. The mud was icy. The mist thickened and the trees huddled. Gorse snaked out around my ankles, fruitless brambles snagged my trousers. I remembered the opening of Dante's *Divine Comedy*: 'In the middle of the journey of our life, I came to myself, in a dark wood, where the clear path was lost.' The mist became fog, the fog something like an old television set's static. Ahead of me something impossible loomed. It looked like a tapered Aztec ziggurat, a slender ruined Borobudur. It must have been hundreds of feet high and I had no idea what it was. As I got closer, I could see on the steep sides of the valley I was in a scree – of washing machines, kitchen sinks, fridges, with bin bags of every colour round about them. Anyone would have thought it was some kind of sacrificial offering. For sword, read vacuum; for torque, toilet seat. The monolith clarified itself. It was the central pillar of what must have been the railway bridge between the towns. The bridge was gone and its support remained. What ruins will we leave?

Scrambling up a suddenly evident set of steps, I emerged into Chapelhall. It had the same Sixties architecture, a sort of shop-worn Bauhaus, and the same spirals of dead ends. I had a nauseous sense of déjà vu. I had been here before. I had actually never been in Chapelhall or Calderbank in my life, but it was almost identical to the council estate I had grown up on as a child before we moved to the countryside. The houses had the same white pebble-dashing, the same alternating mixture of flats, semis and maisonettes. The paths were the same width – supposedly calculated so that two mothers with prams might walk together side by side. There were boulders mounted on little plinths; landscape engineering turned into a simulacrum of public art. These estates, built in the 1960s and 1970s, are achingly faded Utopias. When my parents moved into Heather Court, Easter Langlee, Galashiels, we were the first people ever to live in that house. The estate had been built in two phases: Langlee, latterly Wester Langlee, in the valley; then Easter Langlee on the hill. Wester Langlee houses were harled in brown Dorset Pea, and at the age of four I was firmly convinced that white houses were a sign of moral superiority. As a teenager, and now living in a rural village with the un-Scottishly poetical name of Lilliesleaf, I read *The Great Gatsby* for school, and Fitzgerald's description of 'the city rising up across the river in white heaps and sugar lumps all built with a wish out of non-olfactory money' surreally recollected Easter Langlee and its quartz cube houses.

These places have since acquired reputations: dole, drugs, depression. But in 1973, they were new, even promising places. Is that true? In part, though even in 1973 parts of the estate were referred to as the 'pig-pens'. Langlee was newer than new: even the church, St John's, was new. It did not smell of wet stone and beeswax polish. You would not find a gas mask hidden in the vestry cupboard, as I once did in Lilliesleaf. Its stained glass was challengingly abstract. As I wandered around Chapelhall and Calderbank, I realised that the churches here were among the oldest buildings. Langlee, too, had a few anomalies: Victorian farmhouses and Edwardian villas stranded among the Lego-like modernity, jostled by the underpasses and random playgrounds.

Eventually, through a combination of deciding to keep heading uphill and walking as if I knew where I was going, I found Chapelhall Church. It was an impressive building, grand without being imposing, elegant without being fancy. It was built, I learned, in 1857: a Disruption Church. It had joined with the United Presbyterians in 1900, as part of the United Free Church of Scotland, and then rejoined the Church of Scotland in 1929. I scribbled the name of the minister in my notebook and sloped away. I could easily walk back to Airdrie and catch the train. The mist turned to mizzle, and the drizzle turned to rain.

Nestled into the only available singe seat, I retraced my walk in my memory. What had I been not noticing? I looked at my file of clippings, and pondered the tiny notice in the *Scotsman* which announced the ratification of Nelson's ministry. He was 'at one time jailed for the murder of his mother'. That 'at one time' seems close to forgiving. The manse next to Chapelhall Church was a delightful, desirable building – the Church of Scotland has very specific rules about the number of bedrooms a manse must have, to accommodate hoped-for large families and with a spare room for visiting ministers. *The Little Minister* made much of Gavin Dishart's joy in acquiring a manse to relieve his mother's poverty. The manse in Chapelhall was certainly finer than the homes around it. If there were salmon in the river I did not see them. Then, with the suddenness of something outside of me, I understood. There was a reason for these schemes. They were not an architectural whim, but a social necessity. After the Second World War, the squalid conditions of inner-city Glasgow were deemed intolerable. The 'New Towns' – East Kilbride, Glenrothes, Cumbernauld (where I first lived, before we returned to the Borders), Livingston, Irvine – were supplemented with housing schemes. Those living in toilet-less tenement slums, sleeping top-to-toe with their siblings, were relocated to shining cities on the hills. Of course, the parishioners of Chapelhall and Calderbank chose the Rev. James Nelson. They too had been given a second chance, a reprieve. Those to whom kindness has been extended are the most likely to extend the hand. Or – and the mists encircle – is this my sentimentality, to project onto poorly paid people I will never meet a moral righteousness that I wish were mine?

Ideas are often not inside us, but outwith us. I would not have had that epiphany had I toured Chapelhall and Calderbank on Google Maps; no self-archaeology would unearth what I did not know I needed to know. I determined to return. This had been a sortie, now I needed an expedition. I had done my *avant-garde* and now had to marshal my efforts. But sequestered at home, I did grasp another thing I had overlooked. Chapelhall and Calderbank were no longer a linked pair of parishes. They had gone their separate ways, and both, as I write, are looking for new ministers. Unfortunately, so did Georgina and James Nelson.

The Gospel According to
St Matthew 2:12

*And being warned of God in a dream that they should not return
to Herod, they departed into their own country another way.*

I went back to Calderbank and Chapelhall another way. Instead
of taking the train, I persuaded – or pleaded with – my parents to
drive me there. It is a different journey by road rather than rail. I
had not realised that the major employment opportunities in the
area are all concerned with warehousing, for example. We arrived,
and my imprecations about eating anywhere other than a chain
bakery went unheeded. As we left, we heard on the radio that
fifteen minutes after we bought some sausage-less sausage rolls
and coffee that tasted of burnt water, a young man had turned up
there with a knife and threatened the young woman who was
serving. My dad, in his customary fashion, had been bantering
with the lass. I wondered if, if we had delayed going in, I would
have been brave enough to tackle the poor thug. I doubt it. As for
my dad, I am sure he would have. He has a glare that is worse
than a punch.

The second visit involved people rather than bricks and
mortar. It also involved being inside the buildings rather than
outside of them. Both are handsome churches, and if I were to

make a choice, I found the polyhedral interior of Chapelhall more fascinating and the austere, rectangular, traditional inside of Calderbank more calming. In Chapelhall, there was a photograph of the Rev. Nelson alongside all the other men (and they were all men) who had fulfilled that duty. In Calderbank, there was no image of him.

Everyone I tried to speak to was laconic, with the exception of the minister of Chapelhall, who had found the original petition, of which he was a signatory, asking the Assembly to be generous of spirit. He was about to leave the charge and go into retirement. Although he was straight-backed, there was a kind of stoop around him, as if he regretted leaving. I heard a great many positive things about the Rev. James Nelson while speaking with church members. He was, I learned, particularly sensitive at funerals; was a good preacher; and had been very handy at sorting out manual tasks: a door that needed fixing, lights that had to be replaced, paintwork that required a new lick. Rather than ask for the session to hire a labourer, he would do it himself. His father's joinery skills had evidently been handed down. One person just said, 'He was a good man.' But elsewhere I heard a different story. He was a sarcastic man, prone to flaunting his knowledge of music against the choir. He could be peremptory and presumptuous. He was snide, and thought himself better than others, as if he of all people had any right to do so. Nobody mentioned murder. Nobody mentioned Georgina. Nobody mentioned if he was pious, or holy, or devout, or even forlorn. He was dedicated and dutiful. Maybe that is enough.

I asked where his grave was. It wasn't: he had been cremated. He is one with the grass I walked over and the air I breathed in, I assume.

I had expected people to have differing opinions, but not

polarised ones. There was no way by which the striving good man and the sneaky wicked thing might be reconciled. On one hand there might be legitimate grievances; on the other, naïve forgoing. On one hand there was genuine affection; and on the other sincere revulsion. Why could I not, being a wise man, or wiser than most at least, untangle the conundrum of Nelson? Every emotional part of me wanted him to be a genuine convert, and every intellectual part of me whispered he was a clever fake. In so many ways, I had made the same mistake I always make. I thought it could be thought through. For some people, James Nelson was a steadfast friend and loyal minister; for some he was a chancer ventriloquizing faith.

It is not for me to know. It is not for you to know.

Let us presume he was always more than double. He was not a minister or a murderer, he was not neither nor but both and. In which case he is just like every other human being. We are all multiples: a son to a mother, an uncle to a nephew, an ex-husband to a former wife. Walt Whitman wrote, in *Leaves of Grass*, 'Do I contradict myself? / Very well, then I contradict myself, / (I am large, I contain multitudes.)' Whitman could celebrate what I find encroaching: others, hypothetical selves, alternate *Is*. The double, so prevalent in Gothic fiction, is a curiously comforting notion. It supposes a binary fission, a good and a bad, a light and a dark, a former and a latter, a once and a now, a then and a yet. It has the nicety of being stark. But reality is more complicated. What if we are, as the demon in the Gospels of Mark and Luke taunts, 'Legion: for we are many'? Might anyone bear such multiplicity? Could anyone thole such polyphony? I left an ellipsis in Georgina Nelson's letter because it needed to be read on its own: 'I recall Jim with affection and with sadness, because, for all the "official" forgiveness which the church extended when it granted him permission to become a minister, and for all the support that he received from people who truly believed in the possibility of new beginnings, his past was always with him. It always cast a shadow . . .'

'Official forgiveness': there is wisdom in that formulation. Nelson was technically forgiven, but not, alas, actually. It is like the Scottish judicial system having not two possible verdicts – guilty or innocent – but three: guilty, innocent and 'not proven'. Not proven is not guilty, but nor is it innocent; it is limbo, an idea the Reformation supposedly swept away. There is infinitude in those tapped periods as well. It trails off, as if the thought is greater than language can encompass.

I kept an eye on the news for any stories about Chapelhall and Calderbank. Chapelhall had been united with the Kirk o' Shotts. Nobody was ever publicly named for the bakery robbery. 'Balaclava-clad vandals' superglued the church door shut in Calderbank, in an incident which was being treated as a hate crime. No newspaper carried a story about the calling of a sole nominee to either church.

As we were in the area, my parents decided to divert through Cumbernauld, so that I could see where I had first lived. It was a place of which I had only false memories. I recognised it, after a fashion, as I had seen in it films: *Gregory's Girl*, a sweet rom-com that I watched as a teenager and that convinced me that love might be possible for anyone, even someone with thick glasses and intermittent plooks. I 'remembered' pulling eggs off a supermarket shelf before I was a year old. The shopping trolley had an orange front bar; the eggs were in a clear plastic box. I cheekily stuck out my hand and pulled the whole lot down. Only I didn't. Mum says the eggs were in a green cardboard box, and it was a plain metal bar on the trolley. I had been told the story – Oh! When Stuart smashed all those eggs! – and the story had become the memory. If my memory of one minor incident could be rewritten and rewritten by the telling of it and the retelling of it, then how could I trust anything said about Nelson? Whose memories were reliable? Whose were uninflected by prejudice or love, resentment or admiration?

On the way home, I talked to my dad about church linkages, and the breaking of the links. Our church in Lilliesleaf had once been linked to Bowden and Ashkirk, and then changed to a joined congregation with Ancrum, Crailing and Eckford. Linkages are always emotional businesses for the parishes concerned, he said. He recounted a story about an inland parish and a coastal parish which the Kirk determined would be best served by a single minister, and the legendary response from the farming community: 'They didnae even tell us when the Vikings waur coming.' The separation of Chapelhall and Calderbank would have not, I suppose, been wholly amicable. Dad elaborated on the mean-spirited negotiations they involved: if there were one minister for two parishes, which manse should be sold? Who should receive the profits from the sale – both churches, or the one giving up the minister being a resident? How should the session reflect the numbers of each parish? I had never realised that holiness involved so much bureaucracy.

Nelson must have had to deal with these kinds of utterly mundane decisions as well. John Berryman, in his *Dream Songs*, has the chilling line: 'Life, friends, is boring. We must not say so.' Being a minister is not all about perpetual epiphanies, or endless transcendental oneness with the One. It is about whether or not the church sale is allowed to have a raffle, or if the nativity play happens the week before Christmas or two weeks prior. It is about the slow business of dying and the long business of living.

It is about the Boys' Brigade and the Women's Guild both wanting the Church Hall on a Wednesday afternoon. Nelson was redeemed into boredom, I think. He, at least, already had experience of it.

The visit to Chapelhall and Calderbank made my mum ask a question which I have flinched from since ever and ever since. 'They need a minister – why don't you train?' I could impersonate a clever vicar very well indeed, and especially if it was in a rural parish with nice buildings and a tied house. But that is insufficient. Unless I heard the call that I could preach, and pray, and devote myself to the newborn, the married, the lonely and the dead, in a parish like Calderbank and Chapelhall, I have no right to step forward. Nelson did. He was better than me.

The Book of Job 31:35

Oh that one would hear me! behold, my desire is, that the
Almighty would answer me, and that mine adversary
had written a book.

If I could have granted Nelson one wish, it would be the complete anonymity he wanted, the divine amnesia. But that was never going to happen. On the tenth anniversary of his induction as the minister of Chapelhall and Calderbank, his parishioners might have been surprised to read an article in the *Glasgow Herald* with the inflammatory headline 'A Crime That Is Beyond The Limit'. The author, one Graham Lironi, did not pull his punches. It began: 'If civilisation is a bridge, the Commandment "thou shalt not kill" is its keystone, for it is this tenet which stops civilisation from collapsing into the abyss of anarchy. A decade ago to the day, the Church of Scotland condemned the bridge by removing the moral imperative to comply with this keystone.' Did he know the bridge had been broken in Calderbank and Chapelhall?

The article reprises Nelson's biography, slanted to be as damaging as possible. Lironi refers to Nelson's apparently saying he was 'in it for the money'; mentions resits during his theology degree, the intransigence of his father – who had died eight years beforehand; and insists that the ordination and induction were orchestrated by a 'cabal' of ministers who operated 'secretly'.

295

Lironi questions the Assembly's judgement: 'If there is no limit to forgiveness there is no conscience, no sin, no guilt, no right, and no wrong. The concept of unlimited forgiveness is a means of sanctioning anarchy.' I would disagree with all of this. Forgiveness, even unlimited forgiveness, can happen only if we recognise conscience, sin, guilt and moral distinction. Lironi calls the decision 'absurd' and goes on to insult the congregation: 'Forgiving a murderer is one thing, placing him upon a pedestal to preach about morality and provide spiritual guidance to a flock of comparative innocents is quite another.' The article feels, in places, somewhat padded. At one point he writes, 'Imagine if the Devil appears before you in a puff of smoke – scarlet-skinned, cloven-hooved, horned-headed and pointed-tailed – begs your forgiveness for his evil past, proclaims a conversion to God [I have added a capital on his behalf, since it is lacking in the original], and promises henceforth to lead an exemplary life condemning evil and preaching the gospel of peace, love and true Christian faith. Do you believe him?'

Speaking purely personally, I would be disinclined to believe such a clearly stereotyped image of Satan. But the insinuations in the piece are cumulative. Lironi claims that the Church, in forgiving Lucifer – or Nelson – made them 'paragons of virtue', not fellow sinners. 'We are not who we say we are,' he continues, 'we are what we do.' But as we have seen, this is a problematic argument. Neither intention nor consequence can entirely account for how we make a moral judgement. Lironi also lets slip his prejudices when he writes: 'If I murder a human being I am, and always will be, by definition, a murderer. If that other human being happens to be my mother (my real creator), the fact that I later profess allegiance to a conceptual creator is an ironic irrelevance which does not alter the unpalatable truth.'

Since, it seems, Lironi does not believe in a God, Christian or otherwise, it seems presumptuous to castigate those who do, and the decisions they have made based on their beliefs. He concludes with the words of Oliver Cromwell to the General Assembly in 1650: 'I beseech you, in the bowels of Christ, think it possible you may be mistaken.' Lironi clearly did not question his own stance.

What was remarkable was the outpouring of support for the Rev. Nelson two days later. Three separate letters to the paper addressed Lironi's article. The Rev. Charles Heriot, from Falkirk, noted that if Nelson's motives had been 'crassly materialistic', then he would surely have been weeded out during training. 'Far from undermining the fabric of society were we more ready to forgive as God forgives the fabric of society would be all the stronger. No crime is beyond the limit!' The Rev. James Duncan from Pitlochry wryly notes that, given the level of a minister's stipend, had Nelson's motives been venal they were also naïve. Moreover, if Nelson was not performing adequately as a minister, then the presbytery of Hamilton would certainly have intervened. 'As far as I know, Mr Nelson is carrying out a perfectly good and acceptable ministry,' he writes. Finally, J. B. Cox, one of the original members of the vacancy committee, speaks of a feeling between 'amazement and revulsion'. Nelson has, in the last ten years, 'done nothing to lower my opinion of him or his commitment, only to strengthen it. It is evident that my God of love and forgiveness is not known to Mr Lironi.' The idea that the piece was commissioned because of the ten-year anniversary strikes Cox as 'tenuous' and he darkly asks, 'Could it be that Mr Lironi is only the gun firing someone else's bullet?'

Such support must have been heartening. But the full force of the Kirk was apparent in a letter from the Principal Clerk to the

General Assembly, the Very Rev. James Weatherhead – the same Weatherhead who had spoken during the Motherhood of God debate. His letter forensically unpicks the Lironi article. 'Some cabal! Some conspiracy!' he writes, pointing out that a public debate with over a thousand ministers and elders is hardly backroom skulduggery. 'What the Church did, acting through its supreme court and not through any cabal, was done prayerfully and carefully, after the most meticulous observation of all its relevant procedures, in an open debate informed by theology and pastoral concern.' Even those who had voiced opposition to Nelson's candidature 'pales into insignificance' compared with Lironi's article. Weatherhead also sets out the argument made by James Whyte: 'If the Church had no place for repentant sinners, it would have no place for any of us, for we are all dependent on the divine forgiveness, and we are justified by grace alone . . . To say that the Prodigal Son may become a member of the Church but not a minister is to say that Christians are justified by grace, but ministers by works, and that the ministry is for the elder brother only.'

The letter from the Rev. Duncan ends with a sting: 'By the way, Graham Lironi? Who him?' Who he indeed. There were no other articles with his by-line on the newspaper's database. There was a Graham Lironi who was working in PR. And why publish it then? It did seem, as J. B. Cox said, tenuous to hang the story on an anniversary. There were plenty of other ways such an article could have been commissioned: for example, it could have appeared at any time between 1980 and 1991, given that the Archbishop of Canterbury during that period, Robert Runcie, had earned the Military Cross for his actions in the Second World War. The head of the Church of England had definitely killed people. (I spoke with his son, the novelist James Runcie, who said that his father had been tormented by having had to send men under his command to their deaths, but hadn't been terribly vexed about killing Nazis.)

On a hunch, I looked on Amazon, and found it immediately: published by Black Ace Books, in 1996, a novel, *The Bowels of Christ*, by Graham Lironi. The blurb reads:

> In a world where reality is determined by faith yet Jiminy Cricket is more valid than Jesus Christ, *The Bowels of Christ* is a twisting tale of teenage sex, lies and hillwalking. It begins with the unusual relationship between Carol and Carl – a young couple from the same suburban cul-de-sac who are a negative, or positive, image of one another – and ends with the narrator, who shares his name with the author, pondering the Gospel of the Second Chance. Paralleled by the story of James Nelson, the first convicted murderer to enter the clergy of any Christian denomination, *The Bowels of Christ* invites the reader to address the question: 'Did this really happen?'

I clicked and bought it.

It is a slim volume, 128 pages of relatively large type. The author's name is in lower-case letters, an affectation that always sets me on guard. The cover is half orange and half black, with two cherubic faces mirroring each other. *The Bowels of Christ* has this to say of the author. He is 'a son and a brother and a husband and a father. He's a lover not a fighter. An award-winning journalist, he currently edits two of Scotland's leading business magazines and is a founder member of the avant-punk beat combo The Secret Goldfish.' One cannot be a minister and a murderer, but one can evidently straddle the worlds of capitalism and counter-culture. It is a peculiar novel, with many of the hallmarks of slightly self-indulgent, second-hand avant-gardism: twins, incest, equations and diagrams, the self-referential introduction of the 'author' as character. It actually had very little to do with Nelson: perhaps three pages in total recount the bare bones of his story. Thematically, I suppose, it has very broad similarities, in terms of guilt and repentance, rebellion from authoritarian Calvinism, faith and faithlessness. It has an epigraph from – a wonderful synchronicity! – J. M. Barrie's *Dear Brutus*.

In 1996 Graham Lironi's novel was reviewed. 'So what is the story?' the interviewer asks. 'Using my own name in the book meant that it could be seen as some kind of pseudo-autobiography.' Let's allow the 'pseudo' at least. Describing the book as 'a tale of grievous betrayals and arbitrary come-uppances', the interview eventually says that however ambiguous the book is, the author is not. 'Basically, I think forgiveness needs to have a limit. If anything you can do can be forgiven, it is as if you have got some kind of moral right to do whatever you want. I find that pretty crazy or alarming. But in the book, I am not concerned with the James Nelson case per se – it is really there to raise these sorts of questions, not to ram one particular answer down the reader's throat.' Says the man who wrote an article about how the Church of Scotland obviated its moral duty when it ordained James Nelson.

The article in the *Glasgow Herald* is, I would surmise, an attempt to stir up some controversy around the novel, were adulation not forthcoming. I doubt that it would have generated many sales in the Chapelhall and Calderbank areas. The line I keep rereading is J. B. Cox's concern that Lironi is a cat's-paw, that 'opening the old wounds' is someone else's agenda. It chimes with Georgina Nelson's worry that certain elements of the

Church only ever paid lip service to the idea of forgiveness. I wonder what pressures it put Nelson under if there were a whispering campaign. Perhaps, had he been allowed to toil away in obscurity, things would have turned out differently. But Nelson was not just the subject of scrutiny. He also courted a degree of publicity.

The Second Epistle of Paul the Apostle to the Corinthians 2:5–7

But if any have caused grief, he hath not grieved me, but in part: that I may not overcharge you all. Sufficient to such a man is this punishment, which was inflicted of many. So that contrariwise ye ought rather to forgive him, and comfort him, lest perhaps such a one should be swallowed up with overmuch sorrow.

In May 1987, Nelson stood before the General Assembly, but not as a supplicant: as a scourge. Along with the Rev. George Grubb, later the minister of St Giles' Cathedral in Edinburgh, they presented a proposal that the Church and Nation committee should investigate penal reform. The Kirk, Nelson said, and the country itself, could no longer bear the shame of present sentencing policy and must shake themselves out of apathy and become involved in the issue. At a time, he argued, when parties concerned with penal strictures were so increasingly polarised that the situation was deteriorating, the Church was the only agency through which dialogues could be set up to redress the situation. As it was, 'Overcrowding in prisons was making life intolerable for both prisoners and staff. That would continue until there was a programme of radical reform of sentencing and penal policies backed by adequate resources for the penal system.

Governments of all persuasions had been consistently unwilling to tackle that.' Nelson's own direct experience was of prisons under the Prime Ministerships of Edward Heath, Harold Wilson and James Callaghan; since he was released on parole until he made his 'maiden' speech at the Assembly, Margaret Thatcher had been Prime Minister. It was a period of open conflicts: riots in Brixton in 1981 and 1985, hunger strikes in Irish jails in 1981, the Brighton bombing in the year he had first appeared before the Assembly, the Battle of Orgreave during the miners' strike a few weeks afterwards. Riots in prisons seemed reflections of external antipathies. George Grubb contributed the additional observation that while the courts had two options for punishment – fines and imprisonment – many were imprisoned for non-payment of fines, a sentence never initially imposed by the court. The Assembly decided it was a matter for concern, and set up a 'Working Group' 'to examine some of these issues in a serious fashion, with special attention to underlying assumptions, principles and conflicts, and with a special eye to the possibility of constructive insights coming from the Christian theologian tradition'. It comprised a forensic psychiatrist, an advocate, a retired prison governor, a community minister, a professor of Christian Ethics, a reader in criminology, a prison chaplain, a member of the parole board, a lecturer in Scots Law, a QC who was also a parish minister, a research student, a prison chaplain, a parish minister and former director of a Youth Treatment Centre, a social worker and the Rev. James Nelson, 'Parish Minister, and Life Sentence Prisoner'. Not 'Former Life Sentence Prisoner'. Even as the Church gave duties and responsibilities, it held its lost sheep at the end of a long crook. Even the newspaper article waited – unthinkable three years beforehand – three whole paragraphs before mentioning matricide. Of the panel, it should be noted that only two of the members were not men. Change takes time, after all.

The report of the Working Group was eventually published in 1991, with the punning title *The End of Punishment*, implying both the correct purpose of punishment and looking forward to a point where it would not be necessary. The keynote is sounded early: the word 'vacuum' appears again and again. Imprisonment is described as 'a practice without a policy'. A situation has arisen, they argue, where the traditional objectives of 'retribution, prevention, deterrence and rehabilitation' have been found wanting in practice and in theory. Prison is 'a fiasco in terms of its own purposes'. The report begins by considering the different people involved in the penal system: the victim, the sentencer, the prison governor and officers, the prison chaplain, the psychiatrist, the social worker and probation officer, and finally the prisoners themselves. It then considers, more philosophically and theologically, how alternative models of justice might be developed, and especially the roles of punishment, justice and reconciliation in Christian thinking. Finally, it provides a series of relatively modest initiatives that might move forward the debate. The most fruitful parts of the report concern the cleft between how words are used in different discourses. 'Guilt' in a legal and judicial sense is ontological: guilt is or isn't. The individual is either guilty of the crime, or not. But 'guilt' in a theological sense is a subjective, phenomenological proposition; an internal sense of wrongness, a hope that things were otherwise. We might, from a divine perspective, all be criminals, but even among criminals there are some criminals more criminal than others; especially, it would seem, when white-collar criminals are treated more leniently and yet are less repentant. While not underplaying the necessity of justice, it returns to the idea that justice is something that is performed, not imposed, and that as such it ought to be tempered with mercy. There are social reasons for this, but the religious reasons are more compelling in that they start from the premise that we are all already the recipients of mercy. There is an acute awareness that prison is not something set aside from society, but a part of it; and that many of the most grievous problems emerge when the prisoner leaves 'the system'. They quote Oscar Wilde, himself a former convict, to that end: 'Society takes upon itself the right to inflict appalling punishment on the individual, but when the man's punishment is over, it leaves him to himself. It abandons him at the moment when its highest duty towards him begins.'

The section on the prison chaplains is especially interesting and forward-looking. That the chaplain is in the institution but not of it is described as a licence to 'loiter with intent'. The chaplain was an anomaly, moving between ministering to the inmates and ministering to the officers. One chaplain describes the role as holding that 'no one is scum, no one can be written off. We seem to be dangerous amateurs prowling.' The report makes the startling claim that prison chaplaincies might benefit from having more women in that role, arguing that female chaplains would encourage prisoners to forgo the 'hardman' image – there is a nostalgic sense that even the most hardened of criminals would still refrain from beastliness in front of a lady – and even more open-mindedly suggests that a female chaplain would be better able to deal with homosexuality in prisons. There is a paradox as well, in that prison chaplains often found themselves held at arm's-length by the Church itself and its congregations. They were isolated in that churchgoers seemed to fear their own respectability might be contaminated by contact

305

with the prison chaplain. I wonder how much input Nelson had in these sections.

I wonder even more about that in the section on the prisoners. In the analysis of the prison chaplain, certain statements were directly attributed to the prison chaplain on the Working Group; particularly, I assume, because she was one of the two women. Given how careful the Kirk had been over confidentiality and privacy for Nelson, I would not expect *The End of Punishment* to attribute statements directly to him. The Group visited three prisons – it does not say which. Did Nelson walk back into the place where he had been incarcerated? The report strenuously opposed the 'demonisation' of prisoners, which does sound like the kind of thing he might have said. Another passage reads: 'Whether it is the experience of prison, or of imprisonment, or of the whole judicial process, those who have been sentenced to a term of imprisonment would, I believe, agree that if one word can be used to sum up what is meant in this context, it would be contradiction.' That contradiction, the anonymous contributor elaborates, is that the punishment of imprisonment is not the loss of liberty; it is being in prison and the dehumanising, almost unconscious belittling and vilification that is. 'The experience is that the prisoner does NOT go to prison as the punishment, but the prison is a punishing experience and is an experience of continually being punished.' There is a hint of Nelson's strange sense of humour when, as regards petty tyrannies, slopping out and overcrowding, an unnamed prisoner remarks that 'if the staff behave like zoo keepers, the prisoners will respond by behaving like animals'. There is also a keen observation of hypocrisy from one: a staff member – one of the supposedly honest, industrious and moral individuals – walking out of the canteen with a joint of meat under his arm, 'effectively stealing the prisoners' dinner'. Much is made of the magnifying effect of prison, whereby 'little things' take on 'tremendous significance'. Again, I can imagine him revealing that.

'*Abandonment and hopelessness*' was one summary of the prisoner's experience. Whoever said this also stressed the contractual nature of imprisonment: it is within the prisoner's capacities to refuse to conform, to withdraw goodwill; and there is an edge of threat in saying that a public which demanded longer sentences is now reaping what it has sown in terms of riots. The part which struck me as sounding most like Nelson was a throwaway remark on the problems of probation. The hope of getting it often led to increased anxiety. Moreover, 'there is absolutely no confidence in inmates at all' as those determining probation were 'the very same people who battered them in with these astronomical sentences in the first place'. Given the wife of Nelson's chief opponent, the Rev. Bill Morris, had been on the parole board, it is tempting to see a score being settled in these words. But a temptation and the truth might be very different things.

The recommendations in *The End of Punishment* are not just well considered, they are addressed to a wider set of audiences. Policymakers may think about how restorative justice might be done through contrition expressed by the prisoner to the victim; but Churches are told to look to their own laurels, and reflect truthfully on whether they are doing their duty to those in prison. Before they examined each branch of the judicial system, the authors addressed a brief paragraph to 'you', the reader, who has evidently picked up the book, who must be interested in the findings and who can hopefully learn from the experience. When it came to be published, despite the wealth of topics for discussion, the press relied on an old favourite: what would the Kirk's own ex-con have to say?

The article in the *Scotsman* on 20 September 1991, coinciding with the launch of *The End of Punishment*, is Nelson at his most eloquent. Prison is not just being behind bars: 'I will never be allowed to discard the mantle of murderer, nor will I savour freedom or forgiveness. A life sentence really means life. It goes on for the rest of your life which can be quite onerous. There is not really a sense of being free.' Nelson speaks frankly about the fact that while he has experienced kindness, understanding, empathy and some 'curiosity', there are still those – even within the Church – 'who demonstrate the strongest possible feelings of resentment and anger and dislike'. That said, he commends the fact that 'those who are victims of crime are much less punitive than the system of justice which purports to act in their name'. When talking about his own time in HMP Saughton, he says, 'It is a cumulative effect of so many little degrading things that make it dehumanising. I try not to look back on my time there.' But – for the sake of the Church, the inmates, the victims and the entire system – he evidently had.

My copy of *The End of Punishment* has two curiosities. On page xv, the typo 'justine' – a strange Sadeian slip – has been corrected in the margin with 'c/'; likewise '/t' is added to 'insitution' and 'unjist' is emended with a score-through and 'u/'. Whoever read it read it thoroughly. Between the last page and the back cover is a flyer from 'Guild House', for Room G14: it has an old Edinburgh telephone number. There are some rules on the other side: there is a £5 deposit for a key to your room, a kitchen with hot-water bottles, the hot water takes ten minutes to warm up, in an emergency ring the bell if the Tower front door is locked, take care not to drop the lids on the desks that double as dressing tables too suddenly, and please do not wear stiletto heels or studded shoes in the bathroom. A little rummaging online leads you to a project from the mid-Eighties, when the Women's Guild of the Church of Scotland was running accommodation from Carberry Tower and had a Guild House. I would like to think that this might be Nelson's own copy – he has taken a cheap, Kirk-sanctioned room in advance of the press launch, and spent the night beforehand picking up small errors in the book.

The General Epistle of Jude 1:9

*Yet Michael the Archangel, when contending with the devil he
disputed about the body of Moses, durst not bring against him a
railing accusation, but said, The Lord rebuke thee.*

Neither *The End of Punishment* nor *The Bowels of Christ* made
Nelson into any more of a celebrity than he already was. But
he was celebrity enough, and in 1998 he twice appeared on
television: on the BBC's *Everyman* and on Channel 4's *After Dark*.
Let us be clear: Nelson was not invited onto either programme
because he was a minister, but because he was a murderer. He
did not present *Thought for the Day*, Radio 4's rather sententious
religious slot; nor did Chapelhall and Calderbank appear on
Songs of Praise.

Of the two programmes, *After Dark* is more deliberately
provocative. This is unsurprising as its brief was to be provocative.
Nelson appeared alongside other guests: Georgina Lawton, the
daughter of Ruth Ellis, the last woman to be hanged in Britain;
June Patient, the mother of a murdered teenager and founder of
a charity about such bereavements; Peter Whent, an expert in
victim support; Lord Longford, the author of a report on
pornography and a long-time advocate of the rights of the serial
killer Myra Hindley; David Howden, a man whose daughter
had been murdered; the novelist Patricia Highsmith, author of

The Talented Mr Ripley and *Strangers on a Train*; and Sarah Boyle, the psychotherapist who had treated and married Nelson's doppelgänger, James Boyle. The programme lasted three hours, and Nelson used the phrase which in the last part of his life became a kind of mantra: what he did was 'inexcusable but not inexplicable'. The media's attention was not on Nelson in the aftermath, but rather on Highsmith. *Today* newspaper was critical enough: 'But for sheer oddness, none has outmatched crime writer-cum-New York bag lady lookalike Patricia Highsmith . . . asking a series of staggeringly daft and insensitive questions to poor David Howden, whose daughter was strangled by a maniac as she slept.' Her questions included whether his daughter had been raped and whether the perpetrator had been in contact with her beforehand. Nancy Banks-Smith in the *Guardian* was even more caustic. She describes Highsmith as 'inquisitive as a monkey' and continues, quoting Howden, '"I don't know if you can imagine the scene of my daughter's bedroom. Friends and neighbours had to go and clean that bedroom up. The stains and fingerprints. They had to take the carpet up, sandpaper the floor and get rid of the marks, buy a new carpet and put it down." "What kind of marks?" asked Patricia Highsmith, who will be slaughtered herself some day.' What is remarkable is how absent he is. I had thought that seeing his filmic revenant, a kind of digital wraith, would have been enlightening. Instead, he is almost reluctant, unobtrusive and not the 'hardman' of press speculation. He is, perhaps, almost embarrassed to be there.

Yet the *Everyman* programme is probably even more disturbing. Nelson is described in the programme as an 'expert commentator'. The programme's synopsis and voiceover state that 'the act of taking a life is something that could befall any of us'. What an odd word 'befall' is, with its sense that murder is somehow chancy. I could be a murderer, and so could you. I could be a victim, and so could you. There is a nasty equilibrium, of the perpetrator and the body. Both, it seems, are equal in the eyes of God. But there he is, defying every attempt at my understanding him.

All of this occurs with a different narrative behind it. Nelson had left his wife. He now becomes a series of hyphens – 'the murderer-turned-minister' according to the *Aberdeen Evening News*, in a story headed 'New Wife For Minister Who Killed His Mum'. 'Killer-Minister' according to the *Daily Record*. He had met Nancy Ross 'during a ceremony in his own church'. Given that she was both a divorcee and a widow, one wonders why the paper is so reticent to say which ceremony: a baptism? A marriage? A funeral? Communion? The paper refers to his having 'battered his mother's skull to a pulp' and then goes on to say that Nancy 'arrived on time at 3.30 in a pale blue Rolls Royce. She was wearing a gold brocade jacket over a long cream silk dress with a sweetheart neckline and full dress'. Nelson had, apparently, left the manse at three o'clock in a Mercedes. The newspaper reported that he had stated on television that he 'felt no remorse' over murdering his mother. Not true. He said he had 'no great feeling of remorse or anything like that. I was numb and probably in shock but it wasn't an accident. It never was excusable but it was explicable.'

The years running up to this had seen a drip-feed of stories. The year before, Gillian Glover had written in the *Scotsman* about her experience with Nelson. 'I once sat in a church in Lesmahagow' – I never realised there was a Lesmahagow incident – 'and listened to the Rev. James Nelson, a stern, handsome man who had trained for the ministry after serving a "life"' – oh, the ironic finger quotes of the Nineties – 'prison sentence for the murder of his mother, deliver a service which amounted to little more than a harangue on the subject of forgiveness. "Let anyone among you who is without sin"' – there is an inappropriate comma here, ',' – '"cast the first stone" etc. Fine Christian principles, but a little unnerving when delivered with this level of vehemence and repetition. The sermon was a simple challenge, approximating to "condemn me if you dare, you hypocrites in Sunday hats". So they did not dare . . . Mr Nelson . . . may soon stand at the right hand of God in Elysium for all I know.'

Nelson appearing on television is, in a way, a kind of moral rearmament. You say this about me, but I say something else. At the same time, his most significant supporter, the Rev. James Whyte, had not just become Moderator a decade beforehand, but continued to be a religious presence in the public sphere. His time as Moderator was not uncontentious, particularly as the then Prime Minister, Margaret Thatcher, made a speech to the Assembly. She maintained that the Good Samaritan was able to indulge in his charity only by having been an assiduous worker with plenty of savings. It did not go down well, and was referred to facetiously and factually as 'the Sermon on the Mound'. One of Whyte's duties was to give her a gift. He chose a report on poverty. While Nelson is on television, Whyte will in that year preach about the Lockerbie Disaster. A terrorist incident has catastrophised a small Scottish town. He stands up. He says, 'When Martha greeted Jesus after the death of her brother Lazarus, it was with a word of reproach, even though deep within that reproach there was a pained and protesting faith.' Nelson's sceptic, William Morris, is still in Glasgow. He will never be Moderator. Whyte will go on to preach after the shooting in

Dunblane. Nobody asks Nelson to preach elsewhere.

There was a time when a minister divorcing and remarrying would have been a whiff of scandal, magnified into a tsunami of outrage. The Church of Scotland had, in 1959, revised its rules about divorcees and remarriage. Its statement is classically Presbyterian. I have, for my own reasons, read and reread it unhealthily.

> XXVI. ACT ANENT RE-MARRIAGE OF DIVORCED
> PERSONS (AS AMENDED BY ACTS II 1985 AND
> II 2004) Edinburgh, 26th May 1959, Session 12.
> Notwithstanding anything contained in the Act of 27th
> August 1647 approving of the Confession of Faith or in
> any other enactment of the General Assembly, the General
> Assembly, with consent of a majority of Presbyteries, enact
> and ordain as follows:- 1. A minister of the Church of
> Scotland may lawfully solemnise the marriage of a person
> whose former marriage has been dissolved by divorce and
> whose former spouse is still alive, provided that the said
> minister adhere to the requirements stated hereunder.
> 2. A minister shall not accede as a matter of routine to a
> request for the solemnisation of marriage of persons whose
> marriage has been dissolved by decree of divorce as
> aforesaid. 3. A minister invited to celebrate such a second
> marriage shall, in order to enable a decision to be made,
> take all reasonable steps to obtain relevant information
> which shall normally include the following:- (a) adequate
> information concerning the life and character of the parties
> to be married; here the very greatest caution shall be
> exercised in cases where, for any reason, no pastoral
> relationship exists between the minister and either or

both of the parties concerned; (b) the grounds and circumstances of the divorce case; (c) facts bearing upon the future well-being of any children concerned; (d) whether any other minister of religion has declined to solemnise the proposed marriage; (e) the denomination to which the parties belong; special care shall be taken in cases where one or both parties belong to a denomination whose discipline in this matter may differ from that of the Church of Scotland. 4. A minister shall also consider whether there is danger of scandal arising if the re-marriage is solemnised; at the same time, and before refusing to solemnise the remarriage, the minister shall take into careful consideration the moral and spiritual effect of a refusal on the parties seeking such a marriage. 5. As the determinative factor, a minister shall do all he or she can to be assured that by word and deed there has been sincere repentance where guilt has existed in the past on the part of any divorced person seeking re-marriage. He or she shall also give the most careful instruction, where this is needed, in the nature and requirements of a Christian marriage. 6. A minister shall not be required to solemnise a re-marriage against his or her conscience. 7. Every Presbytery shall appoint certain individuals (who need not be members of the Presbytery concerned) with one of whom ministers in doubt as to the correct course of action may consult if they so desire; in such cases the final decision must rest with the minister who has been asked to officiate. 8. The admission to Communion of persons who have contracted marriage after divorce, and any other matters affecting pastoral care, shall remain the responsibility of the minister and Kirk Session involved.

9. The Acts of Assembly of 1566 and 1576 anent the
re-marriage of divorced persons and all other enactments
of like tenor and effect are hereby repealed. 10. For the
purposes of this Act, the term 'minister' shall be deemed
to include 'deacon'.

The problem here is that Jesus is quite clear. In Matthew's Gospel, Chapter 19, we are told, 'And I say unto you, Whosoever shall put away his wife, except *it be* for fornication, and shall marry another, committeth adultery: and whoso marrieth her which is put away doth commit adultery.' My schoolboy Latin – nominative, accusative, dative, ablative – became rather useful. I was not the 'whosever'. The subject of the sentence was someone other, whereas I had not putteth-ed away anyone and therefore had committeth-ed nothing wrong. I suppose.

Nelson's remarriage is of interest only because he is notorious rather than famous. I have known parishes torn apart by unsubstantiated rumour, let alone actual separation. The miracle of having been loved more than once is sometimes unthinkable.

Who married them? What does it matter. I thought of contacting Nancy Nelson. When I was in Calderbank and Chapelhall I heard different stories – she had left, for who knows where; she was at the choir in a nearby town just the other day. She was not listed in the telephone directory. Was she being protected or forgotten? It transpired that she had written some verses in the People's Bible, a handwritten copy of the King James translation. She had been given the very final verses of Acts of the Apostles: 'And Paul dwelt two whole years in his own hired home, and received all that came in unto him, Preaching the kingdom of God, and teaching those things which concern the Lord Jesus Christ, with all confidence, no man forbidding him.' By coincidence, I had written in that Bible as well. My verses were: 'Therefore said the disciples to one another, Hath any man brought him *ought* to eat? Jesus saith unto them, My meat is to do the will of him that sent me, and to finish his work.' My ex-wife wrote two verses from later – about how the Samaritans believed on the word of a woman. I decided that Nancy deserved her privacy, while I could only be public; that she should allowed quietness while I tried to articulate why this story fascinates and perturbs me. The newspapers referred to Nelson's 'love riddle'. Well, it is.

The Revelation of St John
the Divine 6:8

And I looked, and behold a pale horse: and his name that
sat on him was Death.

The ending is always the same ending. On the first day of August
2005, Nelson discovered whether or not there was a God. He
had retired through ill health – lung cancer – two years
beforehand. His obituaries mention outcry, but not the children
he baptised, the marriages over which he officiated, the funerals
he conducted or the Communions he offered. He 'never
expressed remorse' according to the 'several journalists who
interviewed him', according to the *Fife Free Press*. He 'never
expressed any remorse or regret', according to the *Glasgow Herald*.
His repentance was 'to say the least, equivocal', according to the
Daily Telegraph. Stewart Lamont, who had first revealed the story
of the murderer who wanted to be a minister, said that 'in
retrospect' the Kirk had made a mistake in accepting him for the
ministry. 'I was not aware in my two years of interviews with
him that he had ever expressed remorse,' he said.

Nelson is dying. A sympathetic minister asks him, before
he dies, to get off his ailing, riddled chest the big reveal and
say why he did what he did. 'If you had known my mother,

318

you wouldn't need to ask why.' It's too good a story, in some ways. It's a resolution but not an explanation. He is still going to be an enigma.

Must angst be public? Must grief be performed? Must shame be shown off? Maybe he did repent in silence and privacy and quietness. The Kirk has a long tradition of wanting visible and punitive begging for forgiveness. The 'repentance stool' may not sit beneath the pulpit any more but it waits nonetheless. In his absence he was placed on its absence. One minister said to me that 'we did the right thing for the wrong person'. But isn't that what forgiveness always is? Another said the Church was 'brave, but not wise'. Yet the foolishness of God is sometimes the most required thing. Should they have been 'cowardly, but not fools'?

At the end, he knows he is loved. The God he has sworn to serve is less sanguine. The Great Unrequited, who loves and is not loved in return, welcomes back a weak and strong soul. Perhaps only divorcees understand the nature of God.

'At the time of the controversy', writes the obituarist in the *Glasgow Herald*, 'there were those with the knowledge of James Nelson who believed that instead of arguing that a minister should not be allowed to be a minister, those who opposed Nelson should have asked whether this particular murderer should have been the test case.' If not him, someone else; someone more demonstrably ruined. After he tendered his resignation, Nelson apparently bought a smart car with the proceeds of the advance on his pension. This made some eyebrows rise. But why not, after all? He knew he would not enjoy it very long. A car seems a forgivable little pleasure, as you await eternity. I doubt many ministers are upbraided for not giving all their wealth to the poor in the last, pained years of their lives.

Let us suppose he was not cremated, and I could uncask his

skull and run his brain through many scans. Would I have learned anything about him, about his beliefs, about his thoughts? Unlikely. Let us scrape a bit from his bones and peer into its DNA, look for aberrant and abhorrent variations, make from the marrow a facsimile of the man. Do we learn what happened that night? I doubt it. Here's a thought! He left a hidden diary, in which he talks about his inmost feelings. But diarists lie. He's just telling us his version of him. So even better: Lazarus-like I let him rise from the ground. What does he say? Nothing. What do I ask? Nothing.

Death is supposed to be a conclusion. The unhappening of a person is supposed to summarise their existence. It is also the start of the stories about them. The dead cannot control the way they are told.

Biography is a kind of God delusion. If only everything were known, then everything might be understood, and everything judged. A whole life could be seen to have a structure, an arc and a message. But God does not write biographies. A writer, sitting with the golden scales, balancing so many sins against so many virtues, decides, and there is no appeal. I have realised that I am not God. I cannot judge Nelson. But I can judge myself, and see if I am found wanting.

The first line of one of the notices of Nelson's death states: 'James Nelson was a murderer who was accepted for ministry in the Church of Scotland.' In death he resolves into one thing only, not a difficult doubleness nor a problematic plurality. In 1996 he was asked by the *Daily Record* about his marital circumstances. He replied, 'I have no comment to make.' These are the last words he had in print. I still have something to say.

THE FIRE SERMON

The Gospel According to St John 1:1

In the beginning was the Word, and the Word was with God,
and the Word was God.

There is always an opposite to the opposite. Every dichotomy breeds a secret fissure: twilight is neither night nor day, nor is it dawn or dusk; between dark and light lies the creeping crepuscular and the slow opalescent; black and white ignores the spectrum from ashen and leaden to hoary and slate. These might be considered mere gradations, as if Good and Evil might imperceptibly shade into one another. Might one be two-fifths wicked and three-fifths virtuous? Over and above the moral diapason, there is the skelf, the irritant that is neither either nor or, both and and and not, neither between nor betwixt. What is the opposite of cat? One of my nephews says 'mouse', the other says 'dogs'. What is the opposite of right? My mum says 'left' and my dad says 'wrong'.

St Matthew describes the apocalypse as a sundering of the goats from the sheep. Given the accreted symbolism, this might appear a simple task. After all, the Lord himself refers to himself as the Good Shepherd, who seeks out the lost of the flock, who is at the same time himself the Lamb of God. The goat appears in one of the visions of Daniel, a precursor to the 'king of fierce countenance, and understanding dark sentences'. From Azazel in the apocryphal Book of Enoch and the cloven-hoofed stereotype in Shakespeare (I look down towards his feet, but that's a fable), from the Rider-Waite tarot cards and Aleister Crowley to H. P. Lovecraft to Dennis Wheatley, the goat is the symbol of the Adversary of God, yet the goat and the lamb are frequently not opposed to each other, but identified with each other: in Isaiah 34:6, 'The sword of the LORD is filled with blood, and is made fat with fatness, *and* with the blood of lambs and goats.' The beloved in the Song of Solomon has hair that '*is* as a flock of goats, that appear from Mount Gilead', while her teeth '*are* like a flock *of sheep that are even* shorn'. The goat is the scapegoat, an offering and expiation for sin just as Christ is. Telling goats from sheep is a trickier business than it seems.

Both sheep and goats were sacrificial beasts, given by and for and from a community. But the goat was often the creature that was sent to die in the wilderness and the lamb the one that bent towards the blade in the Temple. Both were offerings, but they were inside and outside, excluded and included, shunned and embraced. They have their differences, but what is different to them?

What is the opposite of the sheep and the goats?

This is Alexamenos worshipping his God. It is a little scribble on a wall that was uncovered in 1856 on the Palatine Hill in Rome, in the Domus Gelotiana, a building that was once owned by Caligula and then became a boarding school for page boys. It shows, presumably, Alexamenos kneeling before a crucified man with the head of a donkey. It is the earliest pagan depiction of a Christian, and it chimes with other references. In Book V of the *Histories* of Tacitus, he mentions that the Jews were led out of the wilderness by an ass, and consequently have an ass-headed idol in the Holy of Holies of the Jerusalem Temple. Tertullian, the third-century theologian, in both his *Apology* and *To the Nations*, refers to the idea that Christians worship a donkey-headed god, and cites a story about an apostate Jew who travelled around showing a picture entitled *Onocoetes* (*The Donkey-Priest*), portraying a Christian with the ears and tail of an ass. Josephus, the Jewish writer and Roman citizen, had to defend his co-religionists against the accusation of onolatry in his speech, *Against Apion*.

The donkey plays a venerable role in Christian symbolism, as any child who has had to suffer singing the dirge 'Little Donkey' at Christmas – despite there being no references to donkeys in the nativity narratives – will know. But on Palm Sunday, in the Gospels of Matthew, Luke and John, Jesus enters Jerusalem on 'the colt of an ass', in order that the prophecy in Zechariah 9:9 – 'Rejoice greatly, O daughter of Zion; shout, O daughter of Jerusalem: behold, thy King cometh unto thee: he *is* just, and having salvation; lowly, and riding upon an ass, and upon a colt the foal of an ass' – might be fulfilled. Moreover, one of the strangest stories in the whole of the Bible features a significant donkey: that of Balaam in the Book of Numbers. Balaam seems to be a mighty prophet, but one who jibs against his duty. He is also a non-Israelite prophet, one of seven recognised in the Rabbinical texts. He is solicited by Balak, the King of the Moabites, to prophesy against Israel, but can speak only the truth, blessing Israel. It seems that despite speaking truth to power, he managed to offend God as well as the monarch. The questionable 'matter of Peor' might involve Balaam recommending intermarriage between Israelites and the Moabites and Midianites, which causes God to strike the Israelites with a plague (it is in this section that Phinehas, the new high priest, is singularly praised for killing a Midianite woman by thrusting a javelin through her). Just as well he didn't consider falling for any Amalekites. In the Book of Joshua, we learn that Balaam died by the sword at the hands of the Israelites. By the time of Revelation, Balaam is a double-dealer, who taught Balak 'to cast a stumblingblock before the children of Israel'. He is an exceptionally difficult figure to interpret. God tells him to go with the Moabites if they ask, and then is wroth when he goes by his own initiative. Nevertheless, all the prophecies he gives are commendatory towards Israel. In trying to understand the passage, many commentators read it as proof that God can use the unworthy for worthy ends.

But that is not the uncanniest aspect of the story. As Balaam travels to Balak, the angel of the Lord thrice appears before him with a flaming sword, and his donkey is the one who tries to avoid the apparition. Balaam beats the donkey three times in return for its intransigence and then: it speaks. 'Am I not thine ass, upon which thou hast ridden ever since *I was* thine unto this day? was I ever wont to do so unto thee?' Balaam's loquacious steed is the only animal in the Bible to speak, with the exception of the serpent in the Garden of Eden. It is the only *virtuous* animal to speak in Scripture. The ass sees more clearly than the human, and is given in turn the human capacity to use language. The story overturns the imagery of the donkey as recalcitrant, stupid, stubborn and unclean. As a grand reversal, as a foolish thing of the world to confound the wise, Balaam's ass stands – or swerves – squarely – or zigzags – in the tradition of Christianity as 'unto the Jews a stumblingblock, and unto the Greeks foolishness'.

The Alexamenos graffito has other peculiarities. It shows, to use the technical term, a theriocephalic object of veneration. The gods of Greece and Rome were not just human in their lusts and rages, they looked like humans. In Egypt and beyond there were the falcon-headed Horus, the serpent-headed Xantico, the jackal-headed Yinepu, the lion-headed Sekhmet, the ibis-headed Thoth, the eagle-headed Nisroch, the goat-headed Mamitu, the dog-headed Bau, the sheep-headed Khnum, the elephant-headed Ganesha and the goat-headed Naigamesha. The graffito suggests that there is something suspiciously foreign about this new and zealous Jesus Cult.

{{And all the hymnals fell!}}

Even more starkly, none of the chimera deities were shown in the process of being executed. Had any of the trainee pages read the Scriptures, it might have struck them that the God of the Israelites and this new, Christian 'Way' was more often than not described as inconceivable. It was the burning bush that did not burn away to Moses, and then the presence that passed by once he had told Moses to avert his gaze. It was *not* a gale and *not* a quake and *not* a flame to Elijah. It was a thing of amber and beryl and wheels and wings with the faces of humans, eagles, oxen and lions, and straight feet the colour of burnished brass and the appearance of a man but also of a fire infolding itself and rings full of eyes to Ezekiel. Even the enemies of God are indescribable entities of iron teeth and many horns, four-headed leopards with the feet of bears, a winged woman clothed in the sun and crowned by stars.

Whatever the wall-scratchers on the Palatine Hill meant, they meant something obviously derogatory but also surreptitiously complex. It is of roughly the same date as the novel by Lucius Apuleius Madaurensis called *The Metamorphosis* and which St Augustine – from the same part of North Africa – called the *Asinus Aureus*, the *Golden Ass*. It features the foolish hero attempting to do magic and becoming a donkey, and who is ultimately returned to human shape by initiation into the Isis Cult, part of whose mythology involved the resurrection of the wife of Isis, Osiris. Apuleius, Augustine and the page boys would have known of the *pons asinorum*, the fifth proposition in Book I of Euclid's *Elements*: although it is about the angles opposite the equal sides of an isosceles triangle being themselves equal, it was known as the bridge of donkeys as it was the proof over which the stupid would stumble. Becoming a donkey, much later, was part of the moral education of Carlo Collodi's Pinocchio; and being turned, for a brief period, into an ass led Shakespeare's Bottom to a kind of enlightenment in *A Midsummer Night's Dream*. As he says, 'I have had a most rare vision. I have had a dream, past the wit of man to say what dream it was: man is but an ass, if he go about to expound this dream. Methought I was—there is no man can tell what. Methought I was,—and methought I had,—but man is but a patched fool, if he will offer to say what methought I had. The eye of man hath not heard, the ear of man hath not seen, man's hand is not able to taste, his tongue to conceive, nor his heart to report, what my dream was.' Bottom is misquoting part of St Paul's First Epistle to the Corinthians: 'But as it is written, Eye hath not seen, nor ear heard, neither have entered into the heart of man, the things which God hath prepared for them that love him.' The speech, which he claims he will have written up by his friend Peter Quince, is similar to Isaiah 64:4, but not exact at all. The donkey is elusive again. It is still, as in G. K. Chesterton's poem, 'the devil's walking parody / on all four-footed things' that nevertheless 'had my hour' and for whom 'There was a shout about my ears / And palms before my feet.'

In the room next to where Alexamenos was pilloried, there is another inscription in a different hand that reads *Alexamenos fidelis* – 'Alexamenos is faithful', or 'Alexamenos the faithful'. Is this Alexamenos's own riposte and retort? Perhaps. It also has no caricature or cartoon lampoon. His faith might have been more verbal than visual.

In the third scene of Goethe's *Faust*, the world-weary intellectual is pondering the opening of John's Gospel, and finds himself perturbed by the phrase 'In the beginning was the Word'.

Not coincidentally, he is sharing his study with a stray dog he and his apprentice Wagner discovered. The dog is, in fact, the incarnated form of Mephistopheles, with whom he will make his fatal bargain. (Reading this as a teenager, I was awfully confused that Goethe describes the hound as a poodle: it seemed too froufrou and cutesy to be the Devil. I had not realised that eighteenth-century poodles were usually used as hunting dogs.) Is it the dog's malign presence that leads Faust to create alternate versions of the phrase, to outdo the Saint himself? Or is Faust's tinkering with the Gospel the initial chink through which darkness can pour? He begins by wondering whether it should not be 'In the beginning was the thought'. This does not satisfy him either: do thoughts create anything? Instead he suggests it should be 'In the beginning was the power'. But unrealised power is not sufficient either. 'The Spirit aids me! Now I see the light! / "In the beginning was the *Act*," I write.' Toying with his philosophy of the prime nature of action, rather than articulation, is the beginning of Faust's downfall.

When I started reading theology, it was stressed that 'word' was inadequate as a translation of the Greek *logos*. It does mean 'word'; but it also means 'speech', 'ground', 'plea', 'reason'. In the work of Heraclitus, Logos was given new precision: it meant the very principle of order and knowledge. Aristotle revised it again, making Logos mean logical argument. It made a kind of poetic sense that the origin of all things was the abstract proposition of all things, and there was a kind of philosophical beauty in the notion that this would be incarnated, made flesh: what would be a word without lips and teeth and tongue and breath to form it; or even the pinkish blob of imprecisely named grey matter to conceive of it?

But the idea of the Logos as Language niggled at me. It seemed to make even more sense when I discovered the work of the linguist Ferdinand de Saussure. In his *Course in General Linguistics*, a book stitched together from his students' notes, he made a key distinction between *langue* and *parole*, themselves concepts inadequately translated as 'language' and 'speaking'. *Langue* was the deep structure of language, its rules and systems. *Parole* was the concrete, individual speech-acts of language users, the phenomenon of the language itself. Saussure's image to convey this was chess. There are the rules of chess – the sixty-four squares, the bishop's diagonal movement, how the king is castled – and there are actual chess games: 1.f3, 1.f3-e5, 2.g4, 2Qh4#. Even more importantly, the sum of all possible *paroles* would not be same as the *langue*. It was a series of metaphors that seemed to me to be profoundly theological.

Langue is God. It is inherently creative. The soul is the *parole*. God is not the sum of all souls, but all souls participate in Godliness. It was participatory and democratic: I can communicate with you even if you don't know the word 'strabismus' and I don't know the word 'catawampus'. *Langue* is both immanent in *parole* and transcendent in itself. When I thought this I was still doing a passable impersonation of an atheist and it seemed to make perfect sense. 'God' was just the psychic residue, the schizophrenic sludge of humans becoming linguistic beings.

The verbal rather than visual God would crop up in unexpected places. I found it in Gerald Manley Hopkins's poem 'Margaret Clitheroe', where he writes of 'The immortals of the eternal ring, / The Utterer, Utterèd, Uttering.' Deft, I thought, a piece of linguistic Trinitarian thinking, and unconvincing. It was hinted at in Emily Dickinson: 'The Brain is just the weight of God— / For—Heft them—Pound for Pound— / And they will differ—if they do— / As Syllable from Sound—'. It glinted in the country

329

clergy of the eponymous poem by R. S. Thomas who 'wrote /
On men's hearts and in the minds / Of young children sublime
words / Too soon forgotten. God in his time / Or out of time will
correct this.'

What is the opposite of the Logos? The most obvious answer
would be silence. But God, quietly, has almost colonised silence.
In the Book of Habakkuk, all the earth is entreated to keep
silence when the Lord is in his holy temple; in Revelation – in
one of the oddest specific details in that oddest of books – when
the Seventh Seal is opened (the previous seals having unleashed
the Four Horsemen of the Apocalypse and the souls of the
martyrs and caused an earthquake that turned the sun black)
there is nothing but 'silence in heaven about the space of half an
hour'. The silence is broken by the angels with trumpets ushering
in even worse disaster. Jesus refuses to reply to Caiaphas and to
Pilate, which amazes both of them. Many later mystics drawn to
the *via negativa* have figured God as silence. St John of the Cross
wrote that 'silence is God's first language'; Meister Eckhart said
that 'nothing is so like God as silence'. Kierkegaard wrote his
paean to faith, *Fear and Trembling*, under the pseudonym Johannes
de Silentio.

If not the absence of spoken language, might the opposite of
Logos be the inability to use language? To use etymology, might
Logos be opposed to the *in-* ('not') *fans* (present participle of *fari*,
'to speak'), the infant? The ludicrous popular image of God
almost makes this attractive: the variously virile, hirsute, stern
Father as opposed to the puking, mewling child. St Paul says,
'When I was a child, I spake as a child, I understood as a child, I
thought as a child; but when I became a man, I put away childish
things.' Paul's child may spake, and we know that children can
use sounds to convey signs: they wail, they giggle, they yawn.

But they never belch, grizzle, belch then coo to indicate a
different idea from coo, grizzle, belch, belch; any more than a
traffic light could decide to shine green and amber simultaneously
to express a wholly new traffic-related concept. Becoming
acquainted with the Logos is a process of maturing. Except that it
isn't. Doesn't Christ instruct us thus: 'Verily I say unto you,
Except ye be converted, and become as little children, ye shall
not enter into the kingdom of heaven. Whosoever shall humble
himself as this little child, the same is greatest in the kingdom of
heaven.' They translate not signs but needs and desires into
sounds. What could be a more perfect example of our relationship
to the Infinite Logos than an expression of ourselves, and its
understanding of us, as simple as a sniffle?

As a child there was a particular set of steps on which I liked
to play. In my memory I am wearing shorts and Clark's sandals,
but that may just be a synecdoche for 'the memory of being a
child'. One day there was a dead bird lying on the step. I would
be lying if I said I knew which kind of bird. I have remembered
it as a robin, remembered it as a blue tit, remembered it as a
chaffinch, remembered it as a sparrow. But it was definitely dead:
it had become an it. In every other respect it was perfectly
birdlike, except for its lack of aliveness. It was some time – in
memory most of an afternoon, in all likelihood probably about
three minutes – before I dared to put the tip of my index finger
on it. Nothing happened, but I had a vague knowledge of the
word 'germs' and went home and scrubbed my finger with a
nailbrush. Of the nailbrush I am certain. The next day, when I
went to look for the dead bird, it was no longer there. I had been
thinking about its deadness, how it couldn't move or fly, and
would certainly still be there. It wasn't and it seemed perfectly
logical that it had gone to heaven. Something like a *Star Trek*

transporter had shimmered it up into the empyrean, where it would be flying and chirping in some manner. That child's faith seems admirable and pitiable in equal measure. It was not shaken when I saw a smashed crow on the road, day after day, becoming a widening circle of tendons, feathers and blackened flesh.

The Logos speaks: who does not hear?

'Their poison *is* like the poison of serpent: *they are* like the deaf adder,' says the Psalmist. Jesus does seem to prefer healing blind people to the deaf, but does do so, once that we know of, as recounted in Mark 7:31–7. It is one of the miracles that he specifically asks not be trumpeted abroad. I might be wrong though: the last miracle before the Crucifixion is the healing of the centurion's ear which Peter has rashly amputated. The Latin for 'deaf' is *surdus*, a word which is difficult to parse. It lingers on in Romance languages – *sourd* in French, *sordo* in Italian, *sordos* in Spanish, *surd* in Romanian, *I shurdhër* in Albanian. It has been suggested that it comes from the Proto-Indo-European word, **swer-*, from which words spun out to mean such diverse things as 'sword' and 'bitter', 'swear' and 'whistle', 'fester' and 'susurrus' and 'buzz'. It seems a word of anger: those who do not hear and do have ears holler and cackle, snicker and whisper, bellow and seethe. The Word meets a cacophony of insolence and insidiousness, braggadocio and braying. The Logos unites and the Surd divides – not through not hearing, but through yammering over it. Surprisingly, although English uses 'deaf' instead, if one tiptoes back to its Proto-Indo-European origin, it is **dheubh-*, a word associated with the barren, confusion, dizziness, the making of smoke and buzzing. The tinnitus of the divine.

In English, *surd* has only a vestigial existence. Mathematics took the term 'surd' to mean a square root which cannot be simplified: the square root of nine is three and of four is two; the square root of three or two is irrational, a string of unending numerals that never reach the infinite. 'Surd' was deployed here in an ancient sense of 'out of tune'. The proportions are broken, the harmonies unstrung, by such an incomprehensible number. It is also retained in 'absurd', from a Latin which literally meant 'discordant' and figuratively means 'foolish', 'incongruous' or 'unheard of'.

It is attributed to Tertullian, and appears to be a paraphrase of a more complex passage. In *De Carne Christi*, he wrote: '*Crucifixus est Dei Filius, non pudet, quia pudendum est; et mortuus est Dei Filius, prorsus credibile est, quia ineptum est; et sepultus resurrexit, certum est, quia impossibile*': 'The Son of God was crucified: there is no shame, because it is shameful. And the Son of God died: it is by all means to be believed, because it is ludicrous. And, buried, He rose again: it is certain, because impossible.' The abbreviated version is *credo quia absurdum*: I believe because it is absurd. Those words have been above my desk as I thought and wrote about this book. I liked how it encapsulated a writer like G. K. Chesterton's approach to faith – why on earth would anybody make this stuff up? – and we were living in absurd days anyway. I had been rereading a lot of the absurdist literature – the plays of Eugene Ionesco, Dino Buzzati's *The Tartar Steppe*, the stories of Nikolai Gogol, the poetry of John Ashbery – which I had loved as a student as much as I flaunted loving them. They seemed more theological than I had thought at the time. They hinted at some transcendental signified beyond and behind reality's improbability. I was also frenetically reading Kierkegaard, for whom the Absurd was the All. In his *Journals* he wrote: 'The Absurd, or to act by virtue of the absurd, is to act upon faith – I must act, but reflection has closed the road so I take one of the possibilities and say: This is what I do, I cannot do otherwise because I am brought to a standstill by my powers of reflection.' In the *Concluding Unscientific Postscript*, he defined it thus: 'What, then, is the absurd? The absurd is that the eternal truth has come into existence in time, that God has come into existence, has been born, has grown up, etc., has come into existence exactly as an individual human being, indistinguishable from any other human being.' The Absurd was the very splinter through which we approached the Divine, not its opposite at all. Of course, at the same time, my marriage was grinding to its sorry close, and nothing seemed as Absurd as the promises I honestly made and failed to keep, and the vows I was proffered that transpired to be dust and ashes.

The Quantum Pope, Benedict XVI, who is still a pope but not the Pope, was very opposed to the idea of the absurdist faith. In 2012 he invoked the phrase to refute it, saying that 'the desire to believe against reason . . . is not a formula that interprets the Catholic faith'. With all due respect – and despite my being a Protestant – he is wrong. It is a misreading of Tertullian, who quite clearly is arguing rationally that improbabilities are improbable. It is also a misreading of the opposite of the *credo quia absurdum*: systematic theology.

After my year with Kierkegaard, I became excessively interested in systematic theology. Although its definitions are various, the most frequently encountered will tend to stress the rationality, coherence and indisputability of faith. I think of it rather differently: systematic theology was an attempt not to prove the existence of God through philosophy, but to show that God was neither inconsistent with nor contrary to philosophy as it was then understood. Aristotle does not have a disproof of God to St Thomas Aquinas; nor does Heidegger deliver a killer blow to belief for John Macquarrie, his first translator and the author of the wonderful *An Existentialist Theology*. Systematic theology is the opposition to the opposition, a kind of beautiful intellectual virus that inhabits the host, proves it is not invasive and begins rewriting its carrier. I spent many days not writing and instead reading Jürgen Moltmann and René Girard, Edward Schillebeeckx and Friedrich Schleiermacher, Alister McGrath and Hans Küng. There is – and readers may if they wish now throw this book across the room – something sublime and thrilling about reading theology. It is serious in an era of the fleeting; it is committed in an age of irony; it is self-deprecating in a time of bloviations. There is a kind of joyfulness I find in reading theology, the same joy as getting that the cryptic crossword clue '0014? (6,5)' is 'double agent' or 'Honestly? No, otherwise (2,3,3)' is 'on the sly'. I would, I fear, have been a rather good systematic theologian. The point is that it would not have made me a better Christian.

The opposite of the opposite and the opposite of the Logos – again? There is no other to God, nothing is other to God, and there is no nothing in which God is absent, even absence. The vacuum rejoices and the void is uplifted and the vacancy feels itself made whole, not hole.

A Lunatic Proof for the Existence of God: if Hugh Everett's multiverse theory, published in '"Relative State" Formulation of Quantum Mechanics' in the *Review of Modern Physics*, vol. 29, 1957, is correct, each point of alteration spawns a new universe. It had a premonition in a short story by Jorge Luis Borges, 'The Garden of Forking Paths', in 1941, and in 1961 its popular incarnation in DC Comics' *The Flash #123*, 'Flash of Two Worlds!' Each choice, each decision, every time a photon is matter or energy, a new universe calves into the Multiverse. So, to take its logic to extremes, if every possibility ever is actualised somewhere in the Multiverse, there must be a Universe with a God. Just not, alas, in this one. Perhaps we hear him creaking around next door, his footsteps heavy in a rackety, otherwise lifeless space, imagining humanity.

Often when I am shaving, I think about God. I think about the fact that thinking about God is remarkably like looking in the mirror, in that the closer one gets to the reflection, the more one's own breath occludes the image. As Porcius Festus, the Roman governor of Judaea, says 'with a loud voice' and no doubt extreme exasperation to St Paul, whose demands for a trial as a Roman citizen are inflaming an already tinder-dry situation, 'thou art beside thyself; much learning doth make thee mad'. I try to remind myself as I lather my face and scrape my skin with a vintage razor I have christened 'Emergency Exit' that Christianity is a question of doing, not believing. I am fairly nonplussed about Pascal's famous wager, which finds an existentialist reincarnation in the *Als ob* – 'As if' – of Hans Vaihinger. For Pascal, it was not insincere to say that one might live as a Christian and lose nothing if there were no God; but to live an un-Christian life and then be confronted with the Almighty was a risk too far. (His insouciance about how easy it is to live as a Christian is almost touching, and yet he lived in a period of outright religious warfare.) For Vaihinger, the choice is the obverse of Melville's Bartleby, who would prefer not to: it's a metaphysical 'might as well'.

The problem is that, as Simon Critchley has eloquently written about and George Price found tragically true, the Gospels are not an easy, or perhaps even possible, ethic by which to live. I have not given away all I have. Martyrdom has not been demanded of me. I see hungry, thirsty, ill, sad people every day of my life and never lift a finger to help them. The Australian philosopher Peter Singer has a wonderful parable about our desensitisation to suffering. Anyone seeing a child drowning in a paddling pool would be considered heinous were they simply to keep sitting in their deckchair. But we know that equal amounts of suffering are being inflicted outwith our vision and we have the financial assets to alleviate those pains somewhat. This is not a question of Buridan's Donkey, which starved because it was stuck between two identical piles of hay and had not the means to choose one over the other. It is our shameful moral apathy.

Might a feasible and new ethic be distilled from the New Testament that was unique to it? The so-called Golden Rule – do unto others as you would be done by, or don't do to others what you wouldn't want to be done to you – can be found in some form in the teachings of the Buddha, Confucius, Plato, Rabbi Hillel and *The Water Babies*. But there is, I think, a kind of ethical architecture in Paul's writing which is both distinctive and beneficial.

Although Paul's very modern sense of self-contradiction is appealing, his understanding of goodness seems often overlooked, especially when certain rebukes, chastisements and denunciations are turned into eternal verities. Jesus is actually much more interesting and uncompromising on sin: I shudder whenever I read the section in the fifth chapter of Matthew's Gospel, in which he maintains that to looketh on a woman to lust after her is morally equivalent to actual adultery, and that whosoever is angry with his brother is as good as a murderer. Paul never presents virtues singly. Most famously he braids together faith, hope and charity, and although the greatest of these is *agape* – that untranslatable word that does not mean erotic love, nor the love we bear friends and family, nor even sympathy, but something more unconditional and generous – none is possible without the

337

others. (I have often wondered if the best translation of *agape* might not be 'agape': to be wondrous and agog at things.) In his Epistle to the Ephesians, Paul gives a blazon of the virtues: the armour of God, 'your loins girt about with truth, and having on the breastplate of righteousness; And your feet shod with the preparation of the gospel of peace; Above all, taking the shield of faith, wherewith ye shall be able to quench all the fiery darts of the wicked. And take the helmet of salvation, and the sword of the Spirit which is the word of God.' My favourite is the section at the end of the Epistle to the Galatians, where he enumerates the 'fruit of the Spirit': 'love [*agape* again], joy, peace, longsuffering, gentleness, goodness, faith, Meekness, temperance: against such there is no law'. Paul, it seems to me, has a unitary theory of virtue. St Thomas Aquinas pointed out that the word 'fruit' is singular. These are not distinct, and each bolsters and supports the other: remove one, and the whole edifice becomes precarious. It is difficult to imagine being gentle without being temperate, or being peaceful without being joyful. The virtues in a sense even aggregate, they have a gravitational pull to each other. One cannot be forbearing without being courageous; nor can one be truly generous without being meek. Their inter-connection even allows us to understand their specific manifest-ations better. 'Longsuffering' is here an older translation; most modern versions prefer 'patience'. But imagine a patience that was not joyful, or a faith that lacked self-control. They would cease to be the virtues they claim: one would be peevishness, the other fanaticism. To practise one is to learn the rest.

It is possible, however, to be a thief but not a blasphemer, a lecher but not prideful, an addict but not a thug, an embezzler but not a murderer. The kingdom of sin is divided against itself, with one exception. Every sin stems from, or will involve thereafter, one particular sin. It was not for nothing that the first thing Adam and Eve did after eating the apple was literally and metaphorically to cover themselves up. It is not coincidental that in John's Gospel the Devil is described as one who 'When he speaketh a lie, he speaketh of his own; for he is a liar, and the father of it.'

A life without a lie is impossible. The Scottish ballad 'Thomas the Rhymer' shows how the poet is stolen away into Elfland, a kind of opposite to the opposition of Heaven and Hell, and at the end of his travails is returned to reality with a particular blessing and curse: he can no longer lie. It means he becomes a prophet rather than a feigning poet, but it also means that he can never say, 'Oh, I'm fine,' in answer to a polite question when the truth is: 'I am depressed, poor, lonely, single and livid.' Thomas is a psychopathic rejection of Jacques Lacan's 'big Other'. We all lie, perpetually, and worst of all to ourselves most of all. But that does not mean that trying to be more truthful is a will-o'-the-wisp. As a virtue, even a small amount of truth will call out to the virtues to assist it: to patience and gentleness, to bravery and fortitude, to humility and fidelity. I write this at a time when we need this more than ever.

And so to truths. The truth, we are told by Jesus, will set us free, and according to my dad, it at least sets us free from keeping our lies in order.

No one can reason their way to God, even if God is not inconsistent with reason. The only 'proof' is an utterly subjective, fundamentally personal event. It is as private as pain. It is something that I have never had, and have felt, since the spiritual arrogance of my childhood, that it is something I was due. God owed me more than owned me. But no transcendental fatted calf was offered. There is a truly affecting scene in W. H. Auden's *For the Time Being* called 'The Temptation of St Joseph', when after Joseph has been assailed by snide innuendoes, he prays. He asks God to give him an answer to the 'tactless wall' and 'pompous furniture'. Gabriel answers, 'No.' He then bargains, asking for 'one reason'. Again the archangel says, 'No.' Finally he pleads: 'All I ask is one / Important and elegant proof / That what my Love had done / Was really at your will / And that your will is Love.' The answer is the same. In an inversion of the traditional narrative, the woman, Mary, receives the revelation and the man, Joseph, has to subsist on faith. It is, in its own way, a kind of gift.

Milton gave some succour: 'They also serve who only stand and wait.' There was almost a frisson of abnegation in being overlooked. My tepid embrace of atheism had chivvied itself up by becoming a negative theopneusty. The real flash of inspiration was a universe singularly devoid of inspiration and light on flashes; it was the thrill of grasping what seemed the truth, without doubt or hesitation. Once I turned apostate on atheism, and even when hedged around by my new bruxism of humility, with ritual instead of recognition and diligent persistence in place of divine epiphany, I would give anything to have one miracle. Nothing theatrical. I don't want the skies to roll up like a charring manuscript or stones to levitate or communion with the dead. Nor do I want the aleatory tricks I have often played on myself: five heads in a row is not a miracle. My grandfather did not recover from one of his heart attacks because I won ten consecutive games of solitaire. My marriage would not have been saved because I saw a buzzard on the same telephone wire twice a day for three days in a row. But one small miracle seems a modest request. Even a solution to the conundrum of James Nelson might have done it, unless the only answer is that we never know anyone, not even ourselves. I figured that out myself a long time ago. A talking donkey would have done. It needn't even have said anything of especial import.

Nelson is not here. I have no answers.

In the absence of God, the Church must be enough for me. Amen.

Acknowledgements

The late Revs. Tom Donald and James Watson are always in my prayers, as kindly and wise men without whom I would never have written this book. I would also like to pay my respects to the Rev. Ian Clark, the Rev. Johnston MacKay, the Rev. Frank Campbell, the Rev. Victoria Linford, the Rev. Kevin Scott, the Rev. Robin McHaffie, the Rev. Una Stewart, the Very Rev. Allan MacLean of Dochgarroch, and Richard Holloway. All of them contributed to my thinking and nudged me along a stony path.

For their conversations about Nietzsche, Kierkegaard, the Early Church and post-structuralist philosophy, I must thank Ewan Morrison, Simon Pulleyn and Peter Burnett.

For all their invaluable work and almost holy diligence, I would like to thank Max Porter, Stephen Guise, Christine Lo and Pru Rowlandson.

Finally, to two friends: Peggy Hughes and Sarah Gundle, whose friendship has been invaluable while writing this. I doubt they will ever know the extent to which they were the rocks on which I whetted the blade of myself.